Women of the
Colorado Gold Rush Era

Women of the Colorado Gold Rush Era

J.v.L. Bell and Jan Gunia

Filter Press, LLC

Women of the Colorado Gold Rush Era
Copyright © 2023 by J.v.L. Bell and Jan Gunia
First Edition

Published by Filter Press, LLC

ISBN: (Paperback): 978-0-86541-010-7
ISBN: (Hardback): 978-0-86541-015-2

Library of Congress Control Number: 2023939955

Cover design: Jordan Ellender
Cover Photographs: Pikes Peak image courtesy of J.v.L. Bell; Amache Prowers, Denver Public Library Special Collections, Z-8879; Mary Cozens, Denver Public Library, Caroline Brancroft papers, WH 1089; Clara Brown, Denver Public Library Special Collections, Z-275; Albina Washburn, Collections of Loveland Museum, ID 2022.19.7; Katrina Murat, History Colorado, Accession #89.451.2581; Augusta Tabor, Denver Public Library Special Collections, X-21992; Elizabeth Byers, Denver Public Library Special Collections, Z-2318; Tsashin, Denver Public Library Special Collections, X-30460

Filter Press, LLC
Westcliffe, Colorado
https://www.filterpressbooks.com/

This book is dedicated to the women of the Colorado gold rush era.
Their lives and accomplishments inspire us.

Table of Contents

List of Figures

Frederick J. Ebert's 1865 map of the Colorado Territory

Courtesy of Denver Public Library Special Collections, Map CG4310 1865.E2

Preface

We have enjoyed reading, exploring, and writing about Colorado's vibrant history throughout our lives, and when we began working on *Women of the Colorado Gold Rush Era*, we entered a new chapter of discovery. We expanded our research methods, visited museums and libraries throughout Colorado that we had not previously visited, and made difficult decisions about which ten women to include in this book.

Julie began the process that led to this book in 2017 with her discovery of Elizabeth Byers' hand-typed manuscript, *The Experiences of One Pioneer* Woman, at Denver Public Library. The manuscript both enthralled and infuriated her. Here was a woman who had arrived in Denver in 1859, who had spent most of the next sixty years living and contributing to the growing city, whose husband had started the *Rocky Mountain News*, and yet there was not a single biography about her. Julie began writing *Elizabeth Byers: Denver Pioneer*, later published as a Filter Press Now You Know Bio, and as she worked on the biography, she wondered about the many other women who came to Colorado with the Pikes Peak Gold Rush. Those women, like Elizabeth Byers, contributed to Colorado's growth by homesteading, running boarding houses, washing clothes, organizing churches and schools, and fighting for the right to own property or to vote; yet they, too, had lives that were as yet untold.

Jan shared Julie's interest in the unsung heroines of the

Pikes Peak Gold Rush and harbored frustration over historians' tendency to spotlight the lives of the flamboyant and glamorous over those who quietly struggled to support their families and to take on the formidable task of transforming rough mining camps into safe communities in which to rear their children. While in grade school, Jan read a newspaper article about Augusta Tabor, and the injustice that pioneer woman suffered sparked Jan's imagination and her desire to know more about Augusta's life, but nothing was available at the time. Decades later, a painting of Baby Doe Tabor spanning the exterior wall of the Colorado Historical Society incensed Jan's sense of injustice once again. Why not, at least, devote half of the wall to a portrait of Augusta? That set Jan on a path of years of extensive research into Augusta's life and a desire to make her story as well known as Baby Doe's.

Over breakfast at a Broomfield, Colorado, café, Julie told Jan about her ideas for a book of biographies about Pikes Peak Gold Rush women and invited Jan to join her on the project. Julie pointed to Jan's research skills and attention to detail as assets in bringing the book to fruition. Jan eagerly accepted the invitation, seeing this as the perfect venue to highlight Augusta Tabor's contributions to the development of Colorado and to champion some of the state's other strong pioneer women whose stories lay hidden in dusty archives. She excitedly thought of a few women she had "met" during her research who were potential candidates for the book.

Together, we began by using the Society of Colorado Pioneers' definition of original pioneers—those arriving no later than December 31, 1860—to limit our choice of women. We soon expanded our criteria to include Hispanic and Native American women who had called Colorado home long before 1860 because we realized the gold rush affected their lives as much as it did those who directly participated in it.

We found studying each of these women became a work of joy, an unbelievably difficult job, and a lesson in researching, researching deeper, and then researching still more deeply. With each biography, we discovered not only the fascinating stories of these women's lives and struggles, but more importantly, how their contributions fused Native American, Hispanic, African American, and Anglo cultures to shape Colorado's distinctive history and identity.

As the book took shape, we strove to include women who represented various races, ethnicities, religions, economic backgrounds, places settled, and lifestyles, but we were hampered by the dearth of information available. Many historians of the late nineteenth and early twentieth centuries largely ignored women or trivialized them as appendages to their husbands. Elizabeth Byers' own husband, William, did not include any women in his 1901 *Encyclopedia of Biography of Colorado: History of Colorado*.[1]

We found that, unlike Elizabeth Byers, most of the women we chose had not left primary documents such as diaries and letters that detailed their lives in their own words. In fact, at least four of the women were illiterate: Amache Ochinee Prowers, Mary York Cozens, Clara Brown, and Tsashin.[2] In addition, the years since 1858 have left many details of these women's lives lost or recounted in various and contradictory ways. Consequently, we dug through newspapers, genealogical data, censuses, contemporaries' letters and accounts, church records, and numerous other sources in hopes of finding mere mentions of the women. Each small nugget of information unearthed was a cause for celebration, but also presented the necessity to determine if the information was fact, fiction, or myth. Each biography became both a research challenge and a sleuthing adventure, and each completed biography an absolute labor of love.

Seven of our featured women arrived in what would become the state of Colorado during the Pikes Peak Gold Rush. In the summer of 1858, the rush began as a trickle of several hundred gold seekers after the Russell party from Georgia discovered paying gold on Little Dry Creek in present-day Englewood. The following year, the trickle of newcomers became an all-out rush, and lode discoveries by George Jackson at Gold Hill and John Gregory at Black Hawk brought approximately one hundred thousand people across the Great Plains in search of fortune. Mary Cozens, Clara Brown, Albina Washburn, Mary Hall, Augusta Tabor, Elizabeth Byers, and Katrina Murat were part of that massive wave of pioneers, and they spent most of the rest of their lives in Colorado, unlike the two-thirds of the hopeful pioneers who eventually turned back. The 1860 United States compiled census reports 34,277 settlers living in or around the Rocky Mountains, with fewer than five percent of them women.[3]

The newly arrived fortune hunters settled on Native American lands, ignoring the treaties between the United States and Indigenous tribes, believing themselves entitled to the land and the minerals hidden in its rocks and soil. Native American women, who had called the Rocky Mountains and Eastern Plains home long before the gold seekers arrived, paid a heavy price, as did Hispanic women living in southern Colorado along the Santa Fe Trail and in the San Luis Valley.

Tsashin, a Ute woman and friend to the White settlers, was forced by the United States government from her mountain homeland in Colorado to an arid reservation far away in northeast Utah. Amache (Ochinee) Prowers, a Southern Cheyenne, suffered the loss of many relatives, including her father, at the Sand Creek Massacre. When Colorado became a territory, Maria Dolores Ballejos, a woman living on a Spanish land grant in the San Luis Valley, found herself and her family subject to new laws that contradicted their way of life, especially regarding property and water rights. To add insult, as a married woman living in the Territory of Colorado, Maria Dolores lost the right to own property.

The Pikes Peak Gold Rush has seldom been documented from a feminine viewpoint. This book is intended to fill that void. The women who made their homes in the Colorado Territory possessed bountiful perseverance and courage that served them well as they faced individual challenges, struggled to keep their homes and families safe, campaigned for their rights to own property and to vote, or simply fought to survive and remain on their homeland. As National Public Radio reporter and bestselling author Cokie Roberts wrote, "History looks very different when seen through the eyes of women."[4]

We are honored to share the biographies of these amazing women.

J.v.L. (Julie) Bell and Jan Gunia

---

[1] William N. Byers, *Encyclopedia of Biography of Colorado: History of Colorado* (Chicago, IL: Century, 1901).

[2] Maria Dolores Ballejos was likely illiterate, but that has not been verified.

[3] Agnes Wright Spring, "Rush to the Rockies, 1859," *Colorado Magazine,* Apr. 1959, 89, 114; and see Encyclopedia Staff, "Colorado Gold Rush," *Colorado Encyclopedia* (website), last modified Nov. 15, 2022, https://coloradoencyclopedia.org/article/colorado-gold-rush; and also *Population of the United States in 1860: Compiled from the Original Returns of the Eighth Census,* (Washington, DC: Government Printing Office, 1864), 548, https://www.census.gov/library/publications/1864/dec/1860a.html.

[4] Cokie Roberts, preface to *Ladies of Liberty: The Women Who Shaped Our Nation* (New York, NY: Harper Perennial, 2009), xvii.

Figure 1.1. Amache Prowers wearing a dark Victorian dress with a lace collar, circa 1870

Courtesy of Denver Public Library Special Collections, Z-8879

Amache Prowers:
A Woman between Cultures

Born on Colorado's Southeastern Plains, 1846

At sundown on November 26, 1864, United States soldiers of Company E, First Colorado Cavalry, arrived at the Prowers' ranch on Caddoa Creek in what is today Bent County and disarmed the men, including Amache Prowers's husband, John. Under the command of Corporal Cook,[1] the soldiers held the residents of the ranch prisoners for several days. They were released only after John Chivington, Commanding Colonel of the Military District of Colorado, and his forces had annihilated the peaceful Cheyenne and Arapaho camped near Sand Creek, about eighty miles to the northeast of the Prowers' ranch. Amache's father and many of her Southern Cheyenne relatives were killed in what came to be known as the Sand Creek Massacre. Years later, Amache was introduced to Colonel Chivington and was asked whether she knew him. According to her daughter Mary, Amache "drew herself up with that stately dignity, peculiar to her people, and ignoring the outstretched hand, remarked in perfect English, audible to all in the room, 'Know Col. Chivington? I should. He was my father's murderer!'"[2]

Born during the summer of 1846, her parents named her Amache, or, in Cheyenne, Ameohtse'e, meaning Walking Woman.[3] She was the daughter of Chief Ochinee, also known as Nahkôhno'kaeste (Lone Bear),[4] and Nahkóha'e (Bear Woman).[5] Her family was part of the Southern Cheyenne tribes that roamed the southeastern plains of present-day Colorado, sometimes traveling into Kansas, Oklahoma, and New Mexico, but often spending time camped near Bent's Fort on the Arkansas River. Amache's father became friendly with the trader William Bent, and he earned the nickname One-Eye, or O'kenêstse (anglicized to Ochinee), after losing an eye while defending Bent from an attack by Kiowa Indians.[6]

Amache was raised as a traditional Cheyenne girl. She learned to cook traditional dishes; to gather roots, berries, and medicinal plants; to dress hides and turn them into clothing and shelter; and to recognize the plants that provided traditional dyes.[7] Like all Cheyenne children, she was an excellent horsewoman and probably received her own horse at an early age. As the daughter of Chief Ochinee, Amache had a high status in her tribe. She would have been skilled in applying quills and beadwork to her family's clothing and have been expected to be modest, chaste, and hardworking.[8]

In 1860, when Amache was around fourteen years old, John Prowers—an employee of William Bent—saw her perform a traditional Cheyenne dance. John had ventured west in 1856, when he was eighteen years old, initially traveling and working for Robert Miller, an Indian agent.[9] Later, he worked at Bent's Fort as a store clerk and as a freighter where he hauled provisions across the Great Plains.[10]

Bent's Fort was established around 1833 by the Bent, St. Vrain & Company to facilitate trade between Saint Louis merchants, Plains Indian tribes, western trappers, and Hispanos

Figure 1.2. John Prowers, Colorado cattleman, Indian trader, and pioneer, circa 1870

Courtesy of Denver Public Library Special Collections, Z-8876

living in Taos and Santa Fe. The brothers William and Charles Bent, along with Ceran St. Vrain, first built their adobe fort along the Santa Fe Trail around twelve miles upstream from the confluence of the Purgatory and Arkansas Rivers. In 1835, William Bent married Owl Woman, the daughter of White Thunder, an important Southern Cheyenne medicine man.

The marriage was a political arrangement, that ensured that William Bent had good relations with the Cheyenne. It also benefited the tribe to have a White man as an advocate and trading partner. The couple seemed happy and had several children.

Bent and his fort prospered, and by the time John Prowers began working there, the original Bent's Fort near the mouth of Huerfano Creek had been replaced by an impressive adobe structure called Bent's New Fort, which was built near Big Timbers along the Arkansas River.

After seeing Amache dance, John fell in love, but to pursue his interest and court the girl, he had to gain her father's approval. Once he had obtained Ochinee's approval, John and Amache observed a traditional Cheyenne courtship, which included giving gifts. Traditionally, the man gave horses to the woman's father or brother, although John might have broken with tradition and offered Amache's family White man gifts such as metal kettles, knives, guns, and ammunition. John also received gifts from Amache's family including a fine spotted pony and beaded clothing probably made by Amache herself.[11] With the blessing of Amache's father, the two married in 1861 in a traditional Cheyenne ceremony. Amache was fifteen years old; John was twenty-three.

A White man marrying a native woman, as William Bent had shown, had many advantages for the man, but history seldom records the effect these marriages had on the Native American wives. Many intercultural marriages, such as Amache's, lasted a lifetime and had profound and positive influences on both the woman and her Native American family. Jack Faragher, a Howard R. Lamar Emeritus Professor of History and American Studies at Yale, is quoted in Harriet Sigerman's book *Land of Many Hands: Women in the American*

West as writing "Indian women with white husbands often played influential roles within their societies. . . . Called "women in between," these wives often were the ones to introduce new products, techniques, and ideas into their tribes."[12]

Amache became "Amy" Prowers, as her husband called her, and she moved into the commissary at Bent's Fort. Their first child, Susan, was born in 1862, and later that year, John took his young family east to Westport, Missouri, where he had been raised. He left Amache and Susan there in the care of his father's aunt and headed back to Bent's Fort with a wagon train of supplies.[13]

Although fluent in Cheyenne, Spanish, and English, Amache remained illiterate her entire life, so there is no personal written record of her experiences in Westport. It is assumed by the authors that John took her to Missouri, at least in part, to have his relations teach her Victorian etiquette and to introduce her to the ways of what he deemed proper society.

In his book, *Boggsville: Cradle of the Colorado Cattle Industry*, C. W. Hurd describes one of Amache's adventures in Anglo Missouri society. According to Hurd, Amache attended a party in her honor for which she dressed in a formal gown with a bustle. As she started down the steps toward the carriage, Amache caught her foot in the bustle and tumbled to the ground.[14] After that experience, Amache refused to wear a bustle and she seldom wore corsets.

Amache's second child, Mary, was born July 18, 1863, in Westport.[15] A few months after her birth, John returned and brought his family back to the Colorado Territory where they settled on the former Caddo Indian Reservation near Big Timbers. Although he continued to work for William Bent, John also began his own cattle ranch—a lifetime pursuit that would make the couple wealthy.

Part of the success of John Prowers's cattle business was due to his ability, as Amache's husband, to graze his cattle on Cheyenne land. In 1861, the Treaty of Fort Wise had been signed between the United States and the Southern Cheyenne, and it included provisions for land to be allotted to individual members of the Cheyenne tribe.[16] In 1863, John Prowers wrote a letter to his brother and sister that included:

> U.S. Surveyors are at work now laying out the Indian land in 40 acres to <u>each and every one</u>, my squaw and baby will get their share and her parents want me to select the whole together which will make about 600 acres of which I can have the use of as much as I want.[17]

The 1849 Abiquiú Treaty and the 1851 Fort Laramie Treaty gave Utes, Cheyenne, Arapaho, and other Native Americans land rights that included most of Colorado's Front Range. The miners and settlers who came during the 1859 Pikes Peak Gold Rush ignored Native American property ownership and made their mining claims on native lands. As more and more miners arrived in the Colorado Territory, formed in 1861, tensions between Native Americans and Anglos rose. By 1863, the Colorado territorial government had stopped Anglos from filing claims on Native American land, upsetting miners who considered the territory theirs.[18] This, along with several skirmishes, caused tensions to flare into conflict. The hostilities embroiled Amache and John along with their corresponding families and cultures.

By August 1864, the conflicts between Native Americans and settlers were so severe that Governor John Evans issued a proclamation that empowered all Colorado Territory citizens to "kill and destroy as enemies of the country wherever

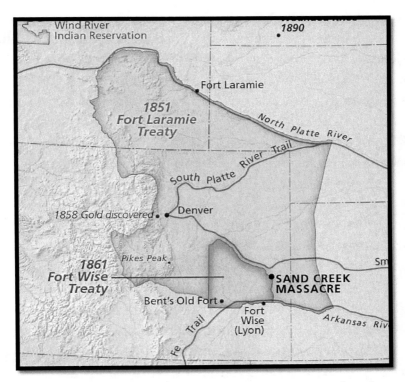

Wind River
Indian Reservation

1890

Fort Laramie

1851
Fort Laramie
Treaty

North Platte River

River Trail

South Platte River

Denver

1858 Gold discovered

Pikes Peak

Sm

1861
Fort Wise
Treaty

SAND CREEK
MASSACRE

Bent's Old Fort

Fort
Wise
(Lyon)

Arkansas Riv

Trail

Fe

Figure 1.3. Cheyenne and Arapaho reservation lands per the 1851 Treaty of Fort Laramie. The tribal lands were reduced significantly by the 1861 Treaty of Fort Wise.

Courtesy of the National Park Service

they may be found, all such hostile Indians."[19] The proclamation caused Major Edward Wynkoop, the commander of Fort Lyon (formerly Fort Wise, a military fort located less than a mile west of Bent's Fort), to command his men to kill any Native Americans sighted near Fort Lyon.

Despite these orders, on September 4, 1864, two Native American prisoners were brought before Major Wynkoop. One of these prisoners was Amache's father, Ochinee. At that time, like most White settlers, Major Wynkoop was no friend of Native Americans. In his autobiography, Major Wynkoop said that before that fateful encounter, he thought Native Americans were "degraded treacherous and cruel," and "that he [the Indian] must make way for civilization or be trampled on, and that he [the Indian] had no rights that we [white men] were bound to respect [such as treaties and land ownership]."[20]

Major Wynkoop chastised the sergeant who had captured Amache's father and his companion, questioning why the prisoners had not been killed on sight. The sergeant defended his actions, saying Ochinee had held up a paper and made the signs of peace. Major Wynkoop questioned his prisoners and learned that Amache's father and his companion, Mah-min-ic, had risked their lives to deliver a peace letter from Chief Black Kettle. When Major Wynkoop asked Ochinee why he'd done this, Amache's father gave a remarkable speech, translated by Fort Lyon's translator, John Smith, that ended with, "I thought I would be killed, but I knew that paper would be found upon my dead body, that you would see it, and it might give peace to my people once more."[21]

Major Wynkoop decided Chief Black Kettle desired peace and that he might be willing to release White prisoners held captive by the tribe. Therefore, Major Wynkoop agreed to follow Ochinee back to Chief Black Kettle's camp where the two leaders met and engaged in peace talks. Ochinee's bravery, along with talks with Black Kettle, permanently changed Major Wynkoop's attitude toward Native Americans. During these talks, several White prisoners were released and Wynkoop began the peace process that eventually led to the 1864 Camp Weld Council near Denver, held on September 28, 1864.

The *Rocky Mountain News*, Denver's first newspaper, described the Camp Weld Council in an article on September 29, 1864: "The council was conducted by His Excellency, Gov.

Evans, in company with Cols. Chivington and Shoup, Maj. Wynkoop." The article describes an "animated speech" by Cheyenne Chief Black Kettle and concludes, "the council broke up with the belief that these chiefs will use their utmost influence to induce their tribes to lay down their arms."[22]

The Native American chiefs who attended the Camp Weld Council were instructed to return, accompanied by Major Wynkoop, and to gather their tribes around Fort Lyon. Under these instructions, the Native Americans were considered prisoners of war and should have been protected as such. Nonetheless, two months after the Camp Weld Council, while Amache, her husband, and her young daughters were held prisoner at their ranch on Caddoa Creek, Colonel Chivington and his forces massacred Ochinee and more than two hundred Cheyenne and Arapaho at Sand Creek, located about thirty miles northeast of Fort Lyon. Because most of the younger Cheyenne and Arapaho men were away hunting, those killed in the massacre were predominantly older men, women, and children.[23]

Even in an era of brutal military campaigns against Native Americans, the Sand Creek Massacre stands out as unjustified slaughter.[24] John Prowers testified at the military inquiry following the massacre, along with Captain Soule, Major Wynkoop, and others. Colonel Chivington and Governor Evans lost their powerful positions but there was little other punishment. In October 1865, the Treaty of the Little Arkansas was signed. This treaty offered reparations to the Cheyenne and Arapaho who had lost family members at the Sand Creek Massacre. Amache and her two oldest daughters, Susan and Mary, were each allocated 640 acres of land.[25] The Prowerses chose valuable land along the Arkansas River, providing John with rich grazing for his growing cattle business.[26]

In retaliation for the massacre at Sand Creek, Plains Indians attacked settlements, farms, ranches, stagecoaches, and freight trains across the Great Plains. The violence went on for several years, until most Plains Indians were killed or forced onto reservations. Amache and her family were spared from attack, both because of Amache's presence and because John Prowers was known to be fair to the Cheyenne and other Native American tribes. Daughter Mary (Prowers) Hudnall described this relationship in a 1945 article published in *The Colorado Magazine*:

> Father was always exceptionally good to mother's people, and they all loved and honored him, paying heed to his advice as to their relations with the white people. The Cheyennes were always welcome at the ranch; father saw that they were well treated and that they had a good present to take along when they returned to the tribe. Many a time I have seen father send out a rider on the range to select a riding horse for one of mother's relatives. Often a band of Indians returning from the hunt, would ride up to the ranch carrying their bows and arrows and ask father to send out a team and wagon to bring in the game they had killed. [27]

In 1866, flooding in the Arkansas Valley rendered Fort Lyon unusable and a new Fort Lyon was built nineteen miles downstream near Boggsville.[28] Since much of the beef raised by the Prowerses was sold to the army, the Prowers family moved their ranch to Boggsville in 1867. Not only did their new home offer better economic opportunities, but it was also closer to the land awarded to Amache and her daughters in the Treaty of the Little Arkansas.

Founded by Tom and Rumalda Boggs in 1866, Boggsville was located two miles southeast of present-day Las Animas.

The small town was a cultural crossroads where Native American, Anglo, and Hispano cultures coexisted. In addition—unusual at that time—it was the women of Boggsville who owned the land around the town. Rumalda Luna (Jaramillo) Bent Boggs was the stepdaughter of William Bent's brother, Charles, and the grandniece of Cornelio Vigil, one of the grantees of the 1843 Las Animas Mexican Land Grant. The Las Animas Land Grant encompassed approximately four million acres and after Cornelio Vigil was killed during the 1847 Taos Revolt, Rumalda Luna, as one of his heirs, petitioned for 2,040 acres. She chose land near the confluence of the Arkansas and Purgatory River, and when it was awarded to her, she and her husband settled there. Unlike Anglo women of that time whose husbands acquired their wives' wealth through marriage, both Amache and Rumalda Luna retained ownership of their lands despite their marriages.[29]

John Prowers built a fourteen-room, two-story adobe house[30] for his growing family and opened a general merchandise store. Dr. William Abraham Bell, working as a photographer for the railroad, visited Boggsville in 1867 and wrote about the Prowers' store in his journal:

> Here we could buy everything—cloths and candles, bowie knives and groceries, canned fruits and Mexican saddles, powder and shot, boots and shoes, caps and crinolines, Worcestershire sauce, whiskey and drinks without end. This well stocked storehouse, raised up in the wilds, for which everything has to be carried hundreds of miles by wagon . . . speaks more for the extraordinary energy and foresight of these Western traders than any panegyric [tribute] I could write.[31]

The Prowers family lived in Boggsville from 1868 until

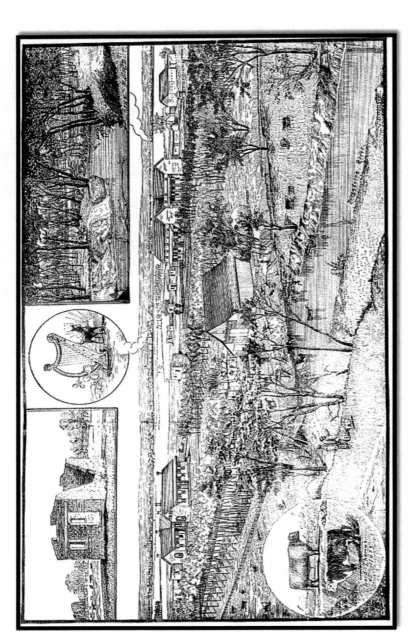

Figure 1.4. Boggsville sketch from the illustrated supplement of the *Bent County Democrat* in the spring of 1888. The Prowers' house is in the background and the Boggs' house is on the left.

Courtesy of the Bent Country Democrat (Las Animas), 1888

1873, during which time Amache gave birth to several more children. In all, Amache and John had nine children: Susan, who died at the age of six; Mary, who married A.D. Hudnall; Katherine, who married A.W. Haws; Inez, who married Glen O. Comstock; John Wesley, Jr., who graduated from Wentworth Military Academy in 1888; Frank (George), who died at the age of ten; Leona, who died at the age of twenty; Ida May, who married Louis F. Horton; and Amy, who was named after her mother.[32] In addition to tending her growing family, Amache helped her husband run their cattle business, manage their trading post, and run their stagecoach station. Amache also remained involved with her Cheyenne family. It was not unusual to see teepee encampments near the Prowers' home.

As might be expected, Amache incorporated many Cheyenne traditions into her Anglo home. Her Cheyenne family was always welcome at the Prowers' ranch and after her father's death, her mother often stayed in Amache's home.[33] In her article in *The Colorado Magazine*, Mary (Prowers) Hundall described how her early life included many Native American traditions:

> Mother clung to many of the Indian customs and we children learned to like them. . . . Every season mother used to gather prickly pears for sweet pickles. She would burn off the stickers, and cook up the pears in vinegar and sugar. They were delicious. She knew all the prairie herbs and their use by the Indians; she gathered mint to make medicine; sage leaves were dried and steeped into sage-tea which she felt was just good for everything.[34]

In 1993, archaeologists excavated the Prowers home in Boggsville. Dr. Bonnie J. Clark, currently an archaeology professor at the University of Denver, was a student in 1993 and wrote her master's thesis for the University of Denver based on the excavation. In "Amache Ochinee Prowers: The Archaeobiography of a Cheyenne Woman," Clark describes finding glass beads and flaked stone tools, indicating Amache continued wearing and making traditional Cheyenne garments. Just as interesting is Clark's discussion of the orientation of the Prowers' home:

> The orientation of the courtyard at the Boggs house makes sense according to the formal layout of the settlement, an arrangement that can be seen in a historic illustration of Boggsville. . . . It faces south and is thus both warmed by the sun and protected from the wind, which often blows from the west. The Prowers courtyard, on the other hand, conforms to neither the site layout nor environmental factors. . . . Facing east as it does, it is almost always in the shade. Taking into account only the traditions of Hispanic and Anglo architecture, the orientation of the Prowers house makes no sense. But if one factors in Cheyenne practice, it becomes much more legible. . . . The Prowers house, with its east-facing courtyard, actually mirrors a Cheyenne encampment.[35]

Both the Boggs' and the Prowers' homes were tattooed adobe, a common nineteenth-century practice wherein the exterior walls are painted with a block design to make them appear, from a distance, to be built from cut stone.[36] The Friends of Boggsville renovated the home and reproduced the tattooed adobe exterior, along with other features that existed when Amache lived in the home.

Boggsville, located on the Santa Fe Trail, thrived during the time Amache and her family lived there. The town became the county seat when Bent County was established in 1870, and

Figure 1.5. Prowers' home in Boggsville, Colorado, 2020

Courtesy of author J.v.L. Bell's collection

John Prowers was appointed county commissioner. However, in 1873, the Atchison, Topeka and Santa Fe Railway reached the area but bypassed Boggsville. The new town of West Las Animas formed along the railroad tracks two miles north of Boggsville. The Prowers family must have realized that West Las Animas, with its railroad commerce, would soon eclipse Boggsville. In the fall of 1873, they moved both their residence and their store to West Las Animas.

As the 1870s progressed, the Prowers family became one of the most influential and wealthy families in Bent County. Amache was an active member of her church and generous to charities. She also participated in the Eastern Star organization. She often was called upon to host parties. In 1875, John Prowers organized the Bent County Bank, and by 1878, he had signed over the deed of their general mercantile store to Amache. She managed the store, expanding its merchandise to include women's fashions, canned goods, and household items.[37]

John Prowers became ill in early 1884. He traveled to Kansas City for medical advice and died there suddenly on February 14, 1884. Amache was thirty-eight years old, a widow with seven surviving children, and the owner of a vast cattle enterprise that included over forty miles of river frontage with eighty thousand acres of fenced land.[38]

For years after her husband's death, Amache successfully ran both the family cattle business and her store in Las Animas, becoming a respected leader in the Upper Arkansas settlements. On October 26, 1890, she married Daniel Keesee, a local stockman and Colorado pioneer.[39] In her book, *Uncommon Men and the Colorado Prairie,* Nell Propst wrote, "Amache Keesee was a beautiful, refined woman and Boston society talked about her with fascination, but also respect and genuine liking."[40] Despite prejudices against her Cheyenne heritage and the biases of the day, Amache conquered Anglo society, but she never forgot her roots.

Historian Dorothy Boyd interviewed Inez (Prowers) Comstock, Amache's fourth child. During this interview, Inez told the story of a dinner party she remembered when she was twenty, five years after her father's death. Amache's half-brother Little Elk and her cousin White River attended this dinner, and after the meal, they all shared a pipe filled "not with tobacco, but with Kisineck, probably the traditional Southern Cheyenne smoke." Inez described how first Little Elk took three puffs, then passed it to White River, who smoked before passing it to Amache, allowing her to take her turn in the ritual. The pipe was then passed on to others in attendance.[41]

Today, many Coloradans know the name Amache only as a

reminder of a dark time in American history. During World War II, Japanese Americans were forcibly imprisoned in the Granada Relocation Center, in southern Colorado, which unofficially became known as Camp Amache, a legacy Amache would surely have hated.

Figure 1.6. Amache Prowers, circa 1860

Courtesy of History Colorado, Denver, Colorado, Accession #89.451.5827

Amache died February 14, 1905, at age fifty-eight, twenty-one years to the day after John Prowers' death. During her life, Amache was a cultural mediator and a sharp, successful businesswoman as well as a wife and mother. In every role, she balanced her Cheyenne culture and her Anglo life, living as a "woman in between." Her many contributions to Colorado have been largely ignored and often minimized. Dr. Bonnie Clark, an expert on Amache Prowers' life, summarized her forgotten contributions to Colorado when she wrote that Amache's historical role "was often trivialized or even absent entirely from the historical records of her time."[42]

---

[1] Mary Prowers Hudnall, "Early History of Bent County," *Colorado Magazine,* November 1945, 237. In this article Hudnall states Captain Cook of Company E, but a roster for the First Cavalry states Corporal Cook, accessed March, 2023, https://sites.rootsweb.com/~scjssawv/Database/Colorado/1stInfant ryRegiment_Roster.html#COE.

[2] Hudnall, "Bent County," 238.

[3] Wayne Leman, Kovaahe, e-mail correspondence with authors, November 2, 2020. Kovaahe is a Cheyenne language expert and curator of the on-line Cheyenne language website: http://www.cheyennelanguage.org.

[4] National Park Service, US Department of the Interior, *Lone Bear and the Sand Creek Massacre,* http://npshistory.com/bro-chures/sand/lone-bear.pdf. Lone Bear's Cheyenne name also has been spelled Náhkôhno'kaestse in Leman's *Cheyenne Dictionary,* http://www.cheyennelanguage.org.

[5] Spelling of the name is from the *Cheyenne Dictionary,* http://www.cheyennelanguage.org, although the spelling differs depending on the reference.

[6] Christopher Gerboth, ed., *The Tall Chief: The Autobiography of Edward Wynkoop*, Monograph 9, (Denver, CO: Colorado Historical Society, 1994), 87.

[7] George Bird Grinnell, *The Cheyenne Indians: History and Society* (Lincoln, NE: Bison Books, 1972), 1:102-26.

[8] Grinnell, *Cheyenne Indians*, 102-26.

[9] Ava Betz, *A Prowers County History* (Lamar, CO: The Prowers County Historical Society Big Timbers Museum, 1986), 67.

[10] Charles Wesley Hurd, *Boggsville: Cradle of the Colorado Cattle Industry* (Las Animas, CO: Boggsville Committee, 1957), 7.

[11] Charles Wesley Hurd, "Romance of Indian Princess and Pioneer John Prowers Affected State's History," *Sunday Pueblo Chieftain*, Mar. 7, 1948, 1B.

[12] Harriet Sigerman, *Land of Many Hands: Women in the American West* (New York, NY: Oxford University Press, 1997), 201.

[13] Galen Moss, *Pioneer History Society of Bent County* (National Register of Historic Places Inventory—Nomination Form, September 12, 1986), 8.

[14] Hurd, *Boggsville*, 66.

[15] Hudnall, "Bent County," 239. In this article, Mary claims to be the oldest child with Susan younger, but birth dates of both children indicate this is an incorrect recollection.

[16] Bonnie J. Clark, "Amache Ochinee Prowers: The Archaeobiography of a Cheyenne Woman," (MA thesis, University of Denver, 1996), 38.

[17] John Prowers, Letter to Brother and Sister from Fort Lyon, 1863, personal collection of Phillip Petersen of La Junta, CO. Text appears in Clark, "Amache Ochinee Prowers," 38.

[18] Clark, "Amache Ochinee Prowers," 41.

[19] "Proclamation," *Rocky Mountain News* (Denver), Aug. 12, 1864, 2, Colorado Historic Newspapers Collection (website), Colorado State Library, coloradohistoricnewspapers.org.

[20] Gerboth, *Tall Chief*, 86.

[21] Gerboth, *Tall Chief*, 89.

22 "Indian Council," *Rocky Mountain News* (Denver), Sept. 29, 1864, 1, Colorado Historic Newspapers Collection (website), Colorado State Library, coloradohistoricnewspapers.org.

23 Frank H. Murkowski, US Senate Report 105-244, Sand Creek Massacre National Historic Site Preservation Act of 1998, July 11, 1998, 2, https://www.congress.gov/105/crpt/srpt244/CRPT-105srpt244.pdf.

24 Clark, "Amache Ochinee Prowers" 44.

25 "Treaty with the Cheyenne and Arapaho," October 14, 1865, Article 5, https://avalon.law.yale.edu/19th_century/char65.asp#art5. Another reference is Carson Bear's article, "Archaeology Reveals the Hidden History of Amache Ochinee Prowers," (https://savingplaces.org/), Saving Places, National Trust for Historic Preservation, August 15, 2018, https://savingplaces.org/stories/archaeology-reveals-the-hidden-history-of-amache-ochinee-prowers#.X3UMTmhKhEY. This indicates that Amache's mother also received an allocation of land, but the authors were unable to confirm this.

26 Carson Bear, "Archaeology Reveals the Hidden History of Amache Ochinee Prowers," (https://savingplaces.org/), Saving Places, National Trust for Historic Preservation, August 15, 2018, https://savingplaces.org/stories/archaeology-reveals-the-hidden-history-of-amache-ochinee-prowers#.X3UMTmhKhEY.

27 Hudnall, "Bent County," 241.

28 Clark, "Amache Ochinee Prowers," 47.

29 Linda Wommack, *Ranching Women of Colorado*, (Cadwell, ID: Caxton Press, 2019), 11-43.

30 Hudnall, "Bent County," 239.

31 William A. Bell, *New Tracks in North America*, (London, England: Chapman and Hall, 1869) 82-83.

32 Betz, *Prowers County*, 68.

33 Clark, "Amache Ochinee Prowers," 35.

34 Hudnall, "Early History of Bent County," 241.

35 Bonnie J. Clark, "Understanding Amache: The Archaeobiography of a Victorian-era Cheyenne Woman," *The Colorado Magazine*, Spring 2021, 16.

[36] Clark, "Understanding Amache," 15.

[37] Linda Wommack, *Ranching Women of Colorado: 17 Legendary Ladies*, (Caldwell, Idaho: Caxton, 2019), 62.

[38] Charles W. Bowman, *The History of the Arkansas Valley, Colorado*, (Chicago, IL: O.L. Baskin & Co., 1881), 880.

[39] "Death of Mrs. Daniel Keesee," *The Lamar Register*, Feb. 22, 1905. 1. The article appeared originally in *Las Animas Leader*, Feb. 17, 1905, 4. Her first name was misspelled Amanche.

[40] Nell Propst, *Uncommon Men and the Colorado Prairie*, (Caldwell, ID: Caxton, 1992), 58.

[41] Clark, "Amache Ochinee Prowers," 77.

[42] Bear, "Archaeology" (https://savingplaces.org/).

Figure 2.1. Mary Cozens, circa 1860-1864, (date based on hair and clothing fashion)

Courtesy of Denver Public Library, Caroline Brancroft papers, WH 1089

Mary Cozens:
Irish Orphan

Arrived in Colorado, May 10, 1859

Born in England but reared in Ireland, Mary Cozens' heart always belonged to Ireland. She immigrated with her family to Canada where—at just twelve years of age—she was orphaned in a strange land without friends or family. She worked as a house servant until presented with the opportunity to join the Pikes Peak Gold Rush. After narrowly escaping being sold into prostitution, Mary arrived in the area of present-day Central City, Colorado. There she met a tall, good-looking deputy sheriff, and her luck took a turn for the better. They married in 1860. Eventually, Mary and her husband established a ranch and stage stop across the Great Divide near the present-day town of Fraser and helped bring Anglo civilization to the wilderness of the high mountain valley.[1]

On the grounds of Windsor Castle, James York and Elizabeth (Cane) York welcomed the birth of their daughter, Mary, on March 17, Saint Patrick's Day, 1830.[2] James and Elizabeth, natives of Ireland, probably thought the day honoring their country's patron saint auspicious for their child's birth. James had a promising future as a gardener at the castle, but Elizabeth hated living in a nation that treated her countrymen poorly and, even more upsetting to her, frowned on Catholicism.[3]

The Yorks returned to Ireland where Mary was reared to be a devout Catholic and a hard worker. Mary's younger brother was born some time before the Yorks decided to immigrate to Canada.[4] Many Irish emigrants chose Canada as their destination, because the passage was less costly than to the United States. Mary's father died en route, likely of cholera, smallpox, or typhus, which ran rampant in the crowded steerage of the ships during the six-week voyage. Mary's mother died three months after they disembarked. It is unclear whether a Catholic orphanage took in Mary's brother or whether a family adopted him, but he survived and later lived in New York.[5]

Left adrift in a foreign country at the age of twelve, with no family or friends and little education, Mary found work as a domestic servant. Although the job paid little, it provided shelter and sustenance. Eventually, she worked her way to New York, and then to Baltimore, where she served a couple named McGee. In 1859, the McGees joined the Pikes Peak Gold Rush and offered Mary continued employment if she accompanied them on their journey westward. The McGees were more considerate than others she had worked for, so she joined them for the opportunity to improve her lot.[6]

She found the early portion of the journey to the goldfields agreeable. However, after they reached isolated country, she overheard the McGees arguing and learned that Mr. McGee intended to rape her and rent her out as a prostitute after they reached the mining camps. She prayed for a means of escape while fending off McGee's escalating advances. Desperate, on the pretense of going to fetch water, she walked away from camp to a deep spot on the Platte River. There, her devout Catholic conscience battled between the choices of life as a de-flowered woman or the mortal sin of suicide.

While praying for an answer to her dilemma, she spotted a man in the willows farther down the river. She ran to him and explained her plight. The man introduced himself as William Green Russell and offered her safe passage to Denver City with his gold-prospecting party.[7] That answer to her prayers, under such dire circumstances, reinforced her already strong faith and set her life's path.

Mary soon learned that Russell was the Georgia miner whose 1858 party's discovery of paying quantities of gold on Little Dry Creek, a tributary of the South Platte River, had spurred the Pikes Peak Gold Rush.[8] Russell had wintered in the East and was on his return trip to the goldfields with a large contingent of men and supplies when Mary came upon him at the river. He told her she could pay for her passage by cooking and doing laundry for himself and some of his men.[9]

Mary and the Russell party arrived in Denver City on May 10, 1859. She chose to continue with the group as they headed into the mountains to prospect. News of John Gregory's discovery of lode gold thirty-four miles west of Denver City soon set Russell's course in that direction. Finding steep and narrow Gregory Gulch swarming with miners, Russell explored nearby areas. On the first of June, Russell and his companions staked claims in a gulch parallel, but south of Gregory's, which soon came to be called Russell Gulch.[10]

Earlier historians disagree about whether Mary York

arrived in the region in 1859 or 1860, but a stock certificate dated December 20, 1889, designates Miss Mary York as owner of one share in the New York Tunneling Company in the Nevada District (one and a half miles southwest of Central City). This documents Mary's presence in the vicinity in 1859.[11]

During the summer of 1859, Mary cooked and did the laundry for some of the Russell party, and they paid her in gold. With the advent of autumn and the first snowfall, Russell packed up to return to Georgia and advised Mary to avoid the harsh mountain winter and find work in Denver.[12]

Instead, Mary moved into an empty cabin in the more populous Mountain City, thus establishing her reputation as the first White woman to settle permanently in what became known as "the richest square mile on earth." Mountain City lay between the present-day towns of Black Hawk and Central City in Gregory Gulch. Horace Greeley, editor of the *New York Tribune*, visited the gulch in the summer of 1859 and described it as "resembling the rungs on a ladder, with one town above the other, so close together that differentiating between them is difficult."[13]

In her cabin, Mary served meals to the miners and laundered their clothes. Work, along with prayer, occupied her early days in Mountain City. She probably attended the first Catholic mass in the district when Father Joseph P. Machebeuf, later bishop of the Denver diocese, visited in the fall of 1860. About two hundred worshippers attended that first service in Sons of Malta Hall. On future visits, Father Machebeuf celebrated mass wherever he could find space, but usually at Hadley Hall, a log building with an upper story that offered the largest gathering space in the area.[14]

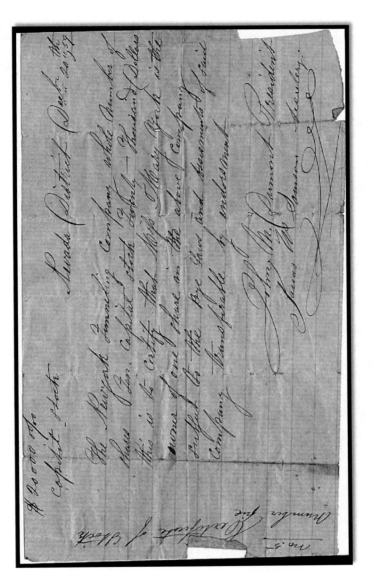

Figure 2.2. Stock certificate of Mary York dated December 20, 1859

Courtesy of History Colorado, Denver, Colorado, William Z. Cozens Collection, Accession MSS 166-FF 18

William Zane Cozens Jr., called "Billy" by friends, began buying his meals at Mary's cabin. He was deputy sheriff of the Gregory mining district and was also a bartender at the saloon owned by Jack Kehler. He was born on July 2, 1830, to William Zane Cozens and Marietta Cozens in L'Orignal,

Upper Canada (later Ontario). In his late teens, he learned the carpenter trade in the northeastern United States. In March 1859, he was plying his trade in Saint Louis and, upon hearing of gold discoveries in the Pikes Peak region, he joined the rush to the Rockies and arrived in Mountain City in June 1859.[15]

Mary and Billy's budding romantic relationship exemplified the adage that opposites attract. Mary was a shy, devout Catholic, and she stood just five feet tall. Gregarious, six-foot-one-inch Billy was a dedicated Mason.[16] Both held strong beliefs. A successful match between a Catholic and a Mason seems at odds because—for centuries—the Catholic Church has banned Masons from receiving Holy Communion, maintaining that their naturalistic faith practices are contrary to the Catholic faith.[17]

Father Machebeuf officiated at Mary and Billy's wedding on December 30, 1860, in Mountain City. Theirs was the first marriage in the mining district and the first performed by Father Machebeuf in what would become northern Colorado.[18]

After their wedding, Billy and Mary probably lived in Mary's cabin. During 1861, their first full year of marriage, Father Machebeuf repeatedly exhorted his parishioners to contribute to a collection to acquire a semi-permanent place of worship. Mary and Billy assisted the priest in procuring a two-story frame house on Pine Street that the church remodeled into a place of worship and priest's residence. Saint Mary of the Assumption Catholic Church now sits on that site.[19]

During that year, Billy first served as sheriff, and then, after losing an election, as deputy sheriff, an occupation made more challenging by the town's rowdiest inhabitants who perpetrated "217 fist fights, 97 revolver fights, 11 Bowie knife fights and one dog fight."[20] The lack of a jail added to the

Figure 2.3. William Zane Cozens, circa 1859

Courtesy of History Colorado, Denver, Colorado, Accession #F-26, 701

difficulty of Billy's job.

The Colorado Territory designated Central City as the county seat of the newly formed Gilpin County on November 1, 1861. In response to the county's need for a courthouse, Billy submitted building plans that received swift approval. In February 1862, he completed the jail on the first floor of the hand-hewn, square-log building that eventually housed both jail and county clerk's office. Billy retained ownership of the building and rented it to the county for thirty-five dollars a month. In March, the county appointed him jailer with an annual salary of $600.[21] This gave the Cozenses a steady income.

Mary gave birth to their first child, William Zane Cozens III, on May 18, 1862.[22] The following year, Billy built a new home for his growing family on land he owned behind the courthouse. The house faced East First High Street. On November 15,1864, Mary and Billy welcomed the birth of their daughter, Mary Elizabeth.[23]

In September 1863, Gilpin County elected Billy sheriff. He concurrently served as a deputy United States marshal. He gained a reputation for being fearless, for he believed in justice and stood his ground, no matter the circumstances. That trait probably left Mary praying for his safe return home each evening. In January 1864, Billy single-handedly faced off an angry vigilante mob threatening a murder suspect and brought the man to trial. After the jury found the culprit guilty, Billy conducted the first legal execution in the region.[24] In all his years of law enforcement, Billy never shot a man. As writer Harry E. Chatfield so aptly put it: "He conquered by the sheer force of his indomitable will every desperado and outlaw within his jurisdiction."[25]

Despite his ability to single-handedly subdue criminals and stave off an angry vigilante mob, family stories say Billy was "rather henpecked by his little Irish wife."[26] Mayme Sturm, a neighbor of the Cozens family, wrote similarly of Mary: "This small woman ruled her stalwart husband and children with an iron hand. Her will was law."[27]

Beginning in January 1865, Mary spent several months alone caring for her two young children while Billy served as captain of Company C with the Colorado Volunteers stationed at Lillian Springs in northeastern Colorado. In retaliation for the Sand Creek Massacre, the Plains Indians had cut off communication, freight transport, and travel between the Colorado Territory and the East. Billy's company provided safe passage for the mail, wagon trains, and stagecoaches between stops on the Overland Trail.[28]

In the spring of 1865, Billy resumed his position as sheriff of Gilpin County and was re-elected the following year.[29] Mary gave birth to their third child, Sarah Agnes, on November 22, 1866.[30]

Central City's economy slowed after placer mining played out. Hard-rock mining proved unprofitable due to the difficulty of extraction combined with the expense of transporting ore a long distance to be processed. Billy sold the jail to Gilpin County for $10,000 in 1868, and the family traveled to the East that spring. By April of the following year, they were back in Central City where Billy served as the town's marshal after he lost the election for sheriff.[31] While the Cozenses were in the East, Nathaniel P. Hill built a smelter at Black Hawk that made the separation of gold from sulfide ores profitable and stimulated Gilpin County's economy.

Around the time of their return to Central City, the Cozens family moved to the new home Billy built on a north hill overlooking the town. In 1870, Mary gave birth to their second son, tiny Alexis. The Cozenses carried Alexis on a pillow during his less than one year of life. He, along with an unnamed daughter, are buried in Central City's Masonic Cemetery. In the 1900 United States Census, Mary stated she had given birth to six children, three of whom lived to adulthood.[32]

While the Cozens family grew, Central City developed from a booming mining camp of tents and log cabins to a settled community of frame buildings peppered here and there with stone or brick structures. By the early 1870s, the town boasted churches, fraternal lodges, professional offices, stores, a school, and a newspaper. It attracted theatrical performances by such acclaimed troupes as that of Jack Langrishe. Even the red-light district took a more subdued tone.[33]

In 1872, the Teller House, an elegant, four-story brick hotel, opened with an opulent inaugural ball and supper. Of more interest to Mary, that same year, Joseph Machebeuf, by then a bishop, laid the cornerstone for a magnificent, double-spired Catholic church.[34]

It was also in 1872 that Mary's family ventured west across the Continental Divide and vacationed in Middle Park. (*Park* is a geographic term referring to a large, flat, mountain valley with few trees. Colorado has three such areas: South, Middle, and North Parks.) They found the isolated and peaceful location near the headwaters of the Fraser River idyllic.

Billy and their son, Will, enjoyed hunting plentiful wild game and fishing in the trout-filled stream. Billy purchased squatter's rights to land on the west side of the river called "The Haystacks" and successfully filed for preemption. (Under the Preemption Act of 1841, a squatter on federal land could purchase up to 160 acres very cheaply if certain requirements were met.) The land's nickname came from the two rotting haystacks left behind by the previous owner, who intended it to be a hay ranch.[35]

Figure 2.4. Saint Aloysius School (top) and partially constructed, roofed-over Saint Mary of the Assumption Church (right), Central City, circa 1879-1900

Courtesy of Denver Public Library Special Collections, X-2801

After the purchase of the Middle Park land, the Cozenses continued to live in Central City. Billy served in law enforcement as a deputy United States marshal, and in April 1874, he became the city marshal.[36] Although only semi-literate herself, Mary saw that her children received both an academic and a religious education. Will boarded at the Jesuits' school in Saint Marys, Kansas. Mary Elizabeth and Sarah attended Saint Aloysius Select and Boarding School built on Gunnell Hill in Central City by the Sisters of Charity of Leavenworth.[37]

A fire in January of 1873 consumed sixteen Central City buildings but proved only a prelude to the great fire of May 21, 1874, which destroyed about 150 structures. The courthouse that Billy had built and the Teller House survived.[38] The Catholic church's wooden structures did not. Mary, along with the other parishioners, resorted to worshipping in the roofed-over, partially-built new church. Its construction had been halted due to financial difficulties, but it boasted a life-size statue of Saint Patrick, the patron saint of Mary's beloved Ireland. Central City's Irish miners donated the statue and called the church Saint Patrick's Cathedral in an attempt to sway Bishop Machebeuf to that name, instead of Saint Mary of the Assumption, but the bishop remained firm.[39] Central City quickly rebuilt most of its buildings, this time in stone and brick.

In 1874, the same year as the fire, Billy began constructing a one-and-a-half-story ranch house on his Middle Park land just east of the Georgetown, Empire, and Middle Park Wagon Road, then under construction. He built the dwelling using six-inch, adze-hewn log planking covered with board-and-batten siding. A roofed porch with majestic mountain views spanned the front of the home and later was a favorite resting spot for Mary and Billy. The house consisted of a parlor, sitting room, kitchen, and dining room on the first floor and six windowless sleeping rooms on the second floor. The sleeping rooms received daylight through transoms above the doors that opened onto a window-lit central hall.[40]

Thought to be the first to establish a homestead in the Fraser Valley, the Cozens family probably moved into their Middle Park ranch house in 1875.[41] Father William J. Howlett, who did not visit northwestern Colorado until five years after the Cozenses settled there, wrote of the region and its people: "Cut off by mountain ranges from railroads and markets, it has been left to herds of cattle and a few venturesome spirits who cared to brave solitude and privation."[42]

Mary and Billy, both forty-five, still possessed their pioneering spirit to leave behind their life in Central City, a town they had helped grow from a rough mining camp into one of the Colorado Territory's largest and most culturally developed cities. When they moved to the isolated wilderness along the Fraser River to take up an entirely different way of life, their three children ranged in age from nine to thirteen. They cleared land for pasture, and Billy built a barn to house workhorses, riding horses, and milk cows.

In 1876, Billy secured the appointment as Fraser's first post-master. His was the only post office between Empire and Hot Sulphur Springs.[43]

Travelers, freighters, and new settlers coming to or returning from Denver or Georgetown over the newly-constructed Berthoud Pass road found the Cozens' ranch a congenial stopping place. Billy's knack for entertaining conversation and Mary's good cooking provided a welcome respite before or after the arduous trip over the steep, switchback wagon road that climbed above eleven thousand feet.

By July 1876, the Cozens' ranch served as a stage stop on the Colorado Stage Company's route between Georgetown and Hot Sulphur Springs. Mary cooked and served the passengers' noon meal, which often featured trout or game. Travelers began stopping at the ranch, whether they came by stage, with the mail, or on their own, and some chose to stay overnight or longer. Women visitors slept in the upstairs bedrooms of the main house, and men were accommodated in the barn's hayloft. Billy added a stage stop building with a new kitchen behind the ranch house and a few years later, he built a post office addition that connected the main house to the stage stop building.[44]

The ranch grew along with its popularity. Billy added a blacksmith shop and another barn to house horses for the stagecoaches and guests. Hunters, fishermen, and vacationers came for weeks at a time, and some spent the whole summer. The Cozenses hired ranch hands and kitchen help. Billy homesteaded adjoining land, built more dwellings to house guests, and eventually developed the ranch into a seven-hundred-acre forerunner of today's dude ranches.

In 1885, *Crofutt's Grip-Sack Guide of Colorado* recommended the ranch to travelers by saying, "Frazer is commonly called 'Cozzens Hotel,' where are provided the best accommodations for tourists in the Park. The hunting and fishing in the vicinity are *par excellence*."[45] The same year, a lady guest at the ranch wrote of her "snug little room," and that the Cozenses were "evidently well to do people; pictures of saints on the walls and books about."[46]

As the Cozens children grew up, they took on some of the chores of running the ranch and stage stop. In 1887, at the age of twenty-two, the oldest daughter, Mary Elizabeth, started a diary she titled "Diary of Fraser haps and mishaps." For a ten-month period, she chronicled bits of the family's daily life. She lamented the toll that the ranch and stage stop exacted on her fifty-seven-year-old parents: "I hope . . . poor father & mother may get a rest this hard work begins to be terrifying — I dread it yet want it because it is our only way of getting a living."[47]

Billy and Will cared for the livestock, farmed, kept up the ranch buildings, hunted, and fished. The women's work, beyond keeping their home running smoothly, revolved around the stage stop/hotel. They cooked and served meals at regular hours, but guests also requested and received meals at unscheduled times, from breakfast before sunrise to supper as late as ten o'clock. The mail carrier often arrived late at night, sometimes with passengers who needed to be fed and bedded down.

The women's chores were not unlike those of other women of the time, but on a larger scale. They cooked more meals per day, cleaned multiple dwellings, hauled more buckets of water from the pump, did a larger volume of linen laundry and ironing, and churned more butter. Their tasks were not confined to indoors. Mary cared for a large flock of chickens, for her daughter's diary notes that "Mama has twenty-seven dozen eggs."[48] Twelve days later, a diary entry records that Mary sought to increase her flock when she set a hen by giving it fertilized eggs to hatch. Daughter Mary Elizabeth also brought beauty to the ranch with her twenty-five hundred-square-foot flower garden, which abounded with a plethora of varieties.[49]

The men and women combined their efforts on some projects. The Cozenses produced potatoes beyond their needs and sold the excess. The men cultivated the large potato field, and daughter Sarah joined them in the harvest. Mary and Billy shared the work of salting and packing a pig.[50]

Winter weather made the family's work more challenging. Fraser, known in modern times as the "icebox of the nation," often records temperatures well below zero degrees Fahrenheit, and Mary Elizabeth noted several days that were in the minus-forties. In December of 1887, she commented, "Cold cloudy & stormy . . . hanging out the clothes is rather a severe penance now a days."[51]

Despite their long workdays on the ranch, the Cozens men found time to contribute to their community. Grand County appointed Billy commissioner and, in 1877, residents elected Will justice of the peace.[52]

After the Cozenses moved to Fraser, Mary yearned for a place to worship and a place where her children could learn her Catholic faith. The nearest Catholic church, Georgetown's Our Lady of Lourdes, stood thirty-five miles away on the far side of treacherous Berthoud Pass, more than eight-hours' travel by horse. After Billy built the new kitchen in the stage-stop addition, Mary met the challenge by transforming her former kitchen into a family chapel with an altar.[53] In the little chapel, Mary and her children prayed and observed the church's holy days. Eventually, the family set up a larger chapel on the main floor of the unused water pump tower, and on the rare occasions when a traveling priest stopped to celebrate mass and hear confessions, they invited Catholics in the area to attend.[54]

Mary successfully reared her children to be devout Catholics. In his article, "A Villa Is Born," Father B. J. Murray wrote of Mary, "Her religious instruction to her family was manifested by the depth of faith imbedded in her children."[55] They not only worshipped and conscientiously observed all the holy days and months, but also reached out from their isolation by regularly corresponding with priests and nuns.

No doubt a deep disappointment to Mary, Billy never converted to Catholicism, but she did not allow it to harm their close relationship.[56] Their daughter noted in her diary that, despite their work-laden life, her papa took her mama for a ride on several occasions and that her parents made an overnight visit to their friends, the Byers family, in Hot Sulphur Springs.

Many people might boast of having been born on the grounds of Windsor Castle, but Mary, like her mother, disliked the English for their disparagement of the Irish—especially Irish Catholics. Throughout her life, she preferred to highlight her Irish upbringing. Ireland was listed as her country of birth on three United States Censuses.[57] On Saint Patrick's Day, 1888, her fifty-eighth birthday, she proudly wore a shamrock, but whether she meant it as an emblem of Ireland or a symbol of the Holy Trinity, or both, is unclear.[58]

In the summer of 1902, a broken wagon wheel proved fortuitous for both the Cozens family and the Jesuit priests from Denver's Sacred Heart College. The clergymen were

Figure 2.5. Cozens Ranch House, post office, and stage stop, Fraser, Colorado, circa 1900

Courtesy of History Colorado, Denver, Colorado,
Accession #PH.PROP.1804

returning from a summer of mountain camping when a wheel on their covered wagon broke, delaying their start over Berthoud Pass. They asked and received Billy's permission to camp in the ranch yard overnight. The next morning, perhaps with a bit of nudging from Mary, Billy invited the priests to set up camp for a few more days on his land across the river. By the time they departed the ranch, they had received an invitation to return the following year for the entire summer, which they did. Thereafter, the Jesuits summered each year on the Cozens' land, and the family enjoyed celebrating mass during the priests' stays.[59]

Mary lost her husband of forty-three years on January 17, 1904, when Billy succumbed to kidney and heart failure. At least ten mourners from Hot Sulphur Springs braved the icy cold to travel to his funeral. After Billy's death, Mary obtained a papal indulgence (a remission of sin granted by the Catholic church) in an effort to save her husband's non-Catholic soul.[60]

A neighbor took over Billy's postmaster position, and the Cozens family vacated the stage stop business, made obsolete by the arrival of the railroad in Middle Park. Will continued the ranch operations, although the family reduced the size of their property by selling several parcels of land.[61]

In 1905 the eighty-acre plot of land on which the Catholic clergy had summered was sold to the Jesuit priests from Sacred Heart College, the forerunner of today's Regis University. A survey prior to the sale did not include the family cemetery where Billy was buried. Mary insisted the cemetery be included before the sale could be finalized. She also stipulated that if the priests ever sold the land, they would transfer the bodies buried there to Denver's Catholic cemetery.[62]

The Jesuits christened their new land Maryvale and set the name in white stones on the bluff overlooking the Cozens' burial plot. In 1908 they constructed a building that housed a chapel, recreation room, dining hall, kitchen, and sleeping quarters for the priests' comfort on their summer retreats.[63]

Late in life, Mary suffered from senility and paralysis. According to the *Middle Park Times* and *The Gilpin Observer*, Mary suffered a bad fall in her home and passed away on November 15, 1909, at the age of seventy-nine. It is unknown why her headstone records her death as March 15, 1909. Father Meyers came from Kremmling to officiate at her funeral in the ranch house.[64]

The Cozens offspring continued to live in the ranch house, and none of the three married. Sarah Agnes died August 8, 1923.[65] The following year, Mary Elizabeth and Will carried out the pledge they had made to their mother to give the ranch—all the remaining four-hundred acres and the house— to Regis College and High School. They wrote to the president of Regis College that "it has long been the wish of our family that our property here, known as the Cozens Ranch, be turned over to Regis College for the use of the Jesuit Fathers, who have been our most kind friends for many years."[66]

Four years later, on December 8, 1928, Mary Elizabeth died of pneumonia at the ranch house.[67] She had requested that after her death, the Jesuit priests watch over her brother, Will, who fought alcoholism. Will spent his remaining years living with the priests at Regis College and summered with them at the ranch. He died in Denver on October 30, 1937.[68]

Mary would have been pleased to know that the Jesuits turned the ranch house into a chapel that served the community from 1955 to 1980. The number of worshippers increased with the growth of the nearby ski-resort of Winter Park until they overflowed the little ranch-house chapel. Services were temporarily held in a movie theater until construction of today's Saint Bernard of Montjoux Church could be completed. Regis University donated land that had been part of the Cozens' ranch to the Archdiocese of Denver for the site of the new church.[69]

Long after Mary's death, it appeared her request for her family to remain buried on church property would not be honored. In September 1987, the Jesuits deeded the ranch house and the small plot of land on which it stands to the town of Fraser, which turned it over to the Grand County Historical Association.[70] That organization had the site placed on the National Register of Historic Places in 1988, and the association later opened the ranch house as a museum. The land transfer to the historical association included the Cozens' cemetery, which meant the graves were no longer on church grounds. Nearby Saint Bernard Catholic Church, however, expressed interest in preserving the cemetery. The historical association agreed to turn it over to the church,[71] and as Mary desired, her family's remains once again rest on church grounds.

In the 1990s, in order to pay for improvements on the Denver campus of Regis University, the Jesuits sold the remainder of the ranch land to a development company. The majority of the former Cozens ranch is now a large residential subdivision.[72]

The Cozenses played a significant part in developing two regions of Colorado. While Billy brought law and order to the booming mining camp of Central City, Mary, the first White woman brave enough to establish permanent residence there, lent her influence to initiate the long process of developing the mining district into a stable town. Her support contributed to the acquisition of a building for the area's first Catholic church, the forerunner of today's Saint Mary of the Assumption Church.

As one of the first homesteading families in Middle Park,

Figure 2.6. Mary and Billy Cozens on their ranch house porch, circa 1900

Courtesy of History Colorado, Denver, Colorado, Accession #47.4. E#11. D#1

the Cozens' impact in that region was even more significant. The post office and stage stop facilitated new settlers and tourists coming into the region, as well as the transport of goods and services to and from Middle Park. Mary offered the first opportunity for Catholic worship in the Fraser Valley. The gift of the ranch to the Jesuits ensured their continued service to the community, and, ultimately, contributed to improvements to Denver's Regis University campus and the building of Saint Bernard of Montjoux Church. Mary Cozens, who came to the raw Pikes Peak region without family, armed only with her strong Irish Catholic faith and her willingness to work hard, forged a substantial legacy in Colorado.

---

[1] Mayme G. Sturm, "Mary York (Cozens), Pioneer Woman in Gregory Diggings," *Colorado Magazine*, May 1945, 107-111. Sturm, a neighbor of the Cozenses in later years, based her article on information told to her by Mary Cozens' adult children.

[2] B.J. Murray, SJ, "A Villa Is Born," *Woodstock Letters* 83, no. 1 (February 1, 1954): 73-74, jesuitonlinelibrary.edu.; and see Sturm, "Mary York (Cozens)," 107.

[3] Sturm, "Mary York (Cozens)," 107.

[4] Sturm, "Mary York (Cozens)," 107-8.

[5] Sturm, "Mary York (Cozens)," 108.

[6] Sturm, "Mary York (Cozens)," 108.

[7] Caroline Bancroft, *Gulch of Gold: A History of Central City, Colorado* (Boulder, CO: Johnson Books, 2003), 46-47; and see Sturm, "Mary York (Cozens)," 109.

[8] Agnes Wright Spring, "Rush to the Rockies, 1859," *Colorado Magazine*, Apr. 1959, 89.

[9] Bancroft, *Gulch of Gold*, 47.

[10] Spring, "Rush," 115.

[11] Stock Certificate, Mary York, 12/20/1859, William Z. Cozens Collection No. 166, FF 18, History Colorado, Denver, CO. Historians disagree as to whether Mary traveled to the gold fields

in 1859 and that it was William Green Russell who rescued her at the river, or if she did not come until 1860, and that it may have been John Gregory who rescued her on his return trip to the diggings. Sturm promulgated the Gregory story (Sturm, "Mary York (Cozens)," 109). Bancroft (*Gulch*, 47) held to the Russell version she had learned from old Central City miners, even after she interviewed Sturm. Bancroft wrote of Sturm's article: "The account contained several bad historical errors but much authentic material" (Bancroft, *Gulch*, xv). Thomas J. Steele, SJ, in his essay "The Cozens Family," in *Fraser Haps and Mishaps: The Diary of Mary E. Cozens*, sided with the Gregory theory. He cited a newspaper article that announced Gregory's arrival in Denver on March 4, 1860, in a party of seventeen men and one woman. Steele theorized that woman was Mary York. However, the party brought eighteen horses, which could indicate the woman in the party made the whole journey with the party and was not picked up along the way. See "Emigrant Arrivals," *Rocky Mountain News Weekly* (Denver, CO), Mar. 7, 1860, 2, Colorado Historic Newspapers Collection (website), Colorado State Library, coloradohistoricnewspapers.org.) Mary's 1859 stock certificate tips the scales in favor of the Russell theory.

[12] Bancroft, *Gulch*, 47-48, 56.

[13] Robert L. Brown, *Central City and Gilpin County* (Caldwell, ID: Caxton, 1994), 74.

[14] The Rev. W. J. Howlett, *Life of the Right Reverend Joseph P. Machebeuf, D.D.* (Pueblo, CO: Franklin, 1908), 291-2.

[15] Capt. James Burrell, "Capt. William Z. Cozens," Biographical Sketches, Gilpin County," *History of Clear Creek and Boulder Valleys, Colorado* (Chicago: O. L. Baskin & Co., 1880), 446-47; and see 1850 US Census, Russell, Saint Lawrence, NY, digital image s.v. "William Cozens," Ancestry.com.

[16] Thomas J. Steele, SJ. "The Cozens Family," in Alice Reich and Thomas J. Steele, SJ., eds., *Fraser Haps and Mishaps: The Diary of Mary E. Cozens,* (Denver, CO: Regis College Press, 1990), 14; see also Discharge Paper, First Regiment Mounted Militia, Co. C, Wm.

Z. Cozens, April 29, 1865, William Z. Cozens Collection No.166, FF 9, History Colorado, Denver, CO.

[17] Father David Endres, "Question of Faith: Catholic Masons?," *Catholic Telegraph*, Feb. 27, 2020, https://www.thecatholictele-graph.com/question-of-faith-catholic-masons/63875; and see David V. Barrett, "Why Can't We Be Freemasons?," *Catholic Herald*, Nov. 9, 2017, https://catholicherald.co.uk/why-cant-we-be-freemasons/.

[18] Marriage Certificate of William Z. Cozens and Mary York, Colorado Subject Collection: Biographical Files, Box 17, William Z. Cozens folder, History Colorado, Denver, CO; and see Howlett, *Machebeuf*, 291.

[19] Howlett, *Machebeuf*, 296-7; and see Thomas J. Noel, *Colorado Catholicism and the Archdiocese of Denver 1857-1989* (Boulder, CO: University Press of Colorado, 1989), 301-2.

[20] Burrell, "Cozens", 447; and see "History of Central City," Gilpin Historical Society (website) https://www.gilpinhistory.org;central-city.

[21] "The Story of Washington Hall," Gilpin Historical Society (website), https://www.gilpinhistory.org/story-of-washington-hall; and see Gilpin County Arts Association (website), https://www.gilpinarts.org>history.

[22] Sturm, "Mary York (Cozens)," 113.

[23] Sturm, "Mary York (Cozens)," 113.

[24] "Wm. Cozens Was Fearless Early Day Peace Officer," *Steamboat Pilot* (Steamboat Springs, CO), Apr. 8, 1932, 2, Colorado Historic Newspapers Collection (website), Colorado State Library, coloradohistoricnewspapers.org; and see Frank Hall, "Death of W. Z. Cozens," *Gilpin Observer*, Jan. 21, 1904, 8, Colorado Historic Newspapers Collection (website), Colorado State Library, coloradohistoricnewspapers.org.

[25] Harry E. Chatfield, "Forgotten Sheriff," *The West*, no date, Grand County Historical Association archives.

[26] Roger W. Cozens to Sid Squibb, Nov. 8, 1979, Grand County Historical Association archives.

[27] Sturm, "Mary York (Cozens)," 111.

[28] Discharge Paper, First Regiment Mounted Militia, Co. C, William Z. Cozens Collection No. 166, FF 9, History Colorado, Denver, CO; and see "Wm. Cozens Was Fearless Early Day Peace Officer," 2.

[29] "Gilpin County Officers," *Rocky Mountain News* (Denver, CO), June 1, 1866, 1, Colorado Historic Newspapers Collection (website), Colorado State Library, coloradohistoricnewspapers.org.

[30] Sturm, "Mary York (Cozens)," 113.

[31] Gilpin Historical Society, "Washington Hall"; and see Burrell, "Cozens," 447; and "Election Notice," *Daily Central City Register*, Aug. 7, 1869, 1, Colorado Historic Newspapers Collection (website), Colorado State Library, coloradohistoricnewspapers.org. See also "Gilpin County Election," *Daily Colorado Miner* (Georgetown, CO), Sept. 15, 1869, 4, Colorado Historic Newspapers Collection (website), Colorado State Library, coloradohistoricnewspapers.org.

[32] Sturm, "Mary York (Cozens)," 110; and Aaron Storms, "Turning Back the Pages: 30 Years Ago-July 29, 1988," *Weekly Register Call* (Central City, CO), July 26, 2018, https://www.weeklyregister-call.com/2018/07/26/turning-back-the-pages-250/. See also Find a Grave (database and images), s.v. "Alexis Cozens," findagrave.com; and see 1900 US Census, Grand Lake, Grand, CO, digital image s.v. "Mary Cozens," Ancestry.com.

[33] Duane A. Smith, *Henry M. Teller: Colorado's Grand Old Man* (Boulder, CO: University Press of Colorado, 2002), 11-12, 24.

[34] Noel, *Colorado Catholicism*, 301.

[35] Sturm, "Mary York (Cozens)," 110; and Heather King Peterson, "Colorado Stagecoach Stations" (MA thesis, CU at Denver, 2002), 176, digital.auraria.edu/AA00004960/00001/190x.

[36] Burrell, "Cozens" 447; and Steele, "Cozens Family," 15.

[37] William Z. Cozens, III to Mary E. Cozens, letter 1873, Wm. Z. Cozens Collection No. 166, FF 2; and see Sturm, "Mary York (Cozens)" 112; and Steele, "Cozens Family," 15.

[38] Brown, *Central City*, 135-6; and see Encyclopedia Staff, "Central City-Black Hawk Historic District," *Colorado Encyclopedia*

(website), last modified August 14, 2022,
https://coloradoencyclopedia.org/article/central-
city%E2%80%93black-hawk-historic-district.

[39] Noel, *Colorado Catholicism*, 302.

[40] Regina M. Black, "Cozens Ranch House," National Park
Service, National Register of Historic Places Registration Form,
May 10, 1988, sec. 7, 1-3,
https://catalog.archives.gov/id/84130595#.XoEhiZ3yWEO.link.

[41] "*Cozens Ranch House: Restoration/Museum*," (Fraser, CO: Grand
County Historical Association, no date), 1; and see Teri Maddox,
"Cozens Ranch House Is Spared," *Sky-Hi News* (Granby, CO),
Apr. 17, 1986, 5, Grand County Historical Association clippings
file.

[42] Noel, *Colorado Catholicism*, 424.

[43] Appointments of U.S. Postmasters, 1832-1971, digital image
s.v. "Wm. Z. Cozens," Ancestry.com; and see *Colorado Encyclopedia*
Staff, "Cozens Ranch," *Colorado Encyclopedia* (website), last modified December 30, 2020, https://coloradoencyclopedia.org/arti-
cle/cozens-ranch.

[44] Peterson, "Stagecoach Stations," 173; and see Black, "Cozens
Ranch House," sec. 7, 2-3; see also "Cozens Ranch House: Restora-
tion/Museum," 1.

[45] George A. Crofutt, *Crofutt's Grip-Sack Guide of Colorado: A
Complete Encyclopedia of the State, Vol. II – 1885* (Omaha, NE:
Overland Publishing, 1885, 94,
https://catalog.hathitrust.org/Record/012239803.

[46] "Pioneering Near Steamboat Springs—1885-1886," *Colorado
Magazine* Apr. 1951, 85.

[47] Reich and Steele, *Haps*, 72.

[48] Reich and Steele, *Haps*, 58.

[49] Reich and Steele, *Haps*, 27, note #9, 78-79.

[50] Reich and Steele, *Haps*, 38, 40.

[51] Reich and Steele, *Haps*, 40.

[52] *Ouray Times* (Ouray, CO), July 28, 1877, 3, Colorado Historic
Newspapers Collection (website), Colorado State Library,

coloradohistoricnewspapers.org; see also Reich and Steele, *Haps,* 33.

[53] Black, "Cozens Ranch House," sec. 7, 2.

[54] Sturm, "Mary York (Cozens)," 112.

[55] Murray, "Villa," 75.

[56] Reich and Steele, *Haps,* 43; and see Murray, "Villa," 75.

[57] Sturm, "Mary York (Cozens)," 108; and also 1870 US Census, Central City, Gilpin, Colorado Territory, digital image s.v. "Mary Cozzens," Ancestry.com; and see 1880 US Census, Frazier, Grand, CO, digital image s.v. "W. Z. Cozens," Ancestry.com; and 1885 Colorado State Census, Grand, CO, digital image s.v. "Mary Cozens," Ancestry.com. Only in the 1880 US Census was Mary's birthplace listed as England; in all the others, it was listed as her preferred Ireland.

[58] Reich and Steele, *Haps,* 55.

[59] Murray, "Villa," 72.

[60] "Death of W. Z. Cozens," *Gilpin Observer* (Central City, CO), Jan. 21, 1904, 8, Colorado Historic Newspapers Collection (website), Colorado State Library, coloradohistoricnewspapers.org; and see Steele, "The Cozens Family," 18; and see Robert C. Black, III, *Island in the Rockies* (Boulder, CO: Pruett Publishing, 1969), 265; also see *"Cozens Ranch House: Restoration/Museum,"* 7.

[61] Black, "Cozens Ranch House," sec. 8, 3; and see Encyclopedia Staff, "Cozens Ranch," *Colorado Encyclopedia* (website) coloradoen-cyclopedia.org; see also "Fraser Items," *Middle Park Times,* Aug. 9, 1912, Colorado Historic Newspapers Collection (website), Colorado State Library, coloradohistoricnewspapers.org.

[62] Murray, "Villa," 72-73, 75.

[63] Sturm, "Mary York (Cozens)," 113; and see Murray, "Villa," 78; and also Steele, "Cozens Family," 18.

[64] "Death Claims Pioneer Woman," *Middle Park Times* (Hot Sulphur Springs, CO), Nov. 19, 1909, 1, Colorado Historic Newspapers Collection (website), Colorado State Library, coloradohistoricnewspapers.org; see also "Noted Pioneer Woman Dies at Advanced Age," *Steamboat Pilot* (Steamboat Springs, CO),

Dec. 1, 1909, 1, Colorado Historic Newspapers Collection (website), Colorado State Library, coloradohistoricnewspapers.org; and see Marie Davies McGrath, "McGrath's Men and Women Who Arrived in What Is Now Colorado Prior to January 1, 1861," 45, typescript, Special Collections and Digital Archives (website), Denver Public Library, https://history.denverlibrary.org/sites/history/files/McGraths_Men_and_Women_Who_Arrived_in_Colorado_Prior_to_January_1861.pdf.

[65] Steele, "Cozens Family," 19.

[66] *"Cozens Ranch Museum and Gift Shop Timeline 1830 – Present: A Time Capsule & Chronology,"* (Fraser, CO: Grand County Historical Association, no date), Cozens Ranch Museum, Fraser, CO; and see "Miss Mary Cozens, Great Friend to Regis, Dies at Fraser," *Brown and Gold* (Regis University, Denver, CO), Dec. 15, 1928, 3, Colorado Historic Newspapers Collection (website), Colorado State Library, coloradohistoricnewspapers.org; Steele, "The Cozens Family," 19-20.

[67] "Miss Mary Cozens, Great Friend to Regis, Dies at Fraser," 3.

[68] Steele, "Cozens Family," 20; also see "Regis Benefactor Buried from Chapel," *Brown and Gold* (Regis University, Denver, CO), Nov. 5, 1937, 1, Colorado Historic Newspapers Collection (website), Colorado State Library, coloradohistoricnewspapers.org.

[69] Black, "Cozens Ranch House," sec. 7, 2-3; Noel, *Colorado Catholicism*, 434-5; Margaret Malsam, "Cozens Ranch Museum Is More Than an Old House," *Beacon Review* (Denver, CO), Feb. 4-17, 1994, Grand County Historical Association clippings file.

[70] Black, "Cozens Ranch House," sec. 8, 3, sec. 10, 1.

[71] Catherine E. Trotter, town planner, "Memo to Mayor Vandernail and the Board of Trustees, Subject: Annexation Agreement Requirement: cemetery conveyance," May 1, 2019, Town of Fraser, Fraser, Colorado (website), https://www.frasercolorado.com/AgendaCenter/ViewFile/Item/1317?fileID=1545.

[72] *"Cozens Ranch Museum & Gift Shop Timeline,"* Cozens Ranch House Museum, Fraser, CO.

Figure 3.1. Clara Brown, circa 1875-1880

Courtesy of Denver Public Library Special Collections, Z-275

Clara Brown:
African American Pioneer

Arrived in Colorado, June 1859

Born enslaved and given no formal education, Clara Brown nonetheless bought numerous properties, became a landlord, and was a successful businesswoman. During her first fifty years of life, she experienced the horrors of slavery, including the unimaginable pain of watching as her husband and children were sold to different masters. She spent the rest of her life searching for her lost family. After she was freed in 1857, she headed west, arriving in Colorado in 1859. She eventually settled in Mountain City (now Central City). Throughout her life, her deep Christian faith guided her, and her generosity made her one of Colorado's most beloved historical figures. At her funeral in October 1885, the Colorado Pioneer Association eulogized her as "the kind old friend whose heart always responded to the cry of distress, and who, rising from the humble position of slave to the angelic type of a noble woman, won our sympathy and commanded our respect."[1]

Numerous books and articles have been written about Clara Brown, yet like most details of her life, even the date of her birth cannot be known with certainty. For an enslaved person—the personal property of another person—oftentimes a birthday was neither recorded nor remembered. Some references say she was born January 1, 1800, near Fredericksburg, Virginia, while others place her birth in 1803, 1804, or 1805 in Spotsylvania County, Virginia, or in Gallatin, Tennessee.[2] It is unlikely that even Clara knew the precise date and location, but she said she had clear memories of the War of 1812 when she was a half-grown girl, perhaps eight to ten years old.[3]

Clara's childhood was spent as one of the enslaved persons of Ambrose Smith. Smith and his family moved to Russellville, Kentucky, in Logan County, bringing Clara and her mother along with the rest of his household.[4] In his book, *Clara, an ex-slave in gold rush Colorado*, Roger Baker cites court records showing that Ambrose Smith purchased "one hundred acres on Big Muddy Creek, in the Russellville area, on April 3, 1820."[5] These records list Mr. Smith as a slave owner.

Clara recalled she was around eighteen years old when she married an enslaved man named Richard, who was also owned by Smith. In the years after this union, she gave birth to four children: a son, Richard, a daughter, Margaret, and twin daughters, Paulina Ann (Palina in some references) and Eliza Jane.[6] Paulina drowned when she was around eight years old. Unfortunately, Clara soon experienced more sadness. When Ambrose Smith died in 1835, Clara and her family were auctioned off with the rest of Smith's property. Each member of Clara's family was sold to a different owner. Assuming Clara was born in 1803 and married at eighteen in 1821, all of her children would have been younger than fourteen. Clara's pain and horror during the sale of her family are unimaginable and unrecorded, although the February 18,

1882, *Denver Republican* describes Clara's memory of that fateful day and what happened to her family:

> Margaret was sold to a man named Bednigo Shelton, who lived near Morgantown, Kentucky. She died several years after she went to that place. Richard, after growing to manhood, was sold so often that his mother could not keep track of him, and finally he was lost sight of. For more than twenty-five years the mother has not heard of her son, and she does not know to-day whether he is dead or alive. The other daughter, Eliza Jane, has been lost for about thirty years, and it is in connection with this daughter that the most romantic and interesting part of old Clara's history is connected. Eliza Jane was sold to a man named James Covington, who lived in Logan county, and in 1852 she left the service of Covington. Whither she went her mother did not then know.[7]

After her family was sold away from her, Clara vowed, "they should never have another [child] out of her body to take away."[8] She never remarried, nor did she have any more children.

The day she lost her entire family Clara was sold to George Brown and she worked as a domestic, cooking and caring for Brown's three daughters.[9] Twenty-one years later, in 1856, George Brown died, and in his will, he specified his slave Clara (or Clary) was to receive $300, a significant sum at that time.[10]

With this money, perhaps augmented by money she'd saved, Clara either bought her own freedom or was assisted in buying her freedom by George Brown's daughters.[11] Either way, in her mid-fifties, Clara was manumitted. She left

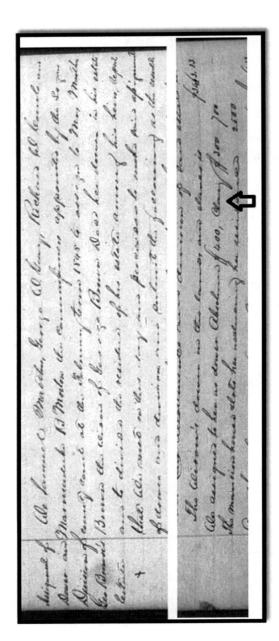

Figure 3.2. George Brown's will, the first known written record of Clara Brown

Courtesy of the Logan County Courthouse in Russellville, Kentucky, Will Book H, pp 34-36. Image pro-
vided by Robin Smith, Archival Services Branch, Kentucky Department of Libraries and Archives

(Kdla.ky.gov)

Kentucky, traveling to Saint Louis, Missouri, and then to Leavenworth, Kansas. During this time, she worked and saved money to acquire everything necessary to open her own laundry business. In 1859, she joined a wagon train and headed to Colorado. In the 1880 *History of Clear Creek and Boulder Valleys*, James Burrell included Clara among his Gilpin County biographies of Clear Creek pioneers. In this biography, he gave details about her journey west:

> Early in 1859, she joined the gold hunting army for Auraria, Cherry Creek, now Denver; she agreeing to cook for a mess of twenty-five men, out of a party of sixty, the conditions being that they transport her stoves, wash-tubs, wash-board and clothes-box, for her services as cook during the trip.[12]

Researchers have offered possible motivations for Clara's move from Kentucky to Saint Louis to Leavenworth and, finally, to what became the Colorado Territory. Sadly, no first-hand record in Clara's own voice has been found to explain her migration. Some believe she was trying to escape restrictive laws regulating the movement and lives of free African Americans. Others speculate that she was searching for her lost family.

Some of Clara's reasons are easily explained. In Kentucky she had no choice. According to Kentucky law, Clara had to leave the state after her emancipation or risk re-enslavement or imprisonment.[13] Heading to Saint Louis, and later to Leavenworth, in search of her lost family is plausible since the late 1850s saw a high influx of free Blacks into these areas. Colorado, in 1859, did not. In 1860, Colorado was not yet a territory and the area's population was represented by combined census figures from the territories of Kansas, Nebraska, New Mexico, and Utah. Compiled 1860 United States Census records for all four territories show that among the forty-six African Americans living in what would become the Territory of Colorado, only nine were female.[14]

Despite the small numbers of African Americans, it is likely Clara headed west to escape prejudices and the growing number of restrictive laws against free Blacks. In addition, unlike Leavenworth, Kansas, the West had few individuals who profited from kidnapping and enslaving free Blacks, as they were allowed to do under the federal Fugitive Slave Act.

Colorado's gold camps also offered opportunities to African Americans that few other places permitted. Although prejudices still existed, several African Americans thrived in Colorado. Mountain man James Beckwourth was well respected, the eloquent Barney Ford owned one of the grandest hotels in Denver, and Lewis Price became wealthy selling real estate. Like these men, Clara successfully crossed racial barriers. Because of her kindness, compassion, and Christian charity—shown to all people regardless of their color or ethnicity—she not only crossed those lines, but she also became beloved by people from all backgrounds and walks of life.

The wagon train that brought Clara to Colorado reached the Cherry Creek settlements around June 1859, making Clara one of the first African American women to settle in the land that would later become the state of Colorado. Starting a new life in the Colorado Territory was difficult for all pioneers. Starting a new life alone as an illiterate, fifty-five-year-old Black woman was remarkable, and it showed unbelievable fortitude. Even more extraordinary was what Clara accomplished while living in Colorado.

During the summer of 1859, thousands of gold seekers rushed to the Pikes Peak region. Most of these newcomers, like Clara, used the settlements of Denver City, Auraria, and Golden City as their jumping-off point for reaching the gold camps in the mountains. As a laundress, Clara found plenty of work. Her religious beliefs brought her into contact with several White men who shared her deep Christian faith.

Almost every article written about Clara mentions her faith. While living in Colorado, she gave generously to numerous churches, independent of their denomination, and when quoted in the newspaper, her words were often interspersed with "Lord, bless yer soul" or "Bless de Lord." Just before her death in Denver, the June 26, 1885, *Denver Tribune-Republican* published the following conversation:

> "You must have been a very handsome girl, Aunt Clara," said the reporter, looking admiringly into the fine old face. "Didn't they always tell you you were good-looking?"
>
> "Lord bless yer soul, Honey, dey did tell me dat, sho' nough, but my mudder she sed purty is that purty does, an' I'se early told not to go much on de good looks. Dey thought more ob de good behavor an' perliteness dem days dan dey does now. Things is different now. Bless de Lord, I wasn't vain when I'se a girl; I relied on His mercy, an' He fetched me frou."
>
> "Aunt Clara, how long has it been since you got religion?" Here a heavenly light seemed to illuminate the dark old face.
>
> "Law me, Darlin', it must 'a been nigh onto fifty years ago. I was nuthin' but a chile when God, He came to, an' took me to find Jesus."[15]

Her Christian faith brought her into contact with the Reverend Jacob Adriance, one of Colorado's earliest ministers. During the Fourth Annual Kansas-Nebraska Methodist Conference, the church sent two pastors to the Rocky Mountains: the Reverend Adriance from Missouri and the Reverend Goode from Kansas. These men arrived in the Cherry Creek area on June 28, 1859, and they held their first service on July third.[16] By July ninth, the *Rocky Mountain News* reported: "On our return from the mountains the other day, we met Elder Goode and Rev. Mr. Adriance, of the Methodist Episcopal church, on a visit to the mines."[17]

The Reverend Adriance kept a personal diary during his time in Colorado, making entries daily. On August twenty-eighth, he noted, "Prayer meetings at my cabin in the evening. From this on we kept up prayer meetings on Thursday evenings at my cabin, or at "Aunt" Clara Brown's cabin, a pious colored lady."[18] Several times in November and December of 1859, Adriance mentions attending a "prayer meeting at Sister Browns."[19] Along with the Reverend Adriance's diary, the local newspaper reported on religious activities, occasionally mentioning Clara. On November 6, 1859, the Reverends Adriance and Goode held their first Sunday School, called the Union Sunday School. The local newspaper reported the school was attended by "twelve children, six adults, an old colored lady known then as Aunt Clara."[20]

The last recording that the Reverend Adriance made about a prayer meeting held in Clara Brown's Denver cabin was on January 10, 1860.[21] Soon thereafter, Clara followed the miners and moved to Gregory Point and then to the mining town of Mountain City (incorporated into Central City in 1869.)[22]

In May of 1859, John Gregory had discovered a rich vein of gold in a valley eight thousand feet above sea level. During 1859 and 1860, more than ten thousand people moved into the area in search of gold. The 1860 compiled United States Census figures for the area included "people from thirty-three states, three territories, the District of Columbia, and twenty-five foreign countries."[23]

Figure 3.3. Mountain City, Colorado, circa 1889

Courtesy of Denver Public Library Special Collections, L-218

It is difficult to imagine what the rough mining town of Mountain City was like when Clara arrived, but one gains a taste of the difficulties she encountered when reading Horace Greeley's description of the area during his sojourn there in the summer of 1859:

> As yet, the entire population of the valley—which cannot number less than four thousand, including five white women and seven squaws living with white men—sleep in tents, or under booths of pine boughs, cooking and eating in the open air. I doubt that there is as yet a table or chair in these diggings, eating being done around a cloth spread on the ground, while each one sits or reclines on mother earth. The food, like that of the plains, is restricted

to a few staples—pork, hot bread, beans and coffee forming the almost exclusive diet of the mountains.[24]

Clara probably traveled to Mountain City by hiring a wagon to carry her belongings and laundry equipment. By May 1862, at a time when free Blacks were seldom allowed to purchase tickets on public transportation, the *Rocky Mountain News* listed Clara's traveling from Central City to Denver in the express stagecoach.[25] On another stagecoach ride between the two cities in 1872, she met Englishman James Thomson, who recorded their encounter in his journal. Thomson's diary is the only contemporaneous record that includes the detail of "two other negresses" traveling on the same wagon train to Colorado with Clara.[26] Historians speculate that if she traveled west with two other women, they might have been Elizabeth Ledbetter and her mother. In 1860, Elizabeth Ledbetter married Jim Beckwourth, and at that time, Ledbetter's mother was described as "the first laundress in Denver."[27]

In Mountain City, Clara set up her laundry business and, by all accounts, was very successful. By October 1860, she had purchased a lot and built a house on it.[28] During the next few years, she worked and invested wisely in the area that soon became known as "the richest square mile on earth."

How did an illiterate, former enslaved woman learn to manage money and to invest wisely? The answer is unknown, but from the investments she made, it is suspected her literate friends helped her. Clara worked hard washing clothing and charging "for blue and red flannel shirts 50 cents, and other clothes in proportion."[29] She purchased shares in mines and bought properties and "in 1864 she was the owner of seven good houses in Central City, sixteen lots in Denver and some good property in Georgetown and Boulder."[30] Rent from these properties would have added to her income and in "a few years she had accumulated property valued at about $10,000."[31]

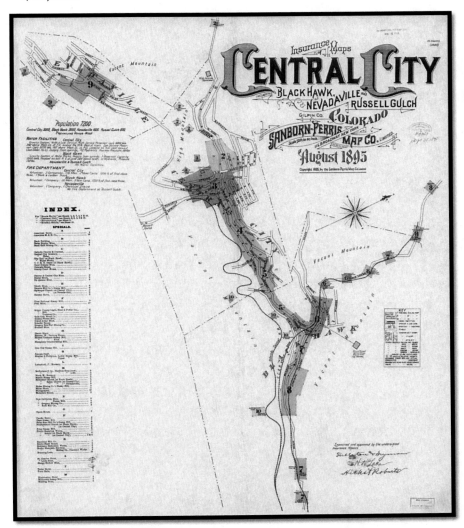

Figure 3.4. The 1895 Sanborn Fire Insurance Map for Central City, Gilpin County, Colorado

Library of Congress, Geography and Map Division, Sanborn Maps Collection

Clara was a shrewd investor and often financially assisted other African Americans, but her numerous friends probably also aided her in financial decisions and investments. Jeremiah Lee and Lorenzo "Professor" Bowman lived in Central City and prospected around Leavenworth Mountain. These two discovered such well-known lodes as the O. K., Argentine, Jenny Lind, and George Law. They also built and ran the Red, White and Blue smelter in Leavenworth Gulch,[32] and by 1867, they had founded the Red, White, & Blue mining company, an organization of African American men operating near Georgetown.[33] Clara is listed as a co-investor on several of their properties.

Barney Lancelot Ford, an escaped enslaved man who arrived in Mountain City in 1860, probably influenced Clara's investments in Denver City. When he couldn't find a place to stay in the mining town, Clara invited him to stay in her cabin. Ford claimed two mines near Mountain City, but he lost them when they were jumped by White miners. He moved to Breckenridge only to again be chased off his mine. A few years later he opened the People's Restaurant in Denver and his prospects improved. He eventually built two luxury hotels, the Inter-Ocean Hotels, one in Denver and the other in Cheyenne, Wyoming. With such a small African American community in Colorado, it is probable he remained in contact with Clara, remembering her kindness and helping her with investments in the Denver area.

In 1864, after the United States Congress enacted a statute enabling a territory to create a state constitution as the first step toward statehood, Coloradans created a constitution, but statehood was rejected in a popular vote. A second constitution was written in 1865, and it contained language specifically barring African American men from voting. This second constitution was passed by popular vote, with only

155 votes turning the scales.[34] Barney Ford, Edward Sanderlin, Henry Wagoner, William Harden, and other influential African Americans were outraged, and they immediately lobbied nationally against Colorado statehood because Black citizens were denied the right to vote. On March 13, 1866, the United States Senate rejected Colorado's statehood bid.[35]

On May 19, 1864, a massive flood destroyed many buildings in Denver, including the City Hall located on Blake Street near Cherry Creek. Denver historian, Jerome Smiley, in his 1901 *History of Denver*, lists the City Hall's iron safe, containing early "town records and various municipal documents," as one of the losses.[36] Clara, along with other Denver landowners, lost leases and deeds to Denver properties, resulting in confusion about lot ownership.[37] She lost ownership of several of her properties, but she may have considered her losses relatively minor compared to the loss of property and life suffered by many Denverites, although as she got older, those lost properties might have made her more financially comfortable.

The Weekly Commonwealth described the Denver flood in an article on May 25, 1864, and included an interesting story about an African American family named Smith who lived near Cherry Creek. It is assumed this was the family of Jack Smith, an African American who had traveled to Colorado with William Byers and Company in the spring of 1859. Smith worked with Byers on the printing press and helped produce the first *Rocky Mountain News*, issued on April 23, 1859.[38] The Smiths, like several Denver residents, were caught in the floodwaters, but they were fortunate and survived. *The Weekly Commonwealth* included the following: "A Negro named Smith, with his wife and five children, were carried away, but through the heroic management and cool courage of Mrs. Smith, the entire family were saved. All honor to the brave hearted woman!"[39]

Despite financial setbacks from the Denver flood and several fires in Central City that affected her property there, Clara remained generous, both with her time and her money. She donated to many churches in Central City, including the Congregational Church, the Presbyterian Church, and the Saint James Methodist Church.[40] She worked with the Reverend Adriance, who often came to Central City to preach, and in 1860, "an organization took place, with twenty-seven church members, whose meetings were held in the house of Aunt Clara Brown, the colored pioneer, on Lawrence street."[41] The meetings resulted in the construction of the first Saint James Methodist Church, a small log church completed late in 1860. Unfortunately, on November 4, 1861, the church burned down.[42] After its destruction, services "were held in the house of Aunt Clara Brown on Lawrence Street."[43]

In 1865, the Thirteenth Amendment to the United States Constitution abolished slavery, making it safe for Clara to travel back to the States. The wealth she'd acquired provided the means for her to earnestly begin searching for her lost family, so she left her home and traveled to Kentucky. There is little written about her activities during her trip east, but on August 7, 1866, the *Rocky Mountain News* published an article titled "A Woman in a Thousand" detailing Clara's return to Colorado:

> Mrs. Clara Brown, (colored) better known to old Coloradians as "Aunt Clara," came here in '59, and by dint of hard labor and perseverance had amassed quite a fortune. Last October the secret of her economy and industry for all these years came to light, and her object apparent. She at that time went east and has since devoted

her time and energies to looking up her numerous progeny; for that purpose she traveled through the length and breadth of Kentucky and Tennessee, gathering together her flock.[44]

Clara returned to Colorado in July 1866 accompanied by "twenty-six relatives and orphans," paying for the passage of all members of her party, at a cost of approximately $4,000.[45] The number of individuals she returned with, along with the cost of the journey, vary with references, as do the identity of these individuals. Burrell refers to the members of Clara's party as "relatives," while the *Rocky Mountain News* article called them her "sons and daughters, with their husbands and wives, and their children." Whether these people were friends, relatives, or orphans, Clara not only paid for their travels, but she also helped get them settled and established, mostly in the Central City and Georgetown areas.[46]

None of the people she returned with was part of her immediate family and soon after her return, she "offered $1,000 reward for the discovery of her lost daughter, Eliza Jane."[47] It was from this point on that her attempts to find her daughter intensified, but years passed without success. Clara returned to her laundry work and was active again in her community and church. In addition, she began financially supporting four young African American women—Margaret Hall, Nancy and Josephine Smith, and Indiana Bell—who were enrolled in Oberlin College in Ohio.[48] Her charity gave them the opportunity to obtain an education, something she had been denied.

Clara's involvement in Denver's first African Methodist Episcopal Church (AME Church) is not documented, probably because she was living in Central City at the time the church was established, but with such a small African

American community in the Colorado Territory, along with her documented travels between Central City and Denver, she certainly must of have been aware of the church and the women who organized it. In 1866, Mary Randolph and Mary Smith founded the church that would later be named the Shorter Community African Methodist Episcopal Church.[49]

Mary Randolph's experiences coming west are an interesting example of the prejudices and difficulties Clara would have had to overcome as an African American. Mary was a free Black, born in 1826 on Staten Island, New York.

Mary came west and "was put off a stagecoach bound for Denver on a bitterly cold day in 1859."[50] Despite having money to pay for her stagecoach ticket, prejudices and laws of the day meant she was not allowed to sit inside the coach. Instead, she had to ride on top with the driver. Somewhere in the vast Kansas prairie, Mary was forced off the stagecoach and deserted without food or water. The next day, another stagecoach picked her up. For the rest of her life, she told the story of having to open and close her umbrella all night long to scare off the coyotes.[51] Like Clara, Mary spent the rest of her life in Colorado, mostly in the Denver area.

Clara's generosity toward others took a toll on her finances, and she is shown to be delinquent in paying her taxes several years in a row. Her generosity, however, wasn't the only cause of her financial difficulties. Although natural disasters destroyed some of her properties or their deeds, Clara complained that most of her losses came from being cheated by White men, a complaint echoed by numerous African Americans living in Colorado. On her stagecoach ride with James Thomson in 1872, he recorded that she said:

> Been much cheated. Has many mining claims taken in payment of debts. Fellow who gave her bill "three months

after death." Judge in Denver who let them "jump" her lots, "guess'd such a number had got their back couldn't give any more," and man at Blackhawk who jumped her lot and wouldn't even pay for log building on it.[52]

Despite these difficulties, Clara and other African Americans in Colorado were faring much better than their brethren in the South. Soon after the Thirteenth Amendment became law, restrictive Black codes were enacted in Mississippi and South Carolina requiring free African Americans to possess written evidence each January to prove their employment for the upcoming year. "Jim Crow" laws gained strength, further restricting rights and movement of freed Blacks in the South. Trying to help other African Americans escape these harsh conditions, Benjamin Singleton, an African American living in Kansas, advertised and encouraged southern African Americans to move to Kansas. In the spring of 1878, thousands of freedmen headed west in search of their own land and a better life, but most had few belongings or resources. Newspapers soon reported on the destitute conditions of these migrants, and communities

Figure 3.5. Ho for Kansas! flier by Benjamin Singleton, 1878

Courtesy of Library of Congress, #98501335

around the world sent their good will and monetary support.

People in Colorado also wanted to help these Kansas African American refugees. On May 9, 1879, *The Denver Daily Tribune* reported on a meeting "For the Relief of the Kansas Movement." In that meeting, influential Blacks and Whites formed a Central Executive Committee to raise money and try to "bring a portion of said emigrants to Colorado."[53] The committee wanted to learn more about the situation and when Clara—then in her seventies—volunteered to investigate, Governor Pitkin, one of the committee members, accepted her offer. Robert Athearn summarized Clara's unusual role in his book, *In Search of Canaan: Black Migration to Kansas, 1879-80*:

> Colorado civic leaders were anxious to learn something of the Kansas situation before committing money to the cause. When "Aunt" Clara Brown, a black woman who was well known in Denver and Central City, offered to investigate the situation, Governor Pitkin agreed at once. He wrote a letter of introduction to St. John [Governor of Kansas], explaining who Aunt Clara was: "She came to Colorado in 1859 & accumulated quite a large fortune, but has spent most of it for the relief of her own race. She is one of the best old souls that ever lived & is respected and loved by all who know her. She goes to Kansas to see the destitute freedmen & to report here upon their condition.[54]

Clara traveled to Kansas as a representative of Governor Pitkin, but her actions there were poorly documented. Once she returned to Colorado in September 1879, the Central City newspaper reported on her trip, stating that of the five thousand or so freedmen who answered Singleton's call, many had by then found employment. In the article, Clara described the refugees as "an industrious and sober class of people, who only ask an opportunity to make an honest living."[55] She felt that they mostly wanted work and if they got that, within another year, most of them would be self-supporting.

The trip took a toll on the elderly woman and by 1880, her health had begun to deteriorate, as had her finances. She moved from Central City to Denver, and in 1884, the *Denver Republican* reported, "Misfortune came upon her in sundry ways, and she was reduced to poverty, having to depend upon those who had known her in other circumstances for aid. Mr. Charles Cheever [Chever] provided a comfortable home for her at 517 Arapahoe street."[56]

Between 1882 and 1885, several articles were written about Clara, some detailing charitable events, while others described her remarkable life and generous acts. A June 26, 1885, *Denver Tribune-Republican* article described Clara as "a tall woman, very aged, yet she does not show the advance of years, save that she is toothless, and consequently her conversation is a little difficult to understand. She has a remarkable face, with high cheekbones, a long, pointed nose and very black eyes. Her cast of features is strong and almost classical, and the hair which curls above her temples is as white as snow."[57]

This article also quotes Clara's view of the conflicts between Native Americans and settlers in the West and her belief about her own heritage: "'You see, I'm part Injun myself, honey . . . an' if I wasn't, why, I'd never been afeared of 'em, poor critters. It's de white folks was to blame in them Indian troubles. Lord bless you, darlin', if de Indians had acted as de whites done, what do you think they'd done to 'em?'"[58]

Despite her frailty and poverty, Clara continued to search for her daughter, Eliza Jane. She "caused letters of inquiry to be sent all over the country. The case was referred to often in the colored churches of Denver, and every time Aunt Clara met strangers, she entreated them to keep a lookout for her daughter."[59] In February 1882, remarkably, her search ended in success. An African American woman who had lived in Denver met Eliza Jane in Council Bluffs, Iowa. After Eliza Jane's identity was confirmed, Clara received the news by letter.[60]

Friends, her church, local businesses, and even the Union Pacific Railroad helped her travel to Council Bluffs, where after more than forty-five-years of separation, Clara was reunited with her lost daughter.[61] The *Council Bluffs Nonpareil* reported on this meeting:

> Yesterday morning, on the Denver Short Line train, Mrs. Brown arrived in Council Bluffs and proceeded to the residence of her daughter. She came up on the street car, and when at the corner of Broadway and Eighth street her long-lost child was pointed out to her, standing on the crossing. With a scream she jumped from her seat, rushed out of the car, and in an ecstasy of joy mother and child were clasped in each other's arms. Unheeding the lookers-on, unheeding the mud in the streets, clasped in each other's arms, they sat down. The sight was one at once amusing and touching. In that embrace the joys and sorrows of a life-time were forgotten, and only the present thought of.[62]

After this joyous meeting, Clara and her daughter, Eliza Jane Brewer, who had given Clara nine grandchildren, returned to Denver.[63] Eliza Jane remained by her mother's side as Clara's health further deteriorated and her finances became grim. Old friends came to her assistance, including the Gilpin County Pioneer Association, which held a benefit dinner for Clara on March 6, 1884. The *Denver Republican* reported on this event by saying, "Aunt Clara Brown was happy yesterday. Wearing a neat calico dress and white apron, with a turban upon her white head, the old lady sat in the lecture room of the City Hall and received all who came to partake of her benefit dinner with a hand shake and warm thanks, and listened with beaming face to their kind words and good wishes."[64]

In September 1884, Barney Ford and Clara Brown were admitted into the Society of Colorado Pioneers.[65] They were the first African Americans accepted into the organization and Clara may have been its first woman member. At the organization's June 1885 meeting, the members "presented Aunt

Figure 3.6. Clara Brown's grave in Denver's Riverside Cemetery, 2020

Courtesy of author J.v.L. Bell's collection

Clara a check for $50. . . . She was honestly happy in being thus remembered by her old friends, and expressed herself in no unfeeling terms regarding the Association's kindness."[66] She attended one last gathering of the association in September of 1885, but then her failing health finally took its toll.

Clara Brown died on October 23, 1885, and she was buried in Denver's Riverside Cemetery. Newspapers across Colorado and individuals of all races paid tribute to her:

> It is seldom that more respect has been paid to the dead than was paid yesterday to the remains of the venerable pioneer negress of whom Colorado has heard so much . . . There were in attendance the Governor, the mayor, and several other prominent dignitaries. The funeral was in the charge of the Colorado Pioneer Association, and everything was done with the most scrupulous regard for order and fitness.[67]

Clara Brown lived during a dark a time in America's history, when African Americans were often considered subhuman, and they could be beaten or killed simply for seeking to live a free life. Clara Brown not only rose above her past as an enslaved woman, but in her fifties, she began a new life in a new country. As a free woman, she served the God she loved, she treated all people—regardless of their color, education, or background—as equals, and she rose above prejudices to become one of Colorado's most beloved pioneers. She was truly, as *the Rocky Mountain News* called her, "A Woman in a Thousand."[68]

---

[1] "Aunt Clara Brown, Resolutions Adopted by the Colorado Pioneer Association—Mourning her Loss," *Denver Tribune-*

Republican, Oct. 30, 1885, 8, Western History and Genealogy, Denver Public Library.

² Tonya Bolden, *Pathfinders: The Journeys of 16 Extraordinary Black Souls* (New York, NY: Abrams, 2017), 42. This page states January 1, 1800, for Clara's birthday. The date probably was taken from Capt. James Burrell's article, "Mrs. Clara Brown," *History of Clear Creek and Boulder Valleys, Colorado* (Chicago, IL: O. L. Baskin & Co., 1880), 443. Other resources list other dates. Roger Baker, in his book *Clara: an ex-slave in gold rush Colorado* (Central City, CO: Black Hawk Publishing, 2003), 1, states: "Clara Brown was born near Fredericksburg, Virginia, on January 1, 1800. Or perhaps it was 1803. And the place of birth might have been Kentucky, or Gallatin, Tennessee. And it might have been 1805 or '06."

³ Roger Baker, *Clara an ex-slave in gold rush Colorado*, (Central City, CO: Black Hawk Publishing, 2003), 3.

⁴ Capt. James Burrell, "Mrs. Clara Brown," Biographical Sketches, Gilpin County, in *History of Clear Creek and Boulder Valleys*, (Chicago, IL: O.L. Baskin & Co., 1880), 443.

⁵ Baker, *Clara*, 4.

⁶ Burrell, "Mrs. Clara Brown," 443.

⁷ "Story of Two Lives: Mother and Daughter Unite After a Separation of Thirty Years," *Denver Republican*, Feb. 18, 1882, 8, Western History and Genealogy, Denver Public Library.

⁸ Marjorie L. Reyburn, *James Thomson in Central City* (Boulder, CO: University of Colorado,1940) 187.

⁹ Baker, *Clara*, 9.

¹⁰ Will of George Brown, Logan County Courthouse, Russellville, KY, Will Book H, 35.

¹¹ "Story of Two Lives," 8. In this newspaper account, Clara was placed on the auction block and sold for $475 to the Brown daughters. Each daughter paid one fourth of Clara's purchase price, leaving Clara to pay the final fourth of $119. Frank Hall, in *History of the State of Colorado*, (Chicago, IL: The Blakely Printing Company, 1889), 1:483, states that upon Brown's death, Clara became "the property of still another purchaser by whom she was manumitted."

[12] Burrell, "Mrs. Clara Brown," 443.

[13] Benjamin Joseph Klebaner "American Manumission Laws and the Responsibility for Supporting Slaves," *The Virginia Magazine of History and Biography* (October 1955), 443–453, http://www.jstor.org/stable/4246165.

[14] "Territory of Colorado," *Population of the United States in 1860; Compiled from the Original Returns of the Eighth Census,* (Washington, D.C.: Government Printing Office, 1864), 546, books.google.com.

[15] "Old Aunt Clara Brown: An Aged Colored Woman Who Crossed the Plains in 1859," *The Denver Tribune-Republican,* June 26, 1885, 2.

[16] Jacob Adriance, 1859 Diary, July 3, 1859, Jacob Adriance Papers, WH4, Box 2, FF 1, Western History and Genealogy, Denver Public Library.

[17] "The Fourth," *Rocky Mountain News* (Denver), July 9, 1859, 2, Colorado Historic Newspapers Collection (website), Colorado State Library, coloradohistoricnewspapers.org.

[18] Jacob Adriance, 1859 Diary, August 28, 1859, Jacob Adriance Papers, WH4, Box 2, FF 1, Western History and Genealogy, Denver Public Library.

[19] Jacob Adriance, 1859 Diary, November 22, December 6, December 13, 1859, and December 27, 1859, Jacob Adriance Papers, WH4, Box 2, FF 1, Western History and Genealogy, Denver Public Library.

[20] "Another Old Timer," unidentified newspaper clipping, Jacob Adriance Papers, WH4, Box 2, FF 8, Western History and Genealogy, Denver Public Library; also see Jerome C. Smiley, ed., *History of Denver: With Outlines of the Earlier History of the Rocky Mountain Country,* (Denver, CO: Th Times-Sun Publishing Company, 1901), 718.

[21] Jacob Adriance, 1860 Diary, January 3 and January 10, 1860, Jacob Adriance Papers, WH4, Box 2, FF 3, Western History and Genealogy, Denver Public Library. "In the evening I was at a prayer meeting at sister Browns."

[22] Burrell, "Mrs. Clara Brown," 443.

[23] Alan Granruth, *The Little Kingdom of Gilpin: Gilpin County, Colorado* (Central City, CO: Gilpin Historical Society, 2000), 2.

[24] Horace Greeley, *Overland Journey, from New York to San Francisco in the Summer of 1859* (New York, NY: C. M. Saxton, Barker & Co., 1860), 122, https://www.google.ca/books/edition/An_Overland_Journey_from_New_York_to_San/qDt1B1y3zJEC?hl=en&gbpv=1.

[25] "From Central City," *The Rocky Mountain News* (Denver, CO), May 28, 1862, 3, Colorado Historic Newspapers Collection (website), Colorado State Library, coloradohistoricnewspapers.org.

[26] Reyburn, *James Thomson*, 187.

[27] LeRoy R. Hafen, "The Last Years of James P. Beckwourth," *Colorado Magazine*, Jan. 1928, 137.

[28] Gregory District Record Book D, 259.

[29] Burrell, "Mrs. Clara Brown," 443.

[30] "Story of Two Lives," 8.

[31] Burrell, "Mrs. Clara Brown," 443.

[32] "Obituary of Jeremiah Lee," *The Gilpin Observer* (Central City, CO), Jan. 14, 1904, 1, Colorado Historic Newspapers Collection (website), Colorado State Library, coloradohistoricnewspapers.org.

[33] Eric Twitty, *Historic Context Interstate-70 Mountain Corridor*, prepared for the Colorado Department of Transportation, (Lafayette, CO: Mountain States Historical and CH2MHILL, 2014), 18, https://www.codot.gov/projects/contextsensitivesolutions/assets-1/docs/pdfs/combined-historic-context-report.pdf.

[34] Eugene H. Berwanger, "Reconstruction on the Frontier: The Equal Rights Struggle in Colorado, 1865-1867," *Pacific Historical Review*, August 1975, 313–29. This article was found in the book *African Americans on the Western Frontier*, edited by Monroe Lee Billington and Roger D. Hardaway, (Boulder, CO: University Press of Colorado, 2001), 39.

[35] Ed Quillen, "Civil rights' role in Colorado statehood," *The Denver Post*, July 31, 2006, https://www.denverpost.com/2006/07/31/civil-rights-role-in-colorado-statehood/.

[36] Jerome C. Smiley, ed., *History of Denver: With Outlines of the Earlier History of the Rocky Mountain Country*, (Denver, CO: The Denver Times, 1901), 371, (website), digital.denverlibrary.org.

[37] Baker, *Clara*, 86.

[38] Robert L Perkin, *The First Hundred Years: An Informal History of Denver and the Rocky Mountain News* (Garden City, NY: Doubleday & Company, 1959), 34.

[39] "Great Flood in Denver. Several Lives Lost!" *The Weekly Commonwealth* (Denver, CO), May 25, 1864, 3, Colorado Historic Newspapers Collection (website), Colorado State Library, coloradohistoricnewspapers.org.

[40] Baker, *Clara*, 36.

[41] Burrell, "Mrs. Clara Brown," 239.

[42] Jacob Adriance, 1861 Diary, Jacob Adriance Papers, WH4, Box 2, FF 5, Western History and Genealogy, Denver Public Library, November 4, 1861, "Great fire in the evening. Church burned. Was up till midnight."

[43] Granruth, *Little Kingdom*, 108 and 128.

[44] "A Woman in a Thousand," *Daily Rocky Mountain News* (Denver, CO), Aug. 7, 1866, 4, (website) Colorado Historic Newspapers Collection (website), Colorado State Library, coloradohistoricnewspapers.org.

[45] Reyburn, *James Thomson*, 187. Different references vary the number of African Americans she brought back to Colorado, citing anywhere between 16 and 34.

[46] Baker, *Clara*, 60.

[47] "Story of Two Lives," 8.

[48] Baker, *Clara*, 60.

[49] "150 Year History of Shorter AME Church, Denver Colorado," *The Christian Recorder*, Dec. 9, 2018, https://www.thechristianrecorder.com/150-year-history-of-shorter-ame-church-denver-colorado/.

[50] "Day Planner," *The Denver Post*, Feb. 2, 2008, https://www.denverpost.com/2008/02/02/day-planner-5/.

[51] Marilyn Lindenbaum, *Discovering Denver: Brick by Brick: Teacher Resource Guide* (Denver, CO: History Colorado, 2012), 10,

https://mollybrown.org/wp-content/uploads/2017/05/Teacher-Packet-ALL-FINAL.pdf.

[52] Reyburn, *James Thomson*, 187.

[53] "The Colored Emigration Subject Agitated. The Meeting For the Relief of the Kansas Movement. Good Speaking and Sensible Ideas," *The Denver Daily Tribune*, May 9, 1879, 4, Colorado Historic Newspapers Collection (website), Colorado State Library, coloradohistoricnewspapers.org.

[54] Robert G. Athearn, *In Search of Canaan: Black Migration in Kansas, 1879-80* (Lawrence, KS: Regents Press of Kansas, 1978), 162.

[55] Baker, *Clara*, 82.

[56] "Aunt Clara Brown: Entertainment Given Yesterday for the Benefit of the Oldest Colored Resident," *Denver Republican*, Mar. 7, 1884, 5.

[57] "Old Aunt Clara Brown," 2.

[58] "Old Aunt Clara Brown," 2.

[59] "Story of Two Lives," 8.

[60] "Story of Two Lives," 8.

[61] "Aunt Clara's Thanks: The Meeting of Aunt Clara Brown and Her Long-Separated Daughter — Their Gratitude to Friends," *Denver Republican*, Apr. 2, 1882, 11.

[62] "After Many Days. Meeting of Aunt Clara Brown, of Denver, and Her Daughter, After Thirty Years Separation," *Denver Republican*, Mar. 4, 1882, 8.

[63] "Aunt Clara's Thanks," 11.

[64] "Aunt Clara Brown: Entertainment Given Yesterday for the Benefit of the Oldest Colored Resident," *Denver Republican*, Mar. 7, 1884, 5.

[65] Baker, *Clara*, 97.

[66] "Old Aunt Clara Brown," 2.

[67] "Clara Brown's Funeral: Touching Tribute to a Well-known Pioneer Woman," *The Daily Register-Call* (Central City), Oct. 29, 1885, 1.

[68] "A Woman in a Thousand," 4.

DENSLOW,   CHICAGO.

Figure 4.1. Albina Washburn, circa 1876

Courtesy from the Collections of the Loveland Museum, ID 2022.19.1.7

Albina Washburn: Radical Reformer

Arrived in Colorado, May 3, 1860

A pioneer in multiple senses of the word, Albina Washburn not only helped open new land for Anglo settlement, but she also sought to open people's minds to political, economic, and social reforms. She and her family came to the Pikes Peak region with the intention of making their living by farming and selling their produce to miners. The Washburns established one of the first successful dairy and fruit farms in what would become the town of Loveland in Larimer County.[1] There was no school, so Albina founded one and briefly served as teacher.[2] She joined the Grange, worked for women's suffrage, organized and managed women's cooperative exchanges, and supported labor unions. In the 1900 United States Census, she listed her occupation as "radical reformer,"[3] an apt description for a woman who spent her life battling against monied corporations and for the common people—especially for women's equality.

Albina Louise Holcomb was born to Laura Abbie and David Holcomb on January 6, 1837, in Tremont, a village southeast of Peoria, Illinois.[4] Records of Albina's childhood are scant, but her exceptional writing skill suggests she received an excellent education.

On January 8, 1853, sixteen-year-old Albina married John Everett Washburn, a man seven years her senior, in Cook County, Illinois. The couple made their home in Freeport, Illinois, where John ran a marble-cutting shop. On April 29, 1855, their daughter, Winona, was born.[5]

Concerns over John's health, which had been impaired by breathing the dust inherent in marble cutting, led to the Washburns' decision to join the throngs heading to the Pikes Peak region. At the end of a seven-week trek in a caravan of horse-drawn wagons, the family arrived in Denver on May 3, 1860.[6] Three days later, in a letter that began with "My Dear Far-off Mother," Albina described their arrival: "Denver was a welcome sight, and as we gradually descended from a bluff road towards a bend in the Platte a right smart chance of new roofs, and the tops of a few brick buildings, greeted our longing eyes." She cautioned her mother that "every letter sent or received at Denver is 25 cents, so if you do not receive many you will know we have not made much."[7]

The Washburns paid ten dollars a month rent for a cabin and land on the west bank of the Platte in Auraria and began dairy farming.[8] Daughter Winona, who was five at the time, later recollected that their first meals were "brown-red Mexican beans and blue Mexican cornmeal."[9] Their home was an earthen-floored log cabin with a dirt and pole roof. A ceiling made of empty flour sacks that were sewn together kept the dirt from falling inside. Winona recalled watching mice run along the cloth and "when they came close to the edge, they fell to the floor with a thump."[10] At the end of June, in another letter to her mother, Albina gave her address as "Mud cabin West Bank of the Platte." She wrote in response to her mother's "beautiful and welcome letter" and implored her to write often.[11]

In 1861, the Washburns moved to Quartz Valley in the Central City area and again set up a dairy farm.[12] There, Albina, homesick and disheartened, wrote in a never-mailed letter to a friend in Freeport, Illinois: "I feel this winter more than ever before since I placed myself under the wing of the Rocky Mountains the pressure of old ties and the drawing of the ever lengthening chain which binds me to former friends. I should like to revisit America." She also expressed concern for the quality of her daughter's education: "I sigh for the excellent schools of Freeport."[13]

Even at that early date, Albina strained at the confines of the woman's sphere. In that same letter, she wrote that if she did return to Illinois for a visit, she would want to earn her own keep by something besides washing and sewing: "I have sometimes had the audacity to imagine that there is something in my head which might be worth to an appreciative public a few dimes, but I don't know." Torn between her dream to return home to the States and her desire to remain by John, whom she affectionately called "Evie," she concluded the letter: "My husband is still sanguine of his wife's success in this country (and so am I) of Colorado. I say if I go, for I fear my own courage would not be equal to the separation from him."[14] Albina chose to remain by her husband's side. Perhaps, writing the unmailed letter helped her sort out her internal conflict.

In 1862, the Washburns packed up once more and moved via ox team to the Big Thompson Valley, fifty miles north of Denver. John briefly partnered with James M. Smith on the latter's farm before acquiring his own 160 acres with a soldier's bounty (a reward of land given for enlistment or service) from the War of 1812.[15] He purchased the log cabin on

Figure 4.2. John Washburn, circa 1876

Courtesy from the Collections of the Loveland Museum,
ID 2022.19.1.8

the land and commenced farming. The cabin stood on the south bank of the Big Thompson River in a section that the town of Loveland now preserves as King's Crossing Natural Area.[16]

John became the Big Thompson postmaster, and he and Albina operated the post office in their home for more than seven years.[17] Albina recalled that the neighbors, gathering in the Washburns' sitting room to await distribution of the mail, became an "impromptu sociable." Writing of the vagaries of the mail delivery, she told of a time when the mail carrier arrived on horseback with the mail tied up in a red handkerchief.[18] On another occasion, when John was away on a two-month business trip, the mail coach arrived late, compelling Albina to get up at two in the morning to send off the mail.[19]

Since there was no school in all of Larimer County, in January 1864, Albina set up a private school on the Big Thompson for her daughter and the neighborhood children. She taught ten students for three months and was paid ten dollars monthly tuition. After her brief teaching stint, the community built a log cabin school, and a succession of other school masters followed Albina.[20]

When it came time to celebrate the Fourth of July in 1864, no United States flag could be found to fly in observance of the occasion. So Albina used blue wool and red and white cotton to sew a flag by hand, and she dated it July 4, 1864. John went to the mountains and cut a pole on which to raise the flag in front of their cabin.[21]

In August 1864, John became a station master on Ben Holladay's Overland Stage Line. Washburn's Crossing, as their property was called after John built a bridge over the Big Thompson River, became the only home station between St. Vrain Creek (today's city of Longmont) and Virginia Dale (a

Figure 4.3. Flag made by Albina Washburn in 1864 is on display at the Fort Collins Museum of Discovery, Fort Collins, Colorado

Courtesy of Fort Collins Museum of Discovery, Fort Collins, Colorado, FC 4367

settlement near the Colorado-Wyoming border). A home station served food, unlike swing stations that only provided fresh horses or mules, so Albina took on the task of cooking for the stage drivers, stock tenders, and passengers.[22]

The United States government had not yet surveyed the land when Albina and John settled along the Big Thompson River. A survey in 1864 determined that the western boundary of their land lay several rods (a rod equals five and a half yards) to the east of what they had thought, and consequently, their cabin sat on the neighbor's property. Since claim jumpers posed a threat to land without a dwelling, John hastily constructed a "slab shanty with a pole and straw roof"[23] within the legal boundaries of the Washburn land. The family moved to the shanty until their new home could be built. Meanwhile, they operated the stage station in their previous home on their neighbor's land. When completed, their new cabin contained living quarters on the main floor and two bedrooms in a low-ceilinged second story. At times, the main floor must have been a very lively place, for it also served as post office and John's courtroom during his two-year appointment as Larimer County judge.[24]

The settlement along the Big Thompson River flourished. In 1867, Andrew Douty built the first grist mill in the county. The popularity of flour milled in Saint Louis, Missouri, led the savvy businessman to name his enterprise the Saint Louis Mill and label his flour sacks "4 X Flour, Made in St. Louis, Colorado." He printed *St. Louis* in large letters in a prominent spot and *Colorado* in tiny letters at the bottom of the sack. Soon, locals called the whole settlement St. Louis and later, Old St. Louis.[25]

In the early 1870s, Albina continued to seek the best possible education for her daughter, Winona. She sent her to Denver to attend the territory's first girls' school, Wolfe Hall. Later, Winona studied at Northwestern University under, among other instructors, Frances Willard, who would become a national temperance and suffrage leader. In 1874, John suffered a serious illness that caused Albina to call Winona home from school. John recovered, but Winona never returned to school because the family's finances had suffered, not only from John's inability to work, but probably from the loss of crops in the 1873 grasshopper plague and the national financial panic the same year.[26]

Albina gave a glimpse into her early 1870s activities that went beyond her role as a farmer's wife in an article she wrote for the June 12, 1875, issue of the *Woman's Journal* titled "Woman Voting in Colorado." Colorado territorial law only required a voter in a school district election to be a taxpaying citizen over the age of twenty-one. So, as Albina related in the *Woman's Journal* article, she asked John to list several ponies

Figure 4.4. Washburn cabin on the Big Thompson River,
Larimer County, Colorado

Courtesy from the Collections of the Loveland Museum, #1158

in her name, and she subsequently paid the tax on the
animals. In 1874, she attended the annual school district
meeting with her husband and voted without anyone's
protesting. She conjectured the lack of protest was due, in
part, to her husband's being a judge and that the attendees
had been caught off guard. The following year, Albina went
to the meeting without John, and attendees protested that a
woman was not a citizen and could not vote. She challenged
the official to consult *Webster's Dictionary*, and he found *citizen*
defined as a person of either sex. She was then allowed to
vote.[27]

In *Woman Suffrage and the Origins of Liberal Feminism in the
United States, 1820-1920*, Suzanne M. Marilley gives Albina's
article, "Woman Voting in Colorado," credit for the national
American Woman Suffrage Association's (AWSA) decision to
send organizers and speakers to support Colorado's

campaign for women's voting rights. At the time, the Colorado Territory's suffragists, like Albina, worked mainly on an individual level or in loosely organized groups. The territory planned a constitutional convention to be held in 1876, and proponents of the women's right to vote sought to have full women's suffrage written into the constitution.[28] With the help of the AWSA, territorial suffragists organized the Colorado Woman Suffrage Association (CWSA) on January 10-11, 1876, and they elected Albina corresponding secretary and John vice-president to represent the Big Thompson district. They also appointed Albina to the committee to present the organization's position to the Colorado Constitutional Convention.[29]

Late in January, Albina, along with the other members of the CWSA committee, addressed the Committee on Suffrage and Elections at the Colorado Constitutional Convention, and they presented a petition, signed by about one thousand residents, requesting that the constitution set voter requirements such that "no distinction be made on account of sex."[30] The women spoke to the injustice of being governed and taxed without representation. Albina referenced voting rights having been extended to include African American men when she stated that "men find it very easy to leave out an objectionable word. The word male is as easily left out as color."[31]

The constitutional convention granted women the right to vote in school elections but postponed the question of full suffrage. It did provide for the general assembly to submit the issue to the state's qualified voters at the state's first general election in 1877, with only a simple majority needed for passage. Albina referenced that small victory when she wrote that it "is the only result of all our effort in behalf of Woman and, as will be seen, calls for renewed and continued effort on our part until we stand equal with our brothers before the law."[32]

Albina, Mary F. Shields, and Alida Avery formed the vanguard of the campaign for passage of the 1877 referendum on Colorado women's suffrage.[33] On October 2, 1876, Albina spoke before the AWSA convention in Philadelphia and successfully rallied the group to support the Colorado effort with funds and speakers. "We plead for reinforcements . . . to scatter the forces of injustice and usurpation, and to place us in possession of our inheritance of freedom."[34]

The following month, at the National Grange Convention in Chicago, Albina failed to convince a committee on women's suffrage to submit a resolution endorsing national enfranchisement of women to the full assembly for consideration, but she laid forth the need for the resolution in her minority report to the assembly. In part, she said:

> They [women] are taxed without representation, their children are taken from them by masculine courts, their husbands and sons are ruined by liquor sold under masculine license, their hours of labor and the wages for that labor are controlled entirely by masculine legislation. Moreover women alone are punished for social crimes in which men are equal partners.[35]

On October 2, 1877, the men of Colorado voted more than two to one against women's suffrage.[36] After their defeat, Albina and Mary Shields turned to the suffrage strategies of temperance leader Frances Willard. Albina had already espoused Willard's methods in her minority report to the Grange in which she proposed that women needed the vote in order to protect their home and family—their accepted social sphere. In 1880, the two women organized a Colorado branch of the Woman's Christian Temperance Union (WCTU) which, as a local charitable organization, offered women a socially acceptable opportunity to grow their leadership skills outside of the home. It also gave Albina, Shields, and other suffragists a forum to quietly instill the necessity for the vote in the minds of more conservative women. Membership in the WCTU grew quickly and auxiliaries formed, but the state would not see another opportunity to vote on suffrage until 1893.[37]

While Albina continued to work for suffrage, change came to her small community. The Colorado Central Railroad laid its tracks, not through St. Louis, Colorado, as the residents had anticipated, but to the west. The depot was completed in December 1877. During that winter, most of the businesses in town put their buildings on skids and moved them a mile northwest to be closer to the depot in the newly established town of Loveland, named for the founder of the Colorado Central Railroad, W. A. H. Loveland.[38] Of course the Washburns and other farmers could not move their established farms, so they faced more difficulty than expected in conveying their produce to the depot for transport to distant markets.

Always active in the farming community, John and Albina joined the Colorado State Grange shortly after its inception in 1874.[39] The Grange promoted farmers' interests and provided their families with a social outlet. On July 27, 1878, Albina, John, daughter Winona, and Winona's husband of three years, Zachary Taylor, represented Big Thompson Grange Number Six at the laying of the cornerstone for Colorado State Agricultural College (today's Colorado State University) in Fort Collins and, as a quartet, performed a Grange song.[40]

John and Albina, as owners of one of Larimer County's first successful dairy and fruit farms, participated in various agricultural associations and often shared their knowledge and experience by presenting papers. During the 1880s and early 1890s, Albina was a popular speaker on far-ranging subjects. She spoke to the Loveland Farmers' Institute on "Domestic Economy," "Household Economy," "Have Our Institutes Been of Any Benefit to the Farmers?," and "What Is the Best Money for the People?," and she was scheduled to present "The Vegetable Garden" but was unable to do so because of illness.[41] She gave "A Woman's View of Forestry" at the inaugural meeting of the Colorado Forestry Association in 1884.[42] Her talks at the state horticultural society's meetings included "Horticulture for Women" and "Cooperative Fruit Markets."[43]

Albina lost her husband on August 15, 1886. John, just fifty-six, died after battling a painful illness for several years. His obituary appeared in Larimer County newspapers as well as Denver's *Labor Enquirer*. The latter article, no doubt penned by Albina, bore the title "A Comrade's Sorrow."[44]

For several years prior to John's death, Albina had been working on a concept for women's cooperative exchanges, and she increased those efforts after his passing. She called it "an experiment in financial reform."[45] In an article in the *Colorado Farmer*, she explained that she wanted to find a way that "women (who were usually moneyless) could obtain honestly the necessaries of life, and more, to make them happy and contented. . . . Why not share with one another what each has to spare?" She described her plan as "cooperative banking with goods instead of money." Each woman would deposit her surplus goods at the exchange and then could withdraw other goods she needed "as we draw money by check which we have deposited in the bank."[46]

In February 1883, Albina temporarily moved to Denver and set up a women's cooperative exchange in a small, rented house on Stout Street. She charged the members a small fee to pay the rent and covered the rest of the expenses herself. The twenty-four members exchanged goods that ran the gamut from pork and beans to poetry books. After three months of running the exchange, Albina returned to her home on the Big Thompson to care for an ailing family member. Unfortunately, no other member of the exchange was willing to take over its management.[47] During the ensuing years, she set up and managed subsequent women's cooperative exchanges in Denver and at her home on the Big Thompson, and mixed-gender cooperative exchanges in Loveland and Fort Collins.[48]

In 1889, Albina continued her drive for women's political rights by running for the only state office open to women, Colorado Superintendent of Public Instruction. She ran on the Union Labor Party ticket and came in fourth in a field of four candidates.[49] She, along with Mary Shields, had persevered to influence women to work for women's suffrage through Colorado's WCTU, and by 1892, that organization had grown to more than a thousand members.[50]

In July of that year, the Larimer County branch of the People's Party elected Albina as a delegate to the party's nominating convention for their Colorado ticket.[51] The party, comprised of mainly farmers and laborers, stood for women's rights to political participation, including suffrage, as evidenced by their allowing women to serve as delegates. Their party platform included free coinage of silver; an eight-hour workday; a child labor law; regulation of freight rates; and the institution of the secret ballot, referendum, and recall. Their candidate for Colorado governor, Davis Waite, won the 1892 election. The party also won the majority in the state senate, but the Republicans maintained control of the house.[52] Under pressure from the suffragists, the new, more reform-minded legislature set a referendum on women's suffrage for November 7, 1893.

Colorado suffragists had quietly built a strong network of supporters since the 1877 referendum, and they were far better prepared to take on the formidable task of convincing the voting men of the state to grant them the right to vote. Albina and Mary Shields' development of the WCTU had armed women with leadership skills and arguments in favor of suffrage. This served them in good stead as they joined with the members of the newly formed Non-Partisan Equal Suffrage Association of Colorado in a door-to-door, grassroots campaign. Colorado newspaperwomen Caroline Nichols Churchill, owner of the feminist *Queen Bee*, and Ellis Meredith, a *Rocky Mountain News* reporter, lent their strong voices to the cause, as did national organization representatives, including WCTU's Frances Willard and Carrie Catt of the National American Woman Suffrage Association.[53] Ironically, an economic crisis also served them well.

A worldwide depression, known as the Panic of 1893, affected Colorado's economy severely. Silver prices dropped significantly, causing mines to close and lay off workers. Railroads filed for bankruptcy, and farm prices bottomed. Runs on the banks forced many to close. Coloradans faced unemployment, homelessness, and hunger.[54] The suffragists promised male voters that women's suffrage would mean more votes for free silver and against monopolies, which the workers and farmers believed would solve their economic woes.[55]

Sadly, in 1893, when the groups that Albina had worked with in the fight for women's rights (Grange, state suffrage associations, WCTU, and People's Party) all came together to marshal votes for Colorado women's suffrage, she sat on the sidelines with her pen her only weapon. In the July 8, 1893, issue of the *Woman's Journal*, she lamented not being actively involved and explained that she was kept at home caring for her invalid mother, who had come to live with the Washburns in the early 1880s, and with household chores "beyond my strength." She said she participated locally by attending and voting at school meetings and running the Women's Cooperative Exchange from her home. She wrote optimistically of the chances for the amendment's passage:

> Be of good cheer, O army of marching women, for Colorado, too, is in the ranks! . . . Suffrage sentiment has grown much of late, and seldom have we a public meeting here that is not more or less tinged with the spirit looking toward woman's enfranchisement.[56]

On November 7, 1893, the men of Colorado, by a majority of fifty-five percent, voted to grant women full suffrage.[57] Caroline Churchill's *Queen Bee* heralded the victory with a front-page headline: "Western Women Wild With Joy Over Colorado Election."[58] Prior to Colorado women's gaining the right to vote, Wyoming and Utah territories had incorporated full suffrage in their constitutions, but Colorado was the first state in which women won the right by referendum.

During Albina's fight for women's and farmers' rights, she had come to believe that the monied class and monopolies were the root of, not only their struggles, but of those of all laborers and that socialism provided the remedy. She based her women's exchanges on socialist principles, and by January 1886, her writing appeared in Denver's *Labor Enquirer*. That newspaper declared itself the "official organ of the Rocky Mountain Social League," an organization whose objectives were "to hold agitation meetings, distribute literature and in all ways aid in the propagation of the doctrines of Socialism."[59]

In December 1887, the *Labor Enquirer* added a "Woman's Column" with Albina as the editor. As an illustration of the content, her January 28, 1888, "Woman's Column" addressed the poor wages, working conditions, and disrespect allotted to female domestic servants and proposed "an honest labor bureau" in Denver to equalize wages.[60] Albina also attended and participated in Social League meetings. At the April 25, 1886, meeting, "Comrade Washburn" read a well-received paper titled "Bulls and Bears."[61]

Albina continued to live on the Loveland farm while she pursued her political activities, participated in agricultural organizations, and managed cooperative exchanges. As late as May 1896, she worked to "perfect the People's Co-operative Exchange plans" (an expansion of her women's cooperative exchange to include men) in Loveland. On July fourth of the same year, she served as a delegate from Larimer County to the People's Party state convention in Denver.[62]

The following year, Albina's daughter, Winona, and her husband moved to Fort Collins so their children could attend Colorado State Agricultural College. The Taylors had six children, but some were grown and living on their own by the time of the move. From oldest to youngest, they were Everett, Nellie, Estes, Laura, Luella, and Clifford.[63] Albina spent that winter at the Taylors' home, and it is believed that she and Winona became charter members of the Fort Collins Unity Church in January of 1898.[64] At the very least, the two women participated in the early years of the church. Albina especially enjoyed working with the choir.[65]

Albina took advantage of her stay in Fort Collins to organize a cooperative exchange in that town. In 1898, the exchange provided a depository for trade items, a dining room, and a reading room. Members held social activities, including a picnic and a rag sewing bee.[66]

At the end of 1899, Albina moved the Fort Collins exchange and reading room to College Avenue, probably to an apartment that she rented as her residence. The 1900 United States Census lists Albina as living at 350 College Avenue in a multi-family building.[67] In early 1900, she invited the workers of the city to join with the farmers at the cooperative exchange: "Come prepared to say not only what you believe, but what you will do to assist your neighbors and be helped yourself."[68]

On January 2, 1902, Albina served as a delegate to a Socialist committee meeting in Denver to organize a Socialist Party state convention.[69] A few months later, her reply to the question: "How Will a Free Society Come and How Will It Operate?" appeared in the *Free Society*, an anarchist newspaper. In the article, Albina, who had devoted so much of her life to gaining the vote for women, posited that voting did not work to change a government that she described as being "in its dotage, administered by a self-appointed regency, variously called Trust, Syndicate, Money, Multi-millionaire; Army, Navy, Party, Power, Law, Necessity, et al. . . ." Instead, she promoted revamping the economic system in much the way she had quietly been doing when she set up cooperative exchanges in Colorado towns. "No weapon was ever so effective, commercially speaking, as the boycott—nor was there ever a remedy for numerous social ills capable of being so peacefully administered." She envisioned a time when all workers would be paid in the product of their labor and wages would be abolished. For instance, coal miners would be paid in coal that they would add to the depository for exchange. She took a practical approach to reaching her ideal world: "But we do not expect to jump from the bottom of the stairs to the top at once. Without haste, if without rest, we will take one step at a time—concentrating perhaps on one great need, then another, until all are won."[70]

Back in the fall of 1898, Albina had visited her nephew in San Diego, and from 1903 to 1909, her name appears in San Diego city directories. The 1910 United States Census for San Diego, California, lists her renting a house on Ingalls Street in that city.[71]

Around 1911, or shortly thereafter, Albina moved back to Fort Collins and lived with her daughter, whose husband had passed away in 1899.[72] On March 3, 1921, Albina passed away at the age of eighty-four. She had attended Unity church services until a few weeks before her death. The Reverend A. Nicholas Kaucher of the Fort Collins Unity Church conducted her funeral service.[73] Her grave lies beside her husband's—at Lakeside Cemetery in Loveland,

Figure 4.5. Washburn family gravestone,
Lakeside Cemetery, Loveland, Colorado, 2020

Courtesy of author Jan Gunia's collection

Colorado.[74]

Albina Louise Washburn wore many hats: first as a Larimer County pioneer, educator, and assistant postmistress, and then, under her self-proclaimed umbrella of radical reformer, as a leader of suffragists, a farmers' advocate, an organizer of cooperative exchanges, and a political activist. The young pioneer wife, who, in 1861, wrote an unsent letter to a friend back home in Illinois expressing her wishes to test her ability to live independently and earn her own keep, spent her life working to give women a voice in their government and an economic system that valued the product of their work. Her writings and her activism led to the fulfillment of some of her own aspirations, as well as those of many Colorado women.

---

[1] Ansel Watrous, *History of Larimer County Colorado* (Fort Collins, CO: The Courier Printing & Publishing Co., 1911), 298, Internet Archive, http://www/archive.org/details/cu31924028878936.

[2] Winona Washburn Taylor, "Notes on the Settlement of the Big Thompson Valley during the Early Part of the 1860's, from Personal Recollections of Mrs. Winona Washburn Taylor," Civil Works Administration Pioneer Interviews, Larimer County PAM 353.18, 96, History Colorado, https://www.historycolorado.org/oral-histories; and see Watrous, *History of Larimer County Colorado*, 129.

[3] 1900 US Census, Fort Collins, Larimer, CO, digital image s.v. "Albina Washburn," Ancestry.com.

[4] "Obituary," [Albina Washburn] *Fort Collins Courier*, Mar. 7, 1921, 2, Colorado Historic Newspapers Collection (website), Colorado State Library, coloradohistoricnewspapers.org. The obituary misspells her maiden name. And see Washburn/Taylor/Holcomb headstone, lot 37, block F, Lakeside Cemetery, Loveland, CO; also see Illinois, U.S., Compiled Marriages, 1791-1850, no image "David H. Holcomb," source: Family History Library, Salt Lake City, UT, microfilm 1314687,

Ancestry.com. David H. Holcomb married Laura A. Case on January 1, 1834 in Tazewell County, IL.

⁵ Cook County, Illinois, US Marriage and Death Indexes, 1833-1889, digital image s.v. "Abina L. Holcomb," Ancestry.com; also see Taylor, "Notes on the Settlement of the Big Thompson Valley," 93; and see Winona Washburn Taylor, "Winona Washburn Taylor," Civil Works Administration Pioneer Interviews, Larimer County PAM 361/30, 280, History Colorado, https://www.historycolorado.org/oral-histories.

⁶ Taylor, "Early Recollections," *Weekly Courier* (Fort Collins, CO), Jan. 23, 1907, 14, Colorado Historic Newspapers Collection (website), Colorado State Library, coloradohistoricnewspapers.org.

⁷ Josephine Payson Clements, "Letters Relate Early Colorado History," *Triangle Review* (Fort Collins, CO), July 27, 1988, 21, livermorewomansclub.org.

⁸ Clements, "Letters Relate Early Colorado History," 21.

⁹ Taylor, "Early Recollections," 14.

¹⁰ Taylor, "Winona Washburn Taylor," 280.

¹¹ Clements, "Letters Relate Early Colorado History," 21.

¹² Taylor, "Early Recollections," 14.

¹³ Clements, "Letters Relate Early Colorado History," 21.

¹⁴ Clements, "Letters Relate Early Colorado History," 21.

¹⁵ Taylor, "Notes on the Settlement of the Big Thompson Valley," 93; and see "Bounty-Land Warrants for Military Service, 1775-1855," National Archives and Records Administration, https://www.archives.gov/files/research/military/bounty-land-1775-1855.pdf. This explains that the US government issued bounty-land warrants to war veterans, both to encourage enlistment and to reward for service. Sometimes the veteran chose to sell his land grant rather than to occupy it.

¹⁶ Taylor, "Notes on the Settlement of the Big Thompson Valley," 93; and see Josephine Payson Clements, "Early Settlers Troubled by Slow Mail," *Triangle Review* (Fort Collins, CO), Apr. 6, 1989, 21, livermorewomansclub.org.

17 U.S., Appointments of U.S. Postmasters, 1832-1971, Larimer County, Colorado Territory, 186, digital image s.v. "John E. Washburn," Ancestry.com. John held the appointment from November 12, 1862 to April 28, 1870.

18 Albina L. Washburn, "Public Sentiment in Colorado," *Woman's Journal* (Boston, MA), July 8, 1893, 212, https://iiif.lib.harvard.edu/manifests/view/drs:49673168$220i.

19 Clements, "Early Settlers Troubled by Slow Mail," 21.

20 Adam Thomas (historian for Historitecture, LLC), "Historical Context" in *In the Hallowed Halls of Learning: The History and Architecture of Poudre School District R-1*, (City of Fort Collins: Poudre School District, August 2004), https://www.fcgov.com/historicpreservation/pdf/psd-historical-context-doc.pdf; and see Taylor, "Early Recollections," 14.

21 Flag made by Albina Washburn, FC 4367, Fort Collins History Connection, https://fchc.contentdm.oclc.org/digital/collection/ma/id/13033/rec/1; and see "Pioneer Flag," *Weekly Courier* (Fort Collins, CO), Aug. 11, 1898, 5, Colorado Historic Newspapers Collection (website), Colorado State Library, coloradohistoricnewspapers.org.

22 Carl McWilliams and Karen McWilliams, historians, *Historic Loveland Residences Cultural Resource Survey* (Loveland, CO: City of Loveland, Community and Strategic Planning Department, May 2010), 8-9, https://irma.nps.gov/DataStore/DownloadFile/578737; and see Taylor, "Notes on the Settlement of the Big Thompson Valley," 94.

23 Taylor, "Notes on the Settlement of the Big Thompson Valley," 94-95.

24 Taylor, "Notes on the Settlement of the Big Thompson Valley," 94-95; see also Clements, "Early Settlers Troubled by Slow Mail," 21; and see "Biography" in Guide to the Papers of the Washburn-Taylor Family, (finding aid mwtc.pdf), Archives and Special Collections, Colorado State University, Fort Collins, CO.

25 Taylor, "Notes on the Settlement of the Big Thompson Valley," 98-99.

26 Taylor, "Winona Washburn Taylor," 282-83; and see "Fort Collins Time Line," Fort Collins History Connection (website), https://history.fcgov.com/timeline/.

27 A. L. W. [Albina L. Washburn], "Woman Voting in Colorado," *Woman's Journal* (Boston, MA), June 12, 1875, 189, https://iiif.lib.harvard.edu/manifests/view/drs:48856487$195i.

28 Suzanne M. Marilley, *Woman Suffrage and the Origins of Liberal Feminism in the United States, 1820-1920* (Cambridge, MA & London: Harvard University Press, 1996), 83-84.

29 Colorado Woman's Suffrage Association Ledger, MSS 1247, 3, 17, 18-19, History Colorado, Denver, CO.

30 Albina L. Washburne, "Annual Meeting, American Woman Suffrage Association, Colorado Report," *Woman's Journal* (Boston, MA), Oct. 7, 1876, 325, https://iiif.lib.harvard.edu/manifests/view/drs:48859470$331i. Apparently the Washburns originally spelled their name with an *e* and later dropped it.

31 "Hearing Before the Committee on Suffrage and Elections," unidentified newspaper clipping pasted in Colorado Woman's Suffrage Association Ledger, 1876-1881, 20.

32 Washburne, "Annual Meeting, American Woman Suffrage Association, Colorado Report," 325, 328.

33 Marilley, *Woman Suffrage and the Origins of Liberal Feminism*, 93.

34 Washburne, "Annual Meeting, American Woman Suffrage Association, Colorado Report," 328.

35 A. L. W. [Albina L. Washburn], "The Grangers on Woman Suffrage," *Woman's Journal* (Boston, MA), Sept. 1, 1877, 280, https://iiif.lib.harvard.edu/manifests/view/drs:48859471$286i.

36 Leslie Karnauskas, "The Road to the Vote," History Colorado (website), November 7, 2019, https://www.historycolorado.org/story/womens-history/2019/11/07/road-vote.

37 Marilley, *Woman Suffrage and the Origins of Liberal Feminism*, 116.

38 "Loveland's Story," Docs & Publications, Loveland Historical Society (website), https://www.lovelandhistorical.org; see also Kenneth Jessen, "Colorado History: Colorado Central Changed

Larimer County," *Reporter Herald* (Loveland, CO), Sept. 7, 2019, re-porterherald.com; and see Stephen J. Leonard and Thomas J. Noel, *Denver: Mining Camp to Metropolis* (Niwot, CO: University Press of Colorado, 1990), 298-299.

[39] Watrous, *History of Larimer County Colorado*, 298.

[40] Taylor, "Winona Washburn Taylor," 284.

[41] "Loveland Institute," *Fort Collins Courier*, Feb. 16, 1882, 3; and see "The Farmers' Institute: Proceeding of the Meeting Held in Loveland, February 5th, 6th and 7th, 1890," *Fort Collins Courier*, Feb. 13, 1890, 6; see also "Loveland's Institute: The Thirteenth Session a Great Success. The Papers All Good," *Leader* (Loveland, CO), Feb. 17, 1893, 1; see "15th Annual Session of the Loveland Farmers Insti-tute," *Loveland Register*, Jan. 24, 1895, 1; and "The Farmers' Council Fire. It Burned Brightly at Loveland Last Week, Bringing out 'Heap Good Talk,'" *Fort Collins Courier*, Jan. 29, 1891, 1. All articles are available at Colorado Historic Newspapers Collection (web-site), Colorado State Library, coloradohistoricnewspapers.org.

[42] "State Forestry Association," *Colorado Miner* (Georgetown, CO), Jan. 3, 1885, 1, Colorado Historic Newspapers Collection (website), Colorado State Library, coloradohistoricnewspa-pers.org.

[43] "State Horticulturists," *Fort Collins Courier*, Jan. 20, 1887, 4,; and see "Local Brevities," *Loveland Register*, Jan. 13, 1897, 1. Both articles are available at Colorado Historic Newspapers Collection (website), Colorado State Library, coloradohistoricnewspa-pers.org.

[44] "J. E. Washburn Dead," [from *The Loveland Reporter*] *Fort Collins Courier*, Aug. 19, 1886, 1; and see "A Comrade's Sorrow," *Labor Enquirer* (Denver, CO), Aug. 21, 1886, 3. Both articles are available at Colorado Historic Newspapers Collection (website), Colorado State Library, coloradohistoricnewspapers.org.

[45] Albina L. Washburn, "Woman's Co-operative Exchange," *Colorado Farmer, Fruit Grower and Live Stock Journal* (Denver, CO), Nov. 5, 1892, 4, Colorado Historic Newspapers Collection (web-site), Colorado State Library, coloradohistoricnewspapers.org.

[46] Washburn, "Woman's Co-operative Exchange," 4.

[47] Washburn, "Woman's Co-operative Exchange," 4.

[48] Washburn, "Woman's Co-operative Exchange," 4; and see Advertisement for "Woman's Co-operative Exchange," *Labor Enquirer* (Denver, CO), Jan. 30, 1886, 1; also see Mrs. A. L. Washburn, "Co-Operative Club Dinner," *Leader* (Loveland, CO), Dec. 2, 1892, 5; and see "Cliff Cottage," *Loveland Register*, May 20, 1896, 8; and see also "Fort Collins Cooperative Exchange," *Fort Collins Courier*, Oct. 22, 1896, 1; "Society Notes," *Fort Collins Courier*, Mar. 10, 1898, 5. All articles are available at Colorado Historic Newspapers Collection (website), Colorado State Library, coloradohistoricnewspapers.org.

[49] "The Vote for State Offices," *Fort Collins Courier*, Jan. 10, 1889, 4, Colorado Historic Newspapers Collection (website), Colorado State Library, coloradohistoricnewspapers.org.

[50] Marilley, *Woman Suffrage and the Origins of Liberal Feminism*, 116.

[51] "Saturday's Convention: The People's Party Hold an Important Meeting," *Leader* (Loveland, CO), July 29, 1892, 1, Colorado Historic Newspapers Collection (website), Colorado State Library, coloradohistoricnewspapers.org; and see Albina L. Washburn, "Colorado Suffrage Items," *Woman's Journal* (Boston, MA), Aug. 27, 1892, 276, https://iiif.lib.harvard.edu/manifests/view/drs:49687854$284i.

[52] Graeme Pente, "Populism in Colorado," *Colorado Encyclopedia* (website), last modified May 4, 2020, https://coloradoencyclopedia.org/article/populism-colorado; and see Carl Abbott, Stephen J. Leonard, and David McComb, *Colorado: A History of the Centennial State*, revised edition (Boulder, CO: Colorado Associated University Press, 1982), 141.

[53] Marilley, *Woman Suffrage and the Origins of Liberal Feminism*, 124. The two national suffrage associations, the National Woman Suffrage Association and the American Woman Suffrage Association merged as the National American Woman Suffrage Association in 1890.

[54] Leonard and Noel, *Denver: Mining Camp to Metropolis*, 103.

55 Marilley, *Woman Suffrage and the Origins of Liberal Feminism*, 146-7.

56 In the 1885 Colorado State Census, District 1, Larimer County, digital image s.v. "Albena Washbourne," Ancestry.com, L. Holcomb, the name of Albina's mother, is listed as living with the Washburns. She is not listed as living with them in the 1880 US Census, Big Thompson, Larimer County digital image s.v. "Albina Washburn," Ancestry.com, so it is assumed Albina's mother moved in with the Washburns after 1880. See also Albina L. Washburn, "Public Sentiment in Colorado," 212.

57 Marilley, *Woman Suffrage and the Origins of Liberal Feminism*, 148.

58 Elizabeth Duncan, "Caroline Nichols Churchill," *Colorado Encyclopedia* (website), last modified September 15, 2020, https://coloradoencyclopedia.org/article/caroline-nichols-churchill.

59 Mrs. A. L. Washburn, "Our Own. The Food, the Clothing, the Comforts and the Luxuries Are the People's. Let Us Exchange with Each Other on the Basis of Liberty, Equality Fraternity. The Reasons Given by Mrs. Washburn for Establishing the 'Women's Co-Operative Exchange,'" *Labor Enquirer* (Denver, CO), Jan. 30, 1886, 1, 4; also see "Socialist Propaganda Fund," *Labor Enquirer* (Denver, CO), Jan. 23, 1886, 3. Both articles are available at Colorado Historic Newspapers Collection (website), Colorado State Library, coloradohistoricnewspapers.org.

60 "Woman's Column," *Labor Enquirer* (Denver, CO), Dec. 24, 1887, 4; and see Mrs. A. L. Washburn, ed., "Woman's Column," *Labor Enquirer* (Denver, CO), Jan. 28, 1888, 4. Both articles are available at Colorado Historic Newspapers Collection (website), Colorado State Library, coloradohistoricnewspapers.org.

61 "The League," *Labor Enquirer* (Denver, CO), May 1, 1886, 1, Colorado Historic Newspapers Collection (website), Colorado State Library, coloradohistoricnewspapers.org.

62 "Cliff Cottage," *Loveland Register*, May 20, 1896, 8; see also "People's Party Convention," *Fort Collins Courier*, July 2, 1896, 1.

Both articles are available at Colorado Historic Newspapers Collection (website), Colorado State Library, coloradohistoricnewspapers.org.

⁶³ Taylor, "Winona Washburn Taylor," 283.

⁶⁴ "Personal," *Fort Collins Courier*, Dec. 2, 1897, 1, Colorado Historic Newspapers Collection (website), Colorado State Library, coloradohistoricnewspapers.org; see also Arthur T. Corey, *The Unitarians in Fort Collins: The First Hundred Years*, 11, Foothills Unitarian Church, https://foothillsuu.org/wp-content/uploads/2019/08/Church-History-The-First-Hundred-Years.pdf.

⁶⁵ "Obituary," [Albina Washburn], 2.

⁶⁶ "Society Notes, *Fort Collins Courier*, Mar. 10, 1898, 5; and see Albina L. Washburn, "Farmer's Picnic Dinner," *Fort Collins Courier*, Apr. 7, 1898, 8; see also Albina L. Washburn, "Personal," *Weekly Courier* (Fort Collins, CO), Sept. 8, 1898, 1. All articles are available at Colorado Historic Newspapers Collection (website), Colorado State Library, coloradohistoricnewspapers.org.

⁶⁷ "City and Country," *Weekly Courier* (Fort Collins, CO), Nov. 23, 1899, 6, Colorado Historic Newspapers Collection (website), Colorado State Library, coloradohistoricnewspapers.org; and see 1900 US Census, Fort Collins, Larimer County, CO, digital image s.v. "Albina Washburn," Ancestry.com.

⁶⁸ Albina L. Washburn, "City and Country," *Weekly Courier* (Fort Collins, CO), Jan. 18, 1900, 3, Colorado Historic Newspapers Collection (website), Colorado State Library, coloradohistoricnewspapers.org.

⁶⁹ "January in Early Fort Collins," blog post, Fort Collins Historical Society (website), https://fortcollinshistoricalsociety.org/2017/06/20/2017-6-20-january-in-early-fort-collins/.

⁷⁰ Albina L. Washburn, "How Will a Free Society Come and How Will It Operate?," *Free Society*, April 6, 1902, 2-3, fairuse.org/free-society/how-will-a-free-society-come-and-how-will-it-operate/.

⁷¹ "Personal," *Weekly Courier* (Fort Collins, CO), Oct. 27, 1898, 1, Colorado Historic Newspapers Collection (website), Colorado State Library, coloradohistoricnewspapers.org; see San Diego, CA,

City Directory, 1903, 378, U.S. City Directories, 1822-1995, digital image s.v. "Albina L. Washburn," Ancestry.com; and also San Diego, CA, City Directory, 1904, 497, U.S. City Directories, 1822-1995, digital image s.v. "Albina L. Washburn," Ancestry.com; also see San Diego, CA, City Directory, 1905, 448, U.S. City Directories, 1822-1995, digital image s.v. "Albina L. Washburn," Ancestry.com; and see San Diego, CA, City Directory, 1906, 541, U.S. City Directories, 1822-1995, digital image s.v. "Albina L. Washburn," Ancestry.com; and see San Diego, CA, City Directory, 1907, 531, U.S. City Directories, 1822-1995, digital image s.v. "Albina L. Washburn," Ancestry.com; see also San Diego, CA, City Directory, 1908, 554, U.S. City Directories, 1822-1995, "Albina L. Holcomb Washburn," Ancestry.com; see also San Diego, CA, City Directory, 1909, 530, U.S. City Directories, 1822-1995, digital image s.v. "Albina L. Holcomb Washburn," Ancestry.com. See also 1910 US Census, San Diego Township, San Diego County, CA, digital image s.v. "Albina H. Washburn," Ancestry.com.

[72] "Loveland," *Weekly Courier* (Fort Collins, CO), July 28, 1911, 4, Colorado Historic Newspapers Collection (website), Colorado State Library, coloradohistoricnewspapers.org; also see "Obituary," [Albina Washburn], 2; and see 1920 US Census, Fort Collins, Larimer, CO, digital image s.v. "Albina Washburn," Ancestry.com; see also Taylor, "Winona Washburn Taylor," 283.

[73] "Obituary," [Albina Washburn], 2.

[74] Larimer County Genealogical Society (website), Larimer County Cementeries 1860-2005 (database), Lakeside Cemetery in Loveland (1860-2002), surname *W* listings, 3. Gravesite visited by authors.

Figure 5.1. Katrina Murat, circa 1855

Courtesy of History Colorado, Denver, Colorado,
Accession #89.451.2581

Katrina Murat:
Mother of Colorado

Arrived in Colorado, November 4, 1858

Blue-eyed, rosy-cheeked, and golden-haired, Katrina (also Catherine, Katerina, and Catharina) Murat liked to be called the "Mother of Colorado" or the "Betsy Ross of the Colorado Territory," despite her German heritage.[1] In November of 1858, she and her husband, "Count" Henry (also Henri) Murat, traveled to what would later become the state of Colorado.[2] Katrina is thought to be one of the first Anglo women to arrive with the Pikes Peak Gold Rush and to settle in the area. She fell in love with the Rocky Mountains and spent most of the rest of her life in Colorado. She sewed the first American flag to fly over the Cherry Creek settlements and is known as Colorado's only countess.

Born Katrina Wolf on August 20, 1824, in Heidelsheim in the Grand Duchy of Baden (now part of Germany), Katrina's family owned a large vineyard that stretched below a spur of the Black Forest.[3] She was the younger of two daughters in a family with "comfortable" circumstances. She loved music and throughout her life sang verses of opera or stanzas from her beloved Goethe or Schiller. Her practical family made sure she was skilled in spinning, weaving, sewing, and cooking—skills that were invaluable during her adventurous life in Colorado.[4]

Katrina died in Palmer Lake, Colorado, in 1910. For years before her death, she was a celebrity of sorts, and reporters often came to interview her about life in Colorado prior to statehood. One woman, Louie Croft Boyd, lived with Katrina for three winters and wrote a biography about her that was published in the *Colorado Magazine* in 1939.[5] In her article, Boyd details Katrina's adventurous experiences. Katrina led a remarkable life, but as with several articles written by reporters who interviewed Katrina in her later years, the accuracy of some of these stories is questionable. Evidence indicates Katrina rewrote pieces of her history, although it is unclear why. The one detail that is consistently reported inaccurately is the story of her meeting and marriage to Henry Murat.

Publications and unpublished writings about Katrina tell a romantic story about how her husband fled France after falling out of favor with the Bourbons, the ruling house at that time.[6] In this version of her story, Henry Murat worked for Katrina's father and fell in love with the lovely Katrina. Before asking for her hand in marriage, Henry showed Katrina's father documents proving he was a count and showing his connection to Joachim-Napoléon Murat.[7] Undeniably, this makes for a romantic story, but according to Henry's obituary

and other historical documents, it does not appear to be true.
Henry Murat died February 8, 1885, and five days after his
death, the *Rocky Mountain News* in Denver published his

Figure 5.2. Henry Murat, circa 1855

*Courtesy of History Colorado, Denver, Colorado,
Accession #89.451.2577*

obituary titled "A Peculiar Pioneer."[8] The obituary states that Murat was Katrina Wolf's second husband and that they married in California, not Germany. Additional sources provide evidence that Katrina's marriage in Germany was to a man named Stolzenberger (the spelling varies in sources as Stolstenberger, Statenberger, and Stolerbergen). Katrina and her first husband married in February 1848 and immigrated to the United States that same year.[9] In 1852, the Stolzenbergers traveled across the United States to San Francisco where her husband died. Katrina then married Henry Murat. San Francisco's *Daily Alta California* of August 20, 1855, announced the marriage of Henry Murat to Katharine Stolerbergen, stating the nuptials were officiated by Rev. N. Thurston.[10]

Why Katrina appears to have changed her past may never be known, although it does make a wonderful historical mystery. Still, two interesting things should be noted. First, the authors were unable to find a record of Katrina Stolstenberger or Katrina Wolf (or any of the numerous spellings of her name) in the 1850 United States Census, although in later census data, Katrina lists 1848 as her arrival date into the United

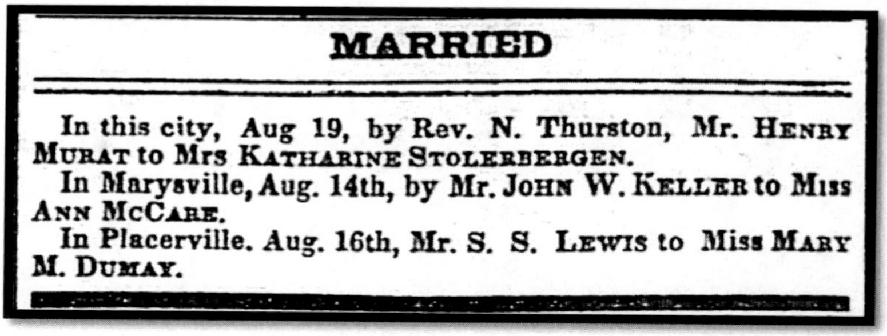

MARRIED

In this city, Aug 19, by Rev. N. Thurston, Mr. HENRY MURAT to Mrs KATHARINE STOLERBERGEN.
In Marysville, Aug. 14th, by Mr. JOHN W. KELLER to Miss ANN McCABE.
In Placerville. Aug. 16th, Mr. S. S. LEWIS to Miss MARY M. DUMAY.

Figure 5.3. This announcement of the marriage of Henry Murat and Mrs. Katharine Stolerbergen appeared in the *Daily Alta California* (San Francisco), Aug. 20, 1855.

Courtesy of the California Digital Newspaper Collection

States. Second, while searching records of 1848-1849 emigrants from Germany, the names Katrina Wolf, Katrina Murat (or any of the numerous spellings of her name) were not found, but a twenty-one-year-old Catharina Stolzenberger, along with her husband, Mathias Stolzenberger, arrived in New York on August 15, 1849, on the ship Leila.[11] If this is indeed the future Katrina Murat, one must question why she, or newspaper articles about her, never mentioned this first husband and why her arrival date was actually 1849.

Perhaps a future biographer will find the truth, or maybe the secret lies in the turmoil existing in her homeland, the Duchy of Baden, at the time she emigrated. During the 1848 French Revolution, there were popular uprisings in Germany, Italy, and Hungary. Insurrection broke out in the Duchy of Baden but was speedily crushed, forcing the rebellion leaders and their supporters to flee. Many of the Germans who emigrated to the United States in 1848-1849 were escaping retribution; perhaps Katrina and her husband, along with Henry Murat, were part of this exodus.[12] Perhaps they knew each other; perhaps Henry Murat was a colleague of Stolzenbergers; or, for a true mystery lover, perhaps Murat and Stolzenberger were indeed the same man. The truth may never be known, but the mystery adds to Katrina's unusual and adventuerous life story.

Two months after Katrina's death, a detailed article about her, written by M. W. Henderson, appeared in *The Trail: A Magazine for Colorado*. Henderson's piece, written in the romanticized, rather flowery language of the day, includes details of Katrina's German marriage: "And here, among the vine-clad hills of Baden-Baden, the fresh young girl, attired in maiden purity, her waist girt with a sash of blue, met her future husband at a dance. They were married during the troublous times succeeding the Revolution of Paris in

February 1848."[13]

What's interesting about this description is that, although the author implies Katrina is marrying Murat, the article does not actually name Katrina's "future husband." The article continues, detailing much of Katrina's life, and it provides one of the few glimpses of her life from 1848 through her travels to California. According to Henderson, after arriving in the United States, the couple moved to Pennsylvania, but as stories of gold discoveries in California spread across the United States, they packed up and headed west.

They joined a wagon train in Leavenworth, Kansas, where Katrina was the only woman traveling with twenty-four men. Like many pioneers who traveled by wagon train in 1852, Katrina experienced both amazing wonders and terrible hardships.[14] She saw huge buffalo herds and Native Americans living nomadic lifestyles, she encountered Mormons heading to their promised land, Zion, and she met trappers, mountain men, and other gold seekers heading to California. At one point along their journey, her wagon train found a dying man who had been deserted by his own party and later rescued by Native Americans. He joined their wagon train, and Katrina nursed him back to health.[15]

Henderson's article never mentions Stolzenberger, but Henry's obituary states that when Stolzenberger died, Katrina inherited the enormous sum of $75,000,[16] over $2.6 million in 2023 dollars.[17] The exact date and location of Stolzenberger's death has not been found, nor is it known how he obtained such wealth, but on August 19, 1855, Katrina married Henry Murat, and soon after their marriage, the couple traveled to Europe. They remained in Europe during 1856 and 1857, and when their funds ran low, they returned to San Francisco.[18]

According to Henry's obituary, he was born in Hanover on October 24, 1824. His father was a surgeon in the French army, and Henry was the family's only child. Little else is known about the family or why Henry chose to immigrate to the United States. His 1864 United States passport application describes Henry as five feet, ten inches tall, with a full face, a florid complexion, a prominent nose, and light hazel eyes. Although Henry claimed he was a French count and a nephew of Joachim-Napoléon Murat, who had been made King of Naples by Napoléon Bonaparte, this aristocratic heritage has never been proven or disproven. Katrina and Henry spent much of their lives being called the Count and Countess Murat.

In the fall of 1858, the Murats joined a wagon train and left San Francisco, traveling toward the Cherry Creek settlements at the base of the Rocky Mountains. They, like other gold seekers, had heard rumors of gold discoveries near Pikes Peak. During this journey, articles describe how a band of Native Americans forced the wagon train to stop so that the natives could see the "white squaw." Katrina, taking her customary afternoon nap, was awakened by her husband and hidden in flour sacks. She remained hidden until the men leading the wagon train gave the Native Americans bacon and flour and convinced them to leave.[19] Years later, Katrina liked to end this story by saying, "Murat was scared."[20]

Katrina and Henry, along with about sixty other settlers, arrived in Montana City in early November of 1858. Montana City was the first permanent settlement on the eastern slope of the Rocky Mountains.[21] It was located near Denver's present-day intersection of South Huron Street and West Evans Avenue, about six miles south of the confluence of the South Platte River and Cherry Creek. When the Murats arrived, the settlement was just a of couple months old and consisted of approximately fifteen crude, semi-permanent log cabins. Each cabin was ten-by-twelve feet in size with dirt floors and roofs made of poles covered with sod.[22]

The Murats built a cabin in Montana City, and Henry opened the first tonsorial temple, or barber shop, in the region.[23] On December 14, 1858, the *Kansas City Daily Journal of Commerce* published a letter Henry wrote that included the following: "My wife is well and getting fat. She looks as blooming and fresh as a maiden, so well the free air of the prairies agrees with her. . . . to-morrow we shall have the cabin done ready for occupancy. . . ."[24]

The Murats, like other Montana City residents, thought they had settled in the primary community in the area, but land speculators closer to the confluence of the South Platte River and Cherry Creek had different plans. North of the confluence, General William Larimer and his party began platting out a new town called Denver City. On the opposite side of Cherry Creek, the Russell brothers, along with their party of Georgians who had first discovered gold in Little Dry Creek, platted out the rival town of Auraria. The towns vied for each new immigrant, hoping to become the predominant town in the area.

Auraria and Denver City soon grew bigger than Montana City. Nolie Mumey wrote in his *History of the Early Settlements of Denver (1599-1860)* that the Montana City miners were out prospecting when "the town builders of Auraria sent ox teams to Montana City, tore down every house in the settlement, and used them to decorate the streets of their own townsite, Auraria."[25] History is vague on the accuracy of this event, yet within a month of their arrival, the Murats moved to Auraria and went into business with David Smoke, opening the area's first hotel, the El Dorado House (also spelled Eldorado House), located on 10th Street, east of Larimer Street.[26]

In 1858, as Christmas approached, Katrina and Henry

planned a holiday party and invited their neighbors, including Uncle Dick Wootton, who brought some of his notorious Taos Lightning whiskey, along with his family. Following German traditions, Katrina decorated a Christmas tree with gingerbread cookies and lit candles on the tree's boughs, which delighted all the new settlers, especially the Rooker and Wootton children, the only youngsters in the settlement.[27]

The El Dorado Hotel opened on February 1, 1859. It was a one-story log cabin approximately seventeen by twenty feet, built from roughly hewn cottonwood logs and chinked with river mud. It had earthen floors, a mud-plastered chimney, and buffalo-robed beds.[28] The structure had a log tower where Count Murat watched for approaching wagon trains. It was on this tower on May 7, 1859 — the day the first Leavenworth & Pike's Peak Express stagecoach arrived in Denver City — that Katrina hung the American flag she had made for the occasion. Hers was the first flag to fly over the Cherry Creek settlements.[29]

To make her flag, Katrina used a red merino skirt she had bought in Paris, a white silk petticoat, and a blue flannel dress. Other Colorado pioneer women, including Mrs. S. M. Rooker, Mrs. Joseph Wolff, Mrs. Albina Washburn, and Mrs. Mary Melissa Hall, would also sew American flags, although what most of these flags looked like is unknown. In 1912, the United States Congress specified the arrangement of the stars in the union (the blue field), but before that time, women such as Katrina sewed their stars into differing patterns and designs according to their own whims. When asked how she made the flag without a pattern, she said, "How could anyone who has seen the flag and loves liberty and freedom forget what it is like? I knew there must be a star for every State and I counted the States at that time."[30] This is probably a reporter's polished rendition of her words since even at the time of her death, Katrina's English was recorded as being gramatically awkward.

One of the men who arrived on the first stagecoach was Libeus Barney of Vermont. He wrote about his travels and sent his letters back east for publication in his hometown newspaper, the *Bennington Banner*.[31] Barney stayed in Denver City, not Auraria, and chose to stay at Denver City's first hotel, Denver Hall, which included a large corral known as the "Elephant Corral."[32] His description of the Cherry Creek settlements gives an interesting view of the world Katrina then called home:

> This marvelous city contains about 150 log cabins, some with roofs, and more without. One hotel, 40 by 200, built of logs and covered with canvas. Here I am stopping at the moderate price of $3 per day. Business is wholly stagnant; money,—coin, I mean,—scarce, and gold dust scarcer.[33]

Although Henry was listed as proprietor of the El Dorado, like many women who settled in Colorado, Katrina was an integral part of her husband's business. Not only was she cook, hostess, and maid, but she also washed miners' laundry. Henry once wrote, "My frau is the first white woman out here and will make money washing clotes which will pay her perhaps 50 centes a piece."[34] Known for her excellent cooking, Katrina's cakes and pies were prized, and during the years she lived in Denver, it is estimated she earned approximately $50,000 (about one million dollars in 2023)[35] selling pies for two dollars and doing laundry.[36]

On April 9, 1859, General Larimer offered the Murats four lots in Denver City, perhaps hoping a woman would bring more respectability to his town. The Murats sold the El Dorado and by the fall of 1859, the El Dorado had become

Henry Humbel's bakery.[37] The Murats built a house on Lawrence Street near Fourteenth Street, and Henry established his barber shop in a building on Fourteenth and Larimer.[38]

During the summer of 1859, Horace Greeley, the well-known editor of the *New York Tribune*, set out on a cross-country trip with plans to investigate the rumors about the Pikes Peak Gold Rush. During his journey, he sent back dispatches describing his travels for publication in his paper. In June of 1859, he wrote that he "had the honor to be shaved there [in Denver] by a nephew (so he assured me) of Murat, Bonaparte's King of Naples—the honor and the shave together costing but a paltry dollar."[39] Katrina added to Greeley's expenses by charging three dollars to wash his clothes. Greeley wrote sarcastically that this new country "harbored at least one person determined to make the best of his opportunities."[40]

Two years later, Henry Murat indirectly responded to Greeley's criticism in a *Rocky Mountain News* article published on December 21, 1861:

> The writer of this, being intimately acquainted with Murat, is requested to state that Murat is surprised that a man who has traveled as much as Horace, should not know that if a barber's services are called to the sick bed, they are worth more than if rendered at his shop. The Count desires me further to state, that in view of the fact that he dressed Horace's wounds, and made his bed, and did not receive as much as a "thank you, sir," he is sorry he did not charge him ten dollars for the shave.[41]

It is hard to imagine how difficult day-to-day living was for women during the early years in the Colorado Territory. In his book, *Beyond the Mississippi*, Albert D. Richardson described Denver as "a strange medley" populated with "Americans from every quarter of the Union, Mexicans, Indians, half-breeds, trappers, speculators, gamblers, desperadoes, broken-down politicians and honest men." He described the Cherry Creek settlements by saying they contained "about one thousand people, with three hundred buildings, nearly all of hewn pine logs. One-third were unfinished and roofless, having been erected the previous winter for speculative purposes."[42] Although a few gold seekers struck it rich, most settlers worked hard in their new home.

Many early Denver settlers, like the Murats, engaged in numerous businesses. In 1861, in addition to being a barber, Henry advertised in the *Rocky Mountain News* as an agent to send goods between Denver and various locations in Germany.[43] Later he advertised as a real estate agent.[44] Katrina's highly successful bakery business contributed to the couple's finances, allowing the Murats to live better than many.

NEW SHAVING SALOON.
I have recently fitted up a fine room on Larimer Street, opposite Apollo Hall, where I shall be happy to wait upon all who favor me with a call.   52   HENRY MURAT.

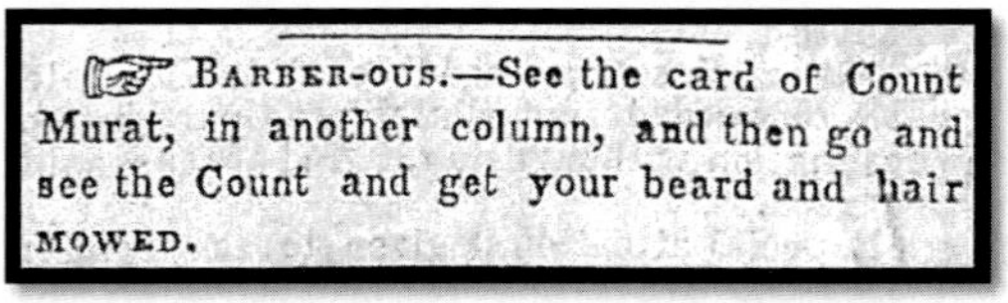

☞ BARBER-OUS.—See the card of Count Murat, in another column, and then go and see the Count and get your beard and hair MOWED.

Figure 5.4. Advertisements, *Rocky Mountain News*, Denver, Colorado, April 18, 1860, 3

Courtesy of Colorado Historic Newspapers Collection

In 1862, the Murats left Denver and traveled to Virginia City, Montana. Before leaving, they sold their house on Larimer Street, describing it for the sale as "one of the most elegant and commodious dwellings in Denver."[45] In Virginia City, the Murats ran a saloon and sundry arcade, probably a gambling hall, until 1864. During this time, it is probable they also visited Denver since they continued to advertise their businesses.[46]

Meanwhile, their Montana venture was so successful they amassed a small fortune. To safely return to Denver with this fortune, Katrina quilted some of the gold dust into her petticoat and secured more gold with heavy leather belts under her skirts.[47] During their trav-

Figure 5.5. Advertisement, *Weekly Commonwealth and Republican*, Denver, Colorado, July 2, 1863, 1

Courtesy of Colorado Historic Newspapers Collection

els, Katrina carried so much gold on her person that the leather belts rubbed against her knee, leaving permanent scars.

The Murats carried their gold dust to New York City and exchanged it for $50,000, over $960,000 in 2023 dollars.[48] They used the money to finance a passport, tickets, and a final journey to Europe. Their passport was issued on December 28, 1864, and it shows a visa issued in Carlsruhe on January 30, 1865, and entry into Salzburg on February 4, 1866.[49] They also are thought to have traveled through northern France, Switzerland, Italy, Austria, Germany, and Russia.

Katrina claimed that while they were in Europe, she saw the Emperor Napoleon III and his wife, Eugenie, and they often played roulette with Count Von Molkt's [assumed Moltke's] sister.[50] During this final European trip, Henry Murat was described as "living the life of a nabob and assuming all the airs of a true Count."[51] The couple spent money lavishly and after a year's extravagance, they returned to Denver, where Henry purchased Mozart Hall, a fine establishment on Larimer Street between Fifteenth and Sixteenth Streets.

Mozart Hall sold liquor but was also known as a billiard and gambling saloon.[52] The July 1, 1868, *Rocky Mountain News* contains an interesting advertisement describing the elegance of Mozart Hall:

> Count Murat invites his numerous friends to call on him at his cool and elegant retreat on the fair ground, where he has the most beautifully arranged rural bar ever seen in Colorado. His arrangements show rare taste and skill, while his wines and liquors are the best ever offered in the city: He has private retreats where one can enjoy Perrin's strawberries and Rhine wine pleasantly and undisturbed by the crowd. The Count's picture adorns the whole scene, while, better than all, the Count himself is there.[53]

Henry's extravagance while running Mozart Hall soon depleted the couple's savings. He eventually lost the business, and over the next twelve years, it was Katrina's income—and the pawning of her remaining jewelry—that kept them afloat. Henry Murat continued to spiral downward, "doing no particular good," and finally, in July 1881, Katrina divorced him.[54] A few months after this divorce, Henry Murat, a homeless drunk, was described in the *Helena Weekly Herald*:

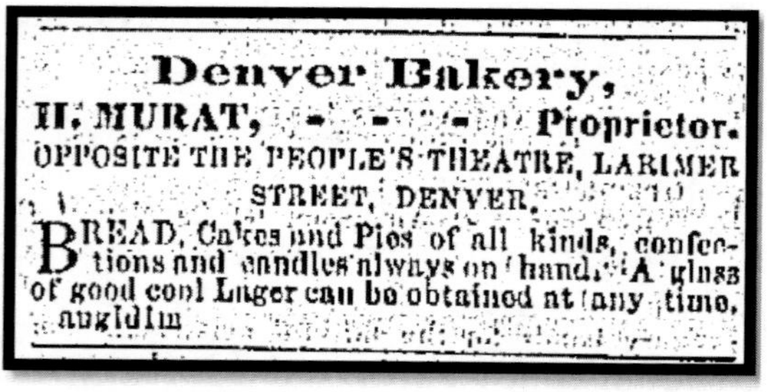

Denver Bakery,
H. MURAT, - - - - Proprietor.
OPPOSITE THE PEOPLE'S THEATRE, LARIMER STREET, DENVER.
BREAD, Cakes and Pies of all kinds, confections and candles always on hand. A glass of good cool Lager can be obtained at any time.
aug1dlm

Figure 5.6. Advertisement, *The Weekly Commonwealth*, Denver, Colorado, November 20, 1862, 4

Courtesy of Colorado Historic Newspapers Collection

Henry Murat, "Count of Colorado," at one time a million-aire and a leader of fashion in the West, and who once spent $300,000 in one visit to Europe, slept recently on the floor of a barber shop in Denver, because the proprietor could not find it in his heart to eject the now shattered old man.[55]

Despite their divorce, when Henry died at the age of sixty-one, on February 8, 1885, Katrina insisted his funeral be held in her home at 603 Lawrence Street.[56] A few years later, in 1887, Katrina, then sixty-three years old, sold her home in Denver and retired to Palmer Lake fifty miles south of Denver.

Katrina settled into an isolated cottage at the foot of Sundance Mountain and spent the next twenty-three years as a beloved figure in the Palmer Lake community. Her neighbors often visited to hear stories about her life during the early gold rush years. One listener described her conversation by saying it was "like old wine, and no one could forget the savour of it."[57]

In Palmer Lake, Katrina lived with a dog named Ring and a pet parrot who sang the popular tune "Two Little Girls in Blue."[58] If her dog wandered too far from home, she would chastise the animal by saying, "Ring, you bad dog, I vill vip you. Lie down, geschwinde!" But soon she would pet her companion and say, "You vill stay at home with Mrs. Murat, yes, you're a good dog, Ringlie, yes."[59] Although Katrina, the so-called "Mother of Colorado," lived in America for more than sixty years, she never lost her thick German accent.

Katrina's fortune was gone, but the Society of Colorado Pi-oneers provided a monthly pension of ten dollars to her in her

Figure 5.7. Katrina Murat, later years, circa 1895

Courtesy of History Colorado, Denver, Colorado,
Accession #89.451.2580

old age. The town of Palmer Lake eventually piped water to
her cottage, giving her free water until she died. Despite her
many hardships, "the spirit of generosity and independence

for which she was noted and her love of the western wilderness, never left her."[60] On March 13, 1910, Katrina Murat died at the age of eighty-five.

To commemorate her extraordinary life and the contributions she made to Colorado, the Denver Chapter of the Daughters of the American Revolution placed a boulder of Silver Plume granite over her grave in Denver's Riverside Cemetery with the following inscription:

In memory of
The maker of the first United States flag
in Colorado
Katrina Wolf Murat
1824-1910[61]

---

[1] Marian McIntyre McDonough, "Pioneer Countess" (unpublished manuscript, Aug. 1970, typescript), 1, Special Collections History Manuscripts and Archives, Carnegie Special Collections, Pikes Peak Library District, Colorado Springs, CO.

[2] "A Peculiar Pioneer," *Rocky Mountain News* (Denver, CO), Feb. 13, 1885, 8, Western History Collection, Denver Public Library. Some references, including Louie Croft Boyd's "Katrina Wolf Murat, The Pioneer," in *Colorado Magazine*, September 1939, 181, list November 3, 1858, for their arrival in Denver, while other references cite November 2. The latter includes Nolie Mumey, *History of the Early Settlements of Denver (1599-1860): with reproductions of the First City Directory, the 1859 Map, the first issue of the Rocky Mountain News, and the Rare Cheery Creek Pioneer* (Glendale, CA: Arthur H. Clark), 48, https://babel.ha-thitrust.org/cgi/pt?id=ucl.32106017228849&view=1up&seq=60.

[3] McDonough, "Pioneer Countess," 1. Various references say 'near Baden-Baden' but the article on Katrina Wolf Murat in the Denver Chapter article in the *Daughters of the American Revolution*

Magazine, August 1917, 83, states Heidelsheim, which the authors believe is more accurate.

[4] M. W. Henderson, "Episodes in the Life of the Countess Murat," *The Trail: A Magazine for Colorado,* May 1910, 13.

[5] Louie Croft Boyd, "Katrina Wolf Murat, The Pioneer," 180.

[6] Augusta Hauck Block, "Christmas in 1858," MSS 2496, Colorado Subject Collection: Biographical Files, Box 55, Augusta Hauck Block folder, History Colorado, Denver, CO; and see Henderson, "Episodes," 14.

[7] Block, "Christmas in 1858."

[8] "A Peculiar Pioneer," 8.

[9] 1900 US Census, Town of Palmer Lake, El Paso, Colorado, digital image s.v. "Katrina Murat," Ancestry.com. This census, along with other references, lists Katrina as immigrating to the US in 1848.

[10] "Married," *Daily Alta California* (San Francisco, CA), Aug. 20, 1855, 2, California Digital Newspaper Collection (website), Center for Bibliographic Studies and Research, University of California, Riverside, http://cdnc.ucr.edu.

[11] 1849 Immigration Records, Ship Leila, Microfilm Roll Number 82, digital image s.v. "Mathias Stolzenberger," Ancestry.com.

[12] "Historical Insights, German Immigration in 1848," (webpage) accessed February 11, 2021, Ancestry.com https://www.ancestry.com/contextux/historicalinsights/german-immigration-1848.

[13] Henderson, "Episodes," 14.

[14] "A Peculiar Pioneer," 8.

[15] Henderson, "Episodes," 14.

[16] "A Peculiar Pioneer," 8.

[17] The equivalent purchasing power of $75,000 in 1855, as of May 17, 2023, was calculated to be $2,615,198 assuming a 2.4% inflation rate, Consumer Price Index (CPI) inflation calculator (webpage), https://www.officialdata.org/us/inflation/1855?amount=750000.

[18] "A Peculiar Pioneer," 8.

[19] McDonough, "Pioneer Countess," 2-3.

[20] Henderson, "Episodes," 15.

[21] Mumey, *Early Settlements*, 47.

[22] Mumey, *Early Settlements*, 47-49.

[23] The Lawrence Street home sale notice in the *Rocky Mountain News* (Denver, CO), May 3, 1862, 3, reads: "Count Murat, of pioneer, public and partisan notoriety, the gentleman who started the first tonsorial temple in this country, at Montana City, a few miles above town, in 1859, and the well known and polite professor of the art, at present on Larimer Street, has one of the most elegant and commodious dwellings in Denver, situated on Lawrence Street, opposite the Brick Church, which he would sell for a family residence on reasonable terms. It is as new and nice looking as a new pin." Article found in the Colorado Historic Newspapers Collection (website), Colorado State Library, coloradohistoricnewspapers.org.

[24] "Henri Murat Letter," *Kansas City Journal of Commerce*, Dec. 14, 1858, Kansas City Public Library, Missouri Valley Special Collections.

[25] Mumey, *Early Settlements*, 49.

[26] McDonough, "Pioneer Countess," 3.

[27] McDonough, "Pioneer Countess," 5; and see Block "Christmas in 1858."

[28] McDonough, "Pioneer Countess," 3.

[29] Mumey, *Early Settlements*, 99-100; and see LeRoy R. Hafen, ed., *Colorado and Its People: A Narrative and Topical History of the Centennial State* (New York, NY: Lewis Historical Publishing, 1948), 2:558.

[30] Grace Deisher, historian, Denver Chapter, Work of the Chapters, *Daughters of the American Revolution Magazine*, August 1917, 82-83, online at Internet Archive, archive.org.

[31] Libeus Barney, *Letters of the Pike's Peak Gold Rush* (San Jose, CA: Talisman, 1959), xi.

[32] Mumey, *Early Settlements*, 113.

[33] Barney, *Letters*, 25-26.

[34] McDonough, "Pioneer Countess," 4.

³⁵ The equivalent purchasing power of $50,000 in 1864, as of June 22, 2023, was $968,557 assuming a 1.88% inflation rate, Consumer Price Index (CPI) inflation calculator (webpage), https://www.officialdata.org/us/inflation/1864?amount=50000.

³⁶ McDonough, "Pioneer Countess," 4.

³⁷ Mumey, *Early Settlements*, 101.

³⁸ "A Peculiar Pioneer," 8.

³⁹ Horace Greeley, *Overland Journey, from New York to San Francisco in the Summer of 1859* (New York, NY: C. M. Saxton, Barker & Co., 1860), 164, https://www.google.ca/books/edition/An_Overland_Journey_from_New_York_to_San/qDt1B1y3zJEC?hl=en&gbpv=1.

⁴⁰ Bill Brenneman, *Miracle on Cherry Creek: An informal history of the birth and re-birth of a neighborhood* (Denver, CO: World Press, 1973), 26-27.

⁴¹ "Denver City," *Rocky Mountain News* (Denver, CO), Dec. 21, 1861, 2, Colorado Historic Newspapers Collection (website), Colorado State Library, coloradohistoricnewspapers.org.

⁴² Albert D. Richardson, *Beyond the Mississippi: From the Great River to the Great Ocean* (Hartford, CT: American Publishing, 1867), 186, online at Internet Archive, (website) archive.org.

⁴³ Advertisement, *Colorado Republican and Rocky Mountain Herald* (Denver, CO), Nov. 2, 1861, 3, Colorado Historic Newspapers Collection (website), Colorado State Library, coloradohistoricnewspapers.org.

⁴⁴ Advertisement, *Weekly Commonwealth and Republican* (Denver, CO), July 2, 1863, 1, Colorado Historic Newspapers Collection (website), Colorado State Library, coloradohistoricnewspapers.org.

⁴⁵ Advertisement, *Rocky Mountain News* (Denver, CO), May 3, 1862, 3, Colorado Historic Newspapers Collection (website), Colorado State Library, coloradohistoricnewspapers.org.

⁴⁶ Advertisement, *The Montana Post* (Virginia City, MT), Nov. 12, 1864, 3, https://chroniclingamerica.loc.gov/lccn/sn83025293/1864-11-12/ed-1/seq-3/.

⁴⁷ Henderson, "Episodes," 16-17.

[48] The equivalent purchasing power of $50,000 in 1864, as of May 17, 2023, was calculated to be $966,124 assuming a 1.88% inflation rate, Consumer Price Index (CPI) inflation calculator (webpage), https://www.officialdata.org/us/inflation/1864?amount=50000.

[49] Henderson, "Episodes," 16.

[50] Henderson, "Episodes," 16.

[51] "A Peculiar Pioneer," 8.

[52] "A Peculiar Pioneer," 8.

[53] Advertisement, *Rocky Mountain News* (Denver), July 1, 1868, 4.

[54] "A Peculiar Pioneer," 8.

[55] "Henry Murat," *Helena Weekly Herald*, Sept. 1, 1881, 4, Chronicling America: Historic American Newspapers (website), Library of Congress, chroniclingamerica.loc.gov.

[56] "A Peculiar Pioneer," 8.

[57] Henderson, "Episodes," 13.

[58] McDonough, "Pioneer Countess," 1.

[59] Henderson, "Episodes," 13.

[60] Marion Savage Sabin, *Palmer Lake: A Historical Narrative* (Denver, CO: Sage Books, 1957), 51-52.

[61] Deisher, *Daughters of the American Revolution Magazine*, 83.

Figure 6.1. Mary Hall, circa 1886

Courtesy of Longyear Museum, Chestnut Hill, Massachusetts, P0626-1

Mary Hall:
Pioneer Healer

Arrived in Colorado, 1860

Unaware her family would soon be torn apart, twenty-two-year-old Mary Nye arrived in the Pikes Peak region in 1860. She traveled with her husband, their two young children, and her father. The following year, Mary's husband, Nathan Nye, not only deserted her but seized their children and took them back East.[1] Bereft, Mary mustered the persistence and fortitude that would serve her well as she faced the many challenges in her life. She built a reputation as a gracious hostess and fine cook at Salt Works Ranch, which she and her second husband, Charles L. Hall, established in a remote section of South Park. In addition, according to her family, she demonstrated her talent for healing when she nursed Hall back to health after he'd been lost without food for nineteen days in the rugged San Juan Mountains.[2] Her inclination to heal others continued when she tended the wounds of Ute Indians injured in an intertribal battle outside her home.[3] Later in life, Mary suffered blindness and lameness. After being cured through the Christian Science faith, she helped bring its practice to Colorado.[4]

Mary was born March 8, 1838, in Genesee County, New York.[5] Four years later, her parents, Ebenezer and Hannah (Barber) Hill, moved their family to a farm in Oakland County, Michigan. Along with her three sisters and five brothers, Mary spent most of her childhood in Michigan. Around 1852, the Hills moved to Johnson, Indiana.[6]

According to family history, in 1855, Mary, at just seventeen, married Nathan Nye, a man seven years her senior. The following year, in Michigan, she gave birth to their daughter, Mary Ella. A son, Hal Byron, followed two years later.[7]

Five years prior to his marriage to Mary, Nathan had joined the California gold rush, but he had returned to Michigan in 1852.[8] Apparently that did not cure him of gold fever. In 1860, he packed up his young family for a trek of more than a thousand miles, likely by oxen-drawn wagon and on foot, to the Pikes Peak region. Mary's father joined them on the journey—a journey that must have been arduous for a mother caring for a four-year-old and a two-year-old.[9]

Following their arrival in the Pikes Peak region, Mary, her husband, and her father all filed mining claims in the California Gulch area near present-day Leadville in August and September of 1860.[10] In December 1860, Mary, her husband, and children were members of a prospecting party that left Denver en route to the San Juan mountains where enterprising Charles Baker claimed to have found large mineral deposits. He dubbed the spot Baker City, even though no town existed. Fourteen years later, the town of Silverton was established there.[11]

Heading south from Denver, the party trekked over the Sangre de Cristo mountains via La Veta Pass to old Fort Garland. Travel proved difficult with severe winter storms that forced some to burn their wagons to stay warm. Roads had to be built and trees cut down to provide forage for the livestock.[12] From Fort Garland, they headed south to find a favorable point to join promoter Baker's new Abiquiu, Pagosa, and Baker City Toll Road that made wagon passage less difficult and profited Baker. Accounts vary as to how far south they traveled before turning northwest and joining the toll road, probably because the party was so large and amorphous that some traveled much more quickly and became separated from the main group, while others joined along the way. The junction may have been at Abiquiu, Ojo Caliente, or present-day Tierra Amarilla, New Mexico, or all of the above. Upon reaching the toll road, they followed it northwest toward Baker City in the San Juans.[13]

Three months after their departure from Denver, about the middle of March 1861, Mary's party arrived on the east bank of the Animas River opposite Pinkerton Hot Springs, about thirteen miles north of present-day Durango. Placer mining did not prove fruitful there, so the group proceeded north into the San Juan Mountains toward the valley surrounding Baker City, known as Baker's Park. The terrain on the west side of the Animas River looked less formidable, so they built a log bridge over the river. It became known as Baker's Bridge.[14]

The impossibility of traveling by oxen through deep snow in the rough, high-mountain region caused the expedition to halt at the base of Castle Rock Peak near Cascade Creek. The women and children remained at that location, dubbed Camp Pleasant, while some of the men ventured out on prospecting and hunting trips. A small group forged ahead to Baker's Park on snowshoes. Deep snow made prospecting impossible and hunting nearly so.[15]

One day two men returned to Camp Pleasant from Baker's Park. They walked on either side of a horse that carried a third man, who was in a severely weakened state. The rider was

Charles L. Hall. He and two other men had been on an unsuccessful trip surveying for gold and had become disoriented when they tried to return to their camp in Baker's Park. Lost for nearly three weeks in the rugged, frozen terrain, Hall and his companions had run out of supplies and had resorted to boiling empty flour sacks and drinking the broth,

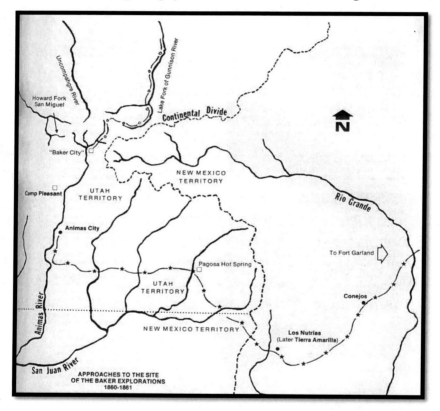

Figure 6.2. Mary likely traveled to the San Juan region via the starred route and then northward to Camp Pleasant, Colorado, the terminus of her journey.

Courtesy of the San Juan County Historical Society, who granted permission for modification of the map in Allen Nossaman, Many More Mountains: Volume 1; Silverton's Roots, 59

eating their buckskin breeches, and devouring a treasure trove of ants discovered beneath a fallen log. When rescued by members of the Baker's Park camp, Hall—near death from starvation and exposure—weighed just forty-eight pounds.[16]

Upon his arrival in Camp Pleasant, some accounts claim Mary took charge of Charles Hall's care and nursed him back to health. Hall recollected that a group of women, none of whom he named, tended him. [17] Either way, that is probably when Charles and Mary came to know each other.

Conditions in camp turned desperate as supplies, including food, became scarce. Meanwhile, Native Americans, displeased with the invasion of miners into their territory, began burning bridges and killing Anglos traveling in small groups. The miners formed several large parties and safely left the area. According to some accounts, the group that included all the women and children left in June to return to Denver. Likely, Mary left in that party.[18] However, a mining claim for Mrs. Mary Nye filed on May 26, 1861, in the Idaho District in Clear Creek County, roughly three hundred miles away, raises the question as to whether Mary was really in Camp Pleasant to nurse Hall back to health and to depart the San Juans in June. The claim next to Mary's was filed five days later by her father, Ebenezer Hill. Since so many sources place Mary in Camp Pleasant at that time, it is probable that her father filed the Idaho District claim in her name without her being there.[19]

Mary's life during the latter half of 1861 remains a mystery. It's not known exactly when her husband, Nathan Nye, took her children from her and left. Were Mary and Nathan still together when she left the San Juans, or had he deserted her there? If Nathan left her in the San Juans, did he leave before Hall, near death, was carried into camp, or did he become jealous when his wife undertook Hall's care? Did she, or they, return to their claims in California Gulch, or did she, or they, join her father in Clear Creek County? No records were found documenting Mary and her father together in Colorado after the May 1861 mining claims. By 1870, probably much earlier, her father had returned to his wife and home in Indiana.[20]

Regardless of the reason Nathan left, the loss of her young children must have been devastating to Mary. She had no legal means to fight for their custody. The common law of England formed the foundation of United States law and gave the father the sole right to choose with whom the children lived.[21] The first Legislative Assembly of the Territory of Colorado adopted that legal tradition when it met in September of 1861 and established the common law of England as the basis for the territory's law.[22]

Nathan left the children in the care of someone back East and soon returned alone to the West. It is doubtful Mary knew where Nathan took her children. Nine years later, the 1870 United States Census records them as living with Nathan's brother Riley Nye in Bloomfield, Michigan.[23]

Some accounts report that right after Nathan deserted Mary, the mining camp where she lived granted her an uncontested divorce, which is credible, because each mining camp established its own judicial system. Later, in March 1863, Mary was granted a divorce from Nathan in the First Judicial District Court for Arapahoe County in the Territory of Colorado.[24]

After leaving the San Juans, Charles Hall pursued mining in California Gulch and on Cache Creek near present-day Granite. No record remains as to how or where Charles and Mary's relationship continued to develop, but they married in late 1861 or early 1862.[25]

The couple settled in South Park, about nineteen miles south of Fairplay, on land that Charles filed a claim for on

Figure 6.3. Charles L. Hall, circa 1886

Courtesy of Clare Fanning, the Antoinette Perry Estate

January 29, 1862. He and Mary built a house with walls of large, adze-squared logs, a corrugated metal roof, a central brick chimney (likely for heating), and a metal pipe chimney (likely for a cookstove). The walls were insulated with 1861 and 1862 newspapers.[26]

Charles saw the area's salt springs as a way to make his fortune, since his gold mining efforts had not proven very successful. Not only did miners desire salt for their tables, but it was used in an ore processing step called chloridization. The transport of salt from the East came at an exorbitant price, and Charles could eliminate that cost by producing it in the Colorado Territory. He obtained a boiler from J. C. Fuller and immediately began production.[27]

The Halls soon learned that they did not hold the sole claim to the salt marsh. The salt drew herds of buffalo and antelope to the area, and Native Americans, consequently, found that a prime hunting ground. They also customarily restocked their salt supply while hunting there. When the Utes arrived, Charles tried to charge them for the salt. The Utes protested to the federal government that the salt belonged to them, and the government ordered Charles to give the Native Americans a specified salt annuity.[28]

In the spring of 1862, Charles Hall's salt went on the market in Buckskin Joe mining camp, and in 1864 sales began in Denver with orders as large as a ton. Leveraging that initial success, Charles convinced wealthy George W. Lane and John Quincy Adams Rollins to invest in his business. The partnership of Rollins, Lane, and Hall incorporated the Colorado Salt Works and soon began plans to expand the operation with Charles as overseer and the other two providing the funds.[29]

Meanwhile, Mary gave birth to the Halls' first daughter, Minnie B. Hall, on May 2, 1863, and to their only son, Charles A. Hall, on July 19, 1865.[30] Life on their isolated homestead must have been lonely and, at times, frightening for Mary. A visitor in 1866 pointed out that the nearest woman lived on a ranch twelve miles distant from the Halls.[31]

In the 1860s, while Charles was away on business and prospecting trips, Mary had to protect herself and children from intruders. One time, she used her rifle to chase off a "desperado" who attempted to kidnap her. On another occasion, feeling threatened by a band of Native Americans, she wielded her butcher knife to keep them at bay. The chief of the band was said to have been so impressed by her bravery that he offered to trade a tribeswoman for her.[32] Mary again demonstrated her courage when she took injured Utes into her home and tended to their wounds after they had battled the Arapaho and the Cheyenne near the Halls' house.[33]

In an August 1865 letter that Charles wrote to Mary, he urged her to "keep up good courage, 'Matty' I think we will come out all right next winter and summer." Whether that referred to Mary's having to protect her family on her own, or to possible financial problems, or both, is unclear. In a postscript, Charles wrote, "Mr. Lane [Charles' business partner] said he would pay you $50." Charles apparently planned to be away for a lengthy time, because he mentioned he had conducted business in Clear Creek and still intended to go prospecting. "I do not know when I will be down. As soon as I can." Charles always wrote affectionately to Mary, as in the closing to this letter: "Kiss Minnie & 'Charlie' for me, & receive a thousand for yourself."[34]

As well as being away from home on business and prospecting trips, Mary's husband also served two legislative terms. He represented Park County in the short-lived state legislature of 1865. Colorado voters approved statehood, adopted a constitution, and elected state officials, but President Andrew Johnson vetoed the enabling act. So, in the following year, Charles represented Park County in the territorial house of representatives, no longer the state legislature.[35]

In the summer of 1866, Charles and his partners, Lane and Rollins, began construction on the expansion of the salt works, the second manufacturing plant in the Colorado Territory.[36] When completed at the end of the year, it included an L-shaped kettle house with a 50-foot-tall chimney; a barn; and a steam-driven, circular sawmill. The kettle house's 125-by-30-foot wing held eighteen 130-gallon kettles, each spanning 4 feet in diameter and weighing roughly a half ton.

The salt water from the spring was boiled in the kettles, then run through a series of evaporating pans, where contaminants were removed from the brine. The kettle wing had a second, ventilated roof called a monitor, which allowed gases from the manufacturing process to escape. The 60-by-25-foot connecting wing stood two stories high and served as the dripping, drying, and sacking facility with storage on the second floor.[37] Construction costs for the new plant were, at a minimum, $50,000, over $950,000 in 2023 dollars.[38]

Figure 6.4. Salt Works Ranch kettle house, South Park, Colorado, late 1800s,

Courtesy of Park County Local History Digital Archive, 144

Prior to Charles' first salt works, salt in the Colorado Territory cost sixty cents a pound due to the cost of transporting it from the East. After construction of the new plant, salt bought at the facility sold for four-and-a-half cents a pound. Salt delivered to Denver cost seven cents, and the charge to Central City was eight cents.[39] By the summer of 1867, the Colorado Salt Works produced two tons of salt per day. In June it sent thirty wagonloads to Denver with a total load of almost one-hundred-thousand pounds.[40]

George Lane withdrew from the partnership in late 1867 or early 1868. Disputes between John Rollins and Charles Hall over operation and ownership of the salt works led to a series of lawsuits that Charles finally resolved by filing a cash homestead claim for the land for agricultural use rather than for mineral rights. He received the land patent in 1881, but by then the salt works were no longer profitable for several reasons. In 1870, completed rail connections to Denver made transport of salt from the East less expensive. The brine at the South Park facility was not concentrated enough to be processed efficiently, and nearby timber to fuel the operation was soon depleted. By 1875, the plant produced little or no salt, and the Halls turned to ranching.[41]

While Charles dealt with the development and demise of the salt works, domestic life went on at a brisk pace for Mary. The sporadic arrival of unexpected travelers in need of food and overnight lodging kept her on her toes.

In the summer of 1866, travel writer Bayard Taylor toured Colorado giving lectures and writing of his experiences for the *New York Tribune*. The small party that accompanied him included well-known painter William Holbrook Beard and *Rocky Mountain News* editor, William N. Byers. While traveling through South Park in July, they were caught in a late afternoon thunderstorm and sought shelter at Salt Works

Ranch. Taylor wrote of their stay in the Halls' home and of Mary's ability as a gracious and efficient hostess:

> The house of Mr. Hall, the superintendent of the works, received our dripping party, so rejoiced to find warmth, food, and protection from the storm, that I am afraid we were not fully aware of the inconvenience we occasioned to our kindly hostess. Ourselves, blankets, saddles, and other traps, almost filled the little cottage; we made a solid circle around the stove; yet, somehow, the bountiful supper was swiftly and quietly prepared, and two strangers who came after us were received with equal hospitality. . . . That night, we filled the sofas, benches, and the floors of the kitchen and sitting room.[42]

That same year, writer and editor Ovando Hollister toured the salt works and praised the fine quality of the food Mary served: "I must not refrain from saying a good word for Mrs. Hall's coffee, cream, butter, raspberry shortcake, wine and jelly, all of it of the sweetest and finest flavor. Also ducks, canvas-backs, roasted and buttered, think of that and weep."[43]

In 1867, Mary acquired a sewing machine, probably the first in all of South Park, which must have been a boon in meeting the challenge of keeping growing children clothed.[44] The Hall family also grew, and the final addition arrived while Mary was traveling between South Park and Denver on the Denver, Turkey Creek, and South Park Wagon Road. On May 30, 1869, Mary gave birth to Mildred Nettie, the Halls' second daughter and third child, at Ellis Ranch, which was located around three to four miles southwest of present-day Conifer. Mrs. Ellis, the road's toll gate keeper, provided a log house at the side of the road as a stopping place for travelers, and that's likely where Mary found shelter for the birth.[45]

The family of five had outgrown their small log home, so in 1872, Charles used earnings from his South Park mining investments to hire a former shipbuilder to construct a two-story, Second Empire style home. Now on the Register of National Historic Places, included as part of the Salt Works Ranch submission, it sits directly in front of the original log house. Characteristic of the style, it boasts a mansard roof and hooded arches over the dormer windows. Two parlors open off the left side of the central hallway, and the right side opens to a formal dining room with a kitchen and pantry behind it. A curved staircase leads to six rooms on the second floor. It was an unusually fashionable and fine home to be built in the rural mountains of the Colorado Territory.[46]

Other buildings constructed about the same time as the ranch house reflect the Halls' decision to change the use of their property from salt production to ranching. They included a barn with attached milking and calving sheds, a springhouse, a well house with a hand pump to supply water to the corrals, and a blacksmith shop.[47]

Visitors' accounts give a glimpse into some of Mary's activities in the early 1870s. She ran a sizeable dairy operation that visitor Annie B. Schenck described in a letter: "Mrs. Hall's dairy is enough to delight one's heart. I went in this evening to see it. It contains about a hundred pans of milk covered with the richest cream, two or three kegs of golden butter and large pans of buttermilk. A cold spring runs through the place, making it cold as ice."[48]

Other visitors noted that Mary was an avid rock collector. An overnight guest in 1872 wrote of Mary's display cabinet full of minerals for which she had been offered $2,000.[49] Artist Eliza Greatorex deemed Mary's collection "very fine."[50] Among other minerals, the collection likely contained jasper, moss agate, other forms of chalcedony, carnelian, trachyte, dendrite, and porphyry that were noted in the area by South Park travelers.[51]

Sometime in the early to mid-1870s, Mary Ella Nye, Mary's daughter from her first marriage, either came to live with the Halls or to visit. On March 1, 1876, she married Robert B. Newitt, who had a ranch on the west side of Trout Creek Pass to the southwest of the Halls' ranch. Mary Ella died later that year on December 23, at the age of twenty, and is buried in Fairplay Cemetery.[52]

In the winter of 1878, Charles, in the hope of prospering from the silver boom, moved to Leadville. It is unclear whether his family moved with him. He went into the liquor and tobacco business, setting up shop on Chestnut Street next to the post office. Correspondence between Charles and Mary

Figure 6.5. Salt Works Ranch house and original log cabin, South Park, Colorado, 2001

Courtesy of History Colorado, Denver, Colorado, Accession #5PA,346,c001

indicates that Mary and the children spent little time in Leadville, if they did move there at that early date. January of 1879 found Mary and the children on a long visit with family in Michigan. Two more Michigan visits followed—one in February 1880 and another in June of the same year.[53]

On January 30, 1879, Charles wrote to Mary on letterhead inscribed "Office of Chas. L. Hall, Dealer in Wines, Liquors, and Cigars." He wrote that he was clearing about seventy-five dollars a day and that he planned to "lay up some money"[54] as soon as he could get out of debt. In an April 17, 1879, letter, Charles implored Mary to come to Leadville.[55] Newspaper articles at the end of that year and in 1880 refer to Mary as a Leadville resident.[56]

In the spring of 1879, Charles, along with George R. Fisher and Dennis Sullivan, established the Leadville Illuminating Gas Company with Fisher and Sullivan as officers. After incorporation papers were filed with the state in April, the company officers were: Horace Tabor, president; Charles L. Hall, vice-president; and William H. Bush, secretary and treasurer.[57] Letterhead for the company in 1880 titles Charles as both vice-president and superintendent.[58] The gas works became operational in time to light the Tabor Opera House on its opening night, November 20, 1879. By the beginning of 1881, the Leadville Illuminating Gas Company served 290 customers and lit ninety streetlamps.[59]

In June of 1880, Charles again went into business with Bush and Tabor when the trio opened the posh Windsor Hotel in Denver.[60] Not long after that, Charles and Mary considered moving to Denver. In an October 8, 1881, letter from Charles to Mary, the move sounds imminent. He wrote that he would be over soon and that he wanted her to accompany him to Denver to get a house and "then we will move down immediately."[61] During the next few years, the Halls moved from one Denver address to another.[62]

Tragedy struck Mary in early 1884. She suddenly lost her eyesight and subsequently injured her foot so badly that she could not walk.[63] Earlier, in April 1880, while staying at the American House in Denver, she had stepped into a hole in the hotel's floor and "injured herself for life."[64] Whether the 1884 crippling was an exacerbation of that previous injury, or a new one, is unclear. Mary had no inkling that the dual tragedy would lead to a major turning point in her life and that of her daughters.

For more than a year, Mary sought treatment for her blindness and lameness. Doctors told her that her eyesight loss was permanent and that her foot injury might require amputation. Not willing to give up hope of a cure for one or both of her ailments, Mary decided to seek the help of New York physicians. In June of 1885, Mary, accompanied by her daughters, twenty-two-year-old Minnie and sixteen-year-old Mildred, boarded a train to the East. They stopped to visit friends in Chicago, where Mary heard of impressive cures through the practice of Christian Science.[65]

Rather than continuing to New York, Mary sought treatment by Roger Sherman, a Christian Science practitioner. While Mary underwent treatment, she and her daughters stayed in a boarding house in Chicago and studied *Science and Health with the Key to the Scriptures* by the founder of the Church of Christ, Scientist, Mary Baker Eddy. After three months, Mary's eyesight problem resolved, and she described it as "the light coming into the eyes."[66] Not long after that, she regained her ability to walk.[67]

Before returning to Denver, Mary and Minnie took the Christian Science Primary Course taught by Bradford Sherman, Roger's father. Successfully completing that class gave Mary and Minnie authorization to heal others through the practice of Christian Science.[68]

Upon their return to Denver, Mary and Minnie began their practice of healing. One of their first successful treatments was administered to a scissors grinder who had been crippled for fourteen years. After three weeks under the care of the Hall women, he threw away his crutches. The striking recovery of both Mary and the scissors grinder generated strong interest in Christian Science in the Denver community. Soon, Mary and Minnie were treating more than one hundred people each day.[69] Their success impressed a medical physician in Denver, Dr. Sanford Hoag. He wrote, "Being a physician I determined to ascertain the genuineness of some of the cures and am convinced that they have accomplished what even the best medical treatment would not have accomplished."[70]

Seeing the need for more qualified practitioners, Mary wrote to Bradford Sherman in Chicago requesting that he come to Denver to teach a Primary Class. At the time she wrote, she had only ten prospective students, so she made a $1,000 deposit (over $31,000 in 2023 dollars)[71] to convince Dr. Sherman it was worth his while to make the trip. Charles admonished her that the money was as good as lost. Mary proved her husband wrong, for she had over one hundred students signed up by the time Dr. Sherman arrived in Denver in December of 1885. With so many students, he had to divide the group and teach classes both day and night.[72]

Bradford Sherman, at the Halls' request, returned to Denver to teach the Primary Class to about forty-five more students in February of 1886.[73] Minnie had begun corresponding with Mary Baker Eddy, telling her of the Halls' successes and seeking Eddy's advice. After Sherman's second class in Denver, Minnie wrote to Eddy that the Halls continued to receive requests for another class. Eddy replied that Minnie

Figure 6.6. La Veta Place, the Denver luxury apartment building where the Halls lived in the late 1880s

Courtesy of Denver Public Library, William Henry Jackson Collections, WHJ-10348

herself should come to Boston and take the Normal Class so she would be qualified to teach the Primary Class.[74]

In May of 1886, Minnie studied the Normal Class under Mary Baker Eddy at the Massachusetts Metaphysical College in Boston. On her return to Denver, at the urging of Eddy, she established the Colorado Christian Science Institute. Chartered on August 23, 1886, it was Colorado's first school to train students to be Christian Science practitioners.[75]

Mary's younger daughter, Mildred, took the Primary Class in January of 1887 and began practicing with Mary, while Minnie ran the institute. In the fall, Mildred started a Christian Science Sunday school in the Hall home at 3 La Veta Place and soon had twenty attendees who ranged in age from four to sixteen.[76]

Mary continued to practice Christian Science healing, as much as her health would allow, for the rest of her life. Minnie taught the Primary Class until 1918 and continued her healing practice until her death in 1952, except for an eight-year break from 1888 to 1896. Mildred quit her public practice of healing in the 1890s.[77]

While the Hall women sought a cure for Mary and organized their Christian Science practice and institute, Mary's husband and son continued their careers, which kept them away from the family's Denver home most of the time. Her husband searched out mining investment opportunities and finally reaped significant results in the Milo mine group in the Ten Mile District in Summit County and the Rose group in Ouray. In 1892, he expanded his mining interests with his opening of the Mammoth Mine in Arizona, which yielded minerals valued at $800,000.[78] He also continued his legislative career, representing Lake County for a four-year term in Colorado's senate from 1883 through 1886.[79]

When Mary's son, Charles A. Hall, turned twenty-one in 1886, he took over the family's South Park ranch. He continued in that capacity until 1892, when he moved to Arizona to oversee his father's mining operations.[80]

In March of 1899, Mary suffered an illness and never fully recovered. That month her son wrote letters from Goldfield, Arizona, to her and to his sisters expressing his concern. On March 27, he cajoled his mother to rest: "I do hope dear Mother that you will not be too ambitious and work, for you certainly should take more rest." He added, "Be contented to let the younger ones of the household do the work while you play lady, and boss."[81] Three days later, he wrote to his sister Minnie to repeat his concern and add his apparent belief in traditional medicine:

I am very sorry to hear of dear Mother being so poorly and hope that it is only a temporary complaint of no serious nature. Now do not allow your faith in C.S. [Christian Science] to prevent you from calling in a M.D. and seeing if some thing could be learned from their experience in such cases and dear mother relieved by some of natures remedies. Give her every attention possible for she is so ambitious that she will over tax her strength as soon as she feels she is improving.[82]

A letter written by Mary's son and signed by both her son and husband on May 21 indicated that Mary was feeling better. They encouraged her to take rides in the open air to improve her strength.[83] By June 19, Mary had taken a turn for the worse. She could not raise her head and wrote while lying on her back. She expressed concern for the hard work that her care caused her daughters, especially in the effort expended to try to keep Mary cool with a palm leaf fan. Her fervent desire to see her son once more is evident: "Charlie dear I love you so dearly, and last night I dreamed you knelt down by the cot that I lie on and we had a good hug & cry."[84]

In a letter to her son on July 6, Mary wrote she was feeling better and implied she had taken his advice to seek traditional medical care. "I had a very good night and did not have to take a tablet & have not taken one since two o,c [o'clock] yesterday. I believe I am doing all you could expect of me."[85]

At the age of sixty-one, Mary passed away on July 17, 1899. She is buried at Fairmont Cemetery in Denver. Her husband followed her in death on August 15, 1907, and is buried next to her.[86]

Mary and Charles contributed significantly to the development of South Park and Colorado. Their well-known hospitality in that sparsely populated region of Park County facilitated travel and encouraged settlement. The salt works was a pioneering industry, being just the second manufacturing plant in the Colorado Territory.[87]

Salt Works Ranch, one of the first agriculture properties in Park County, is a lasting legacy and remains in the hands of Hall family descendants. Mary's youngest daughter, Mildred, owned the ranch in 1911 when she married rancher Thomas McQuaid. He took over the ranch's operations and eventually increased its size to eighty-thousand acres. Although now reduced in size, the ranch, designated both a Colorado Centennial Farm and a National Historic Place, is still in business.[88]

With great fortitude, Mary transcended the grief caused by the desertion of her first husband and the seizure of her children, protected herself and her family from man and beast on an isolated ranch, and faced the challenges of blindness and lameness. As a young woman in the wilds of the San Juan Mountains, she displayed her natural inclination to heal others. Later in life, after being cured through Christian Science, she and her daughters established the practice of Christian Science in Denver to treat the afflicted. Mary not only healed others, but she also facilitated bringing teachers to instruct more people in Christian Science practice. Mary exemplified the pioneer spirit by carving a home for her family in an isolated region and by bringing her religion to Denver.

---

[1] "Mrs. Mary Melissa Hall," in *History of Colorado*, comp. Wilbur Fiske Stone (Chicago, IL: S. J. Clarke, 1919) 4:211-12; and see "Mary Melissa Hall, C.S.," Pioneer Gallery (webpage), Longyear

Museum, Chestnut Hill, MA, https://www.longyear.org/learn/pio-neer-index/hall-mary-m/; The Nye children, Ella and Hal, are listed in the 1870 US Census as living with Nathan Nye's brother Riley Nye in Michigan. See 1870 US Census, Bloomfield, Oakland County, MI, digital image s.v. "Ella Nye," Ancestry.com.

² Allen Nossaman, *Many More Mountains: Volume I: Silverton's Roots: An Illustrated History of the Earliest Exploration in the High San Juans of Southwestern Colorado and of the Settlement and Founding of Silverton, Colorado* (Denver, CO: Sundance, 1989), 1:46, 63, 65, and 67; and see photo of Bakers Bridge sign erected by DAR in 1930, 13.08.56, "Local History Timeline 1860, The Baker Party" (webpage), La Plata County Historical Society Animas Museum (website), accessed May 2, 2023, https://www.animas-museum.org/online_exhibits/Timeline/baker.html. The sign listed "Nate Nye and Family" as members of the 1861 Baker party. Also see John J. Lipsey, *The Salt Works in Colorado's South Park* (Colorado Springs, CO: J. J. Lipsey, Western Books, 1959), 4; and see "Human Endurance Without Food," *The Denver Republican*, July 21, 1897, 2, History Colorado, Denver, CO.

³ "Mrs. Mary Melissa Hall," in Stone, *History of Colorado*, 4:211; see also Tracie Etheredge, *An Inventory of the Papers of the Charles L. Hall Family*, Collection Number 285: *a holding of the Library of the Colorado Historical Society Denver, Colorado 80203* (Denver, CO: Colorado Historical Society, 1992) 5, History Colorado (website); and see Encyclopedia Staff, "Park County," *Colorado Encyclopedia* (website), last modified December 27, 2022, https://coloradoencyclopedia.org/article/park-county.

⁴ "Charles L. Hall," in *History of Colorado*, comp. Wilbur Fiske Stone (Chicago, IL: S. J. Clarke, 1919) 4: 207-11; see also "Mrs. Mary Melissa Hall," in the same volume; and see Etheredge, "Inventory," 2, 5-6; and see three letters: Mary Melissa Hall to Mary Baker Eddy, March 31, 1886, 223A.37.008; Minnie B. Hall DeSoto to Mary Baker Eddy, January 1, 1886, 223A37.001; and Stanford Hoag to Mary Baker Eddy, January 22, 1886, 678A.76.001, Mary Baker Eddy Papers (website), mbepapers.org.

[5] "Mrs. Mary Melissa Hall," in Stone, *History of Colorado*, 4: 211; and see Etheredge, "Inventory," 9.

[6] "Hill, Ebenezer," in *Counties of La Grange and Noble, Indiana, Historical and Biographical* (Chicago, IL: F. A. Battey, 1882), 298-99.

[7] Public Member Trees database, Ancestry.com, McPheeters Combined Master Tree, digital images s.v. "Nathan B. Nye," family tree posted by KeithMcPheeters508, unidentified transcription, "Pioneer of 1850 Dies at Gold Hill," and unidentified newspaper clipping, Nathan Nye obituary, accessed March 30, 2023. See also Find a Grave (database and images), s.v. "Ella Nye Newitt," findagrave.com; also see Find a Grave (database and images), s.v. "Hal Byron Nye," findagrave.com.

[8] "Pioneer of 1850 Dies at Gold Hill," McPheeters Combined Master Tree, digital image s.v. "Nathan B. Nye," Ancestry.com.

[9] Etheredge, "Inventory," 5; and see "Mrs. Mary Melissa Hall," in Stone, *History of Colorado*, 4:211.

[10] Nathan B. Nye, claim No. 86, FF 32; M. M. Nye, claim No. 98, FF 32; and E. Hill, claim No. 119, FF 31, Charles L. Hall Family Papers, MSS 285, History Colorado, Denver, CO.

[11] Nossaman, *Many More Mountains*, 1:46, 63; and see photo of Bakers Bridge sign, La Plata County Historical Society, Animas Museum (website).

[12] Frank Hall, *History of the State of Colorado: Embracing Accounts of the Pre-historic Races and Their Remains; The Earliest French, Spanish and American Explorations; The Lives of the Primitive Hunters, Trappers and Traders; The Commerce of the Prairies; The First American Settlements Founded; The Original Discoveries of Gold in the Rocky Mountains; The Development of Cities and Towns, with the Various Phases of Industrial and Political Transition, from 1858 to 1890* (Chicago, IL: Blakeley, 1889), 2:193.

[13] Hall, in his *History of the State of Colorado* [. . .] 2:193, states the turning point was Abiquiu, where Baker's toll road began and supplies could be obtained. A later volume, Frank Hall, "La Plata County," in *History of the State of Colorado* [. . .] (Chicago, IL: Blakeley, 1895), 4:167, gives Ojo Caliente, to the northeast of Abiquiu, as the turning point; see also Nossaman, *Many More*

Mountains, 1:59, which shows Los Nutrias (present-day Tierra Amarilla), to the north of Abiquiu, as the settlement nearest the party's turning point.

14 "La Plata County: Early History of Southwestern Colorado," *Durango Herald,* Jan. 1, 1888, La Plata County Historical Society, Animas Museum, Durango, CO; and see Hall, "La Plata County," in *History of the State of Colorado,* 4:167; also see photo of Baker's Bridge sign, La Plata County Historical Society Animas Museum (website).

15 "La Plata County: Early History"; and see Hall, "La Plata County," in *History of the State of Colorado,* 4:167.

16 "Human Endurance," 1-2; and see Stone, "Charles L. Hall," in *History of Colorado,* 4:210.

17 Nossaman, *Many More Mountains,* 1:67; also see Virginia McConnell Simmons, *Bayou Salado: The Story of South Park,* rev. ed. (Boulder, CO: University Press of Colorado, 2002), 208; and see Lipsey, *The Salt Works in Colorado's South Park,* 4. See "Human Endurance," 2. In this article, Charles L. Hall recollected that he was improving until one of the women gave him milk that caused him to bloat. After that, a doctor in camp ordered the women to only feed him a watery gruel, and under that regimen, his condition deteriorated. He gives Ben Eaton credit for going to the Animas valley and obtaining potatoes which he baked, buttered, and fed to Hall, resulting in his final recovery. This part of Hall's story lacks credibility, because the whole camp was starving but would not have been if supplies were so easily obtained.

18 "La Plata County: Early History"; and see Hall, "La Plata County," in *History of the State of Colorado,* 4:167.

19 Mrs. Mary Nye claim No. 35, FF 32 and E. Hill, claim 36, FF 31, Charles L. Hall Family Papers, MSS 285, History Colorado, Denver, CO.

20 1870 US Census, Johnson Township, La Grange County, IN, digital image s.v. "Ebenezer Hill," Ancestry.com.

21 Mary Ann Mason, *From Father's Property to Children's Rights: The History of Child Custody in the United States* (New York, NY: Columbia University Press, 1994), 14.

²² LeRoy R. Hafen, "Colorado's First Legislative Assembly," *Colorado Magazine*, March 1943, 46.

²³1870 US Census, Bloomfield Township, Oakland County, MI, digital image s.v. "Ella Nye," Ancestry.com.

²⁴ Webster Lithgow, "A Westward Wind Part 2: Colorado," (webpage), December 17, 2021, 4, Longyear Museum (website), Chestnut Hill, MA, https://www.longyear.org/learn/research-archive/a-westward-wind-part-2-colorado. See also "Mary Melissa Hall, C.S.," Pioneers Gallery (webpage), Longyear Museum (website); and see "Civil Cases," *Weekly Commonwealth* (Denver, CO), Mar. 19, 1863, 1, Colorado Historic Newspapers Collection (website), Colorado State Library, coloradohistoricnewspapers.org.

²⁵ Stone, "Charles L. Hall," in *History of Colorado*, 4:210-11; and see Simmons, *Bayou Salado*, 208.

²⁶ R. Laurie Simmons and Thomas H. Simmons, historians, "Salt Works Ranch," National Park Service, National Register of Historic Places Registration Form, December 18, 2000, sec. 7, 5, sec. 8, 17, https://netgallery.nps.gov/GetAsset/9080e579-5869-42a2-9573-c320db02bf04.

²⁷ Simmons, *Bayou Salado*, 208-9; and see R. Laurie Simmons and Thomas H. Simmons, "Colorado Salt Works," National Park Service, National Register of Historic Places Registration Form, September 1, 2000, sec. 8, 5, https://npgalllery.nps.gov/GetAsset/a76ac5dc-923b-4a06-8db9-d3faef125918; and see Ovando J. Hollister, "Editorial Correspondence: Colorado Salt Works," *Daily Mining Journal* (Black Hawk, CO), Oct. 20, 1866, 1, Colorado Historic Newspapers Collection (website), Colorado State Library, coloradohistoricnewspapers.org.

²⁸ Simmons, *Bayou Salado*, 208.

²⁹ Simmons and Simmons, "Colorado Salt Works," sec. 8, 5-6.

³⁰ Stone, "Mrs. Mary Melissa Hall," in *History of Colorado*, 4:211.

³¹ Hollister, "Editorial Correspondence," 1.

³² Stone, "Mrs. Mary Melissa Hall," in *History of Colorado*, 4:211; and see Simmons, *Bayou Salado*, 208.

[33] Stone, "Mrs. Mary Melissa Hall," in *History of Colorado*, 4:211; see also Etheredge, "Inventory," 5; and see Encyclopedia Staff, "Park County," *Colorado Encyclopedia* (website), last modified November 14, 2020, https://coloradoencyclopedia.org/article/park-county.

[34] Charles L. Hall to Mary Hall, August 23, 1865, FF 4, Charles L. Hall Family Papers, MSS 285.

[35] Legislator History Database, s.v. "Charles L. Hall," Legislative Council Staff (webpage), Colorado General Assembly (website); and see Gerhard Peters and John T. Woolley, "Andrew Johnson, Veto Message Online," (webpage) *The American Presidency Project* (website), https://www.presidency.ucsb.edu/documents/veto-message-439.

[36] Lipsey, *The Salt Works in Colorado's South Park*, 3.

[37] Simmons and Simmons, "Colorado Salt Works," sec. 7, 2; and see Hollister, "Editorial Correspondence"; see also Lipsey, *The Salt Works in Colorado's South Park*, 19-20.

[38] Simmons and Simmons, "Colorado Salt Works," sec. 8, 6. The equivalent purchasing power of $50,000 in 1866, as of May 17, 2023, was calculated to be $953,971 assuming a 1.9% inflation rate, Consumer Price Index (CPI) inflation calculator (webpage), https://www.officialdata.org/us/inflation/1866?amount=50000.

[39] Hollister, "Editorial Correspondence"; and see "Colorado Salt," *Rocky Mountain News* (Denver, CO), Dec. 4, 1866, 4, Colorado Historic Newspapers Collection (website), Colorado State Library, coloradohistoricnewspapers.org.

[40] Park County Timeline (webpage), Park County Local History Archives (website), https://www.parkcoarchives.org/online-resources/timeline/; and see "Mountain Items," *Rocky Mountain News* (Denver, CO), July 3, 1867, 1, Colorado Historic Newspapers Collection (website), Colorado State Library, coloradohistoricnewspapers.org; also see Simmons and Simmons, "Colorado Salt Works," sec. 8, 7.

[41] Simmons and Simmons, "Colorado Salt Works," sec. 8, 9-10.

[42] Bayard Taylor, (1867), 1989, *Colorado: A Summer Trip*, ed. William W. Savage, Jr. and James H. Lazalier, (Niwot, CO: Univ. Press of Colorado), xiii, xvii-xviii, and 139.

[43] Hollister, "Editorial Correspondence," 1.

[44] Simmons, *Bayou Salado*, 211.

[45] Simmons, *Bayou Salado*, 212-13; and see Noah LeGault told to James R. Harvey, "The Old Bradford Hill Road," *Colorado Magazine*, November 1936, 208-9; also see Cathleen Norman, *Historic Contexts Report: 1999-2002 Cultural Resource Survey of Unincorporated Jefferson County* (Lakewood, CO: Preservation Publishing, 2004), 19, Historical Publications (webpage), Jefferson County Colorado (website).

[46] Simmons and Simmons, "Salt Works Ranch," sec. 7, 2, 5, sec. 8, 15.

[47] Simmons and Simmons, "Salt Works Ranch," sec. 7, 7-10.

[48] Annie B. Schenck, ed. Jack D. Filipiak, "Camping Vacation, 1871," *Colorado Magazine,* Summer 1965, 197.

[49] J. E. Liller, "A Trip in the Rocky Mountains," from *Out West,* reprinted in *Weekly Gazette* (Colorado Springs, CO), Sept. 26, 1872, 4, https://www.newspapers.com/image/15257575.

[50] Eliza Greatorex, *Summer Etchings in Colorado* (New York, NY: G. P. Putnam's Sons, 1873), 82.

[51] Liller, "A Trip," 4; and see Hollister, "Editorial Correspondence."

[52] Public Member Trees, database, Ancestry.com, "McPheeters Combined Master Tree," posted by KeithMcPheeters508, digital image s.v. "Mary Ella Nye," Marriage Record Report, Division of Vital Statistics, State of Colorado; and see Find a Grave (database and images) s.v. "Ella Nye Newitt."

[53] Charles L. Hall to Mary Hall, January 30, 1879, FF 4; Charles L. Hall to Mary Hall, February 20, 1880, FF 7; and Charles L. Hall to Mary Hall, June 4, 1880, FF 7, Charles L. Hall Family Papers, MSS 285, History Colorado, Denver, CO.

[54] Charles L. Hall to Mary Hall, January 30, 1879, Family Papers.

[55] Charles L. Hall to Mary Hall, January 30, 1879, Family Papers; and see Charles L. Hall to Mary Hall, April 17, 1879, FF 4, Charles L. Hall Family Papers, MSS 285, History Colorado, Denver, CO.

[56] Don L. Griswold and Jean Harvey Griswold, *History of Leadville and Lake County, Colorado* (Boulder, CO: Colorado Historical Society in cooperation with University Press of Colorado, 1996), 1:421. This cites the *Daily Chronicle* (Leadville, CO), Dec. 24, 1879, as including Mrs. C. L. Hall among the "Carbonate City ladies" who were to hostess Christmas dinners. And see "State News," *Gunnison News*, July 24, 1880, 3, Colorado Historic Newspapers Collection (website), Colorado State Library, coloradohistoric-newspapers.org.

[57] "The Leadville Gas Company," *Leadville Weekly Herald*, Jan. 1, 1881, 4, Colorado Historic Newspapers Collection (website), Colorado State Library, coloradohistoricnewspapers.org; and see Griswold and Griswold, *History of Leadville and Lake County, Colorado*, 1:202, 243.

[58] Charles L. Hall to Mary Hall, February 20, 1880, FF 7, Hall Family Papers.

[59] Griswold and Griswold, *History of Leadville and Lake County, Colorado*, 1:398-400; and see Edward Blair, *Leadville: Colorado's Magic City* (Boulder, CO: Pruett, 1980), 71; also see "The Leadville Gas Company."

[60] Stone, "Charles L. Hall," in *History of Colorado*, 4:211.

[61] Charles L. Hall to Mary Hall, October 8, 1881, FF 7, Charles L. Hall Family Papers, Mss00285.

[62] Envelopes addressed to Mary in FF 7 and FF 8 of the Charles L. Hall Family Papers, Mss00285, show her living at four different Denver addresses between 1880 and 1884.

[63] "Mary Melissa Hall, C.S.," Pioneers Gallery (webpage), Longyear Museum (website); and see Minnie B. Hall Perry, "Sight Restored," *Christian Science Sentinel* August 22, 1901, 818, https://sentinel.christianscience.com/issues/1901/8/3-51sight-re-stored.

[64] "State News," 3.

[65] Perry, "Sight Restored"; and see "Mary Melissa Hall, C .S.,"; and see William O. Bisbee, "Minnie B. Hall De Soto: Christian Science in Colorado," October 7, 2013, Longyear Museum (website), https://www.longyear.org; also see Lithgow, "A Westward Wind," 5; and see "Mrs. Minnie B. Hall Murphy, C. S. D.," in *History of Colorado*, comp. Wilber Fiske Stone (Chicago, IL: S.J. Clarke, 1919), 4:206. Contrary to the other sources cited above, in "Sight Restored," Minnie B. Hall Perry, Mary's daughter, wrote that Mary went directly to Chicago for Christian Science treatment, while all the other sources give the version that she originally intended to seek medical treatment in New York. The authors conclude that Perry abbreviated the story for the purposes of the cited article.

[66] Perry, "Sight Restored."

[67] "Mary Melissa Hall, C.S." Pioneers Gallery (webpage), Longyear Museum (website); see also Caroline D. Noyes to Mary Baker Eddy, August 15, 1885, 304.43.024, Mary Baker Eddy Papers (website), Mary Baker Eddy Library, Boston, MA, mbepapers.org; and see Minnie B. Hall DeSoto to Mary Baker Eddy, January 1, 1886, 223A.37.001, Mary Baker Eddy Papers (website), Mary Baker Eddy Library, Boston, MA, mbepapers.org; see also Perry, "Sight Restored."

[68] Minnie B. Hall DeSoto to Mary Baker Eddy, January 1, 1886; and see Bisbee, "Minnie B. Hall De Soto"; see also "What Is Christian Science Primary Class Instruction?" (webpage), *Christian Science* (website), christianscience.com.

[69] Minnie B. Hall DeSoto to Mary Baker Eddy, January 1, 1886; and see Stone, "Mrs. Minnie B. Hall Murphy, C. S. D.," 4:206; also see Bisbee, "Minnie B. Hall De Soto."

[70] Sanford Hoag to Mary Baker Eddy, January 22, 1886, 678A.76.001, Mary Baker Eddy Papers (website), Mary Baker Eddy Library, Boston, MA, mbepapers.org.

[71] The equivalent purchasing power of $1,000 in 1885, as of May 17, 2023, was calculated to be31,274 assuming a 2.53% inflation rate, Consumer Price Index (CPI) inflation calculator (webpage), https://www.officialdata.org/us/inflation/1885?amount=1000.

[72] Lithgow, "A Westward Wind," 6.

[73] Lithgow, "A Westward Wind," 6.

[74] Stone, "Mrs. Minnie Hall Murphy, C. S. D."; and see Bisbee, "Minnie B. Hall DeSoto."

[75] Bisbee, "Minnie B. Hall DeSoto."

[76] Caroline D. Noyes to Mary Baker Eddy, August 15, 1885. The text links Mildred N. Hall's name to a short biography. See also M. Nettie Hall, "Juvenile Token," *Christian Science Journal* 5, no. 7 (October 1887), 371.

[77] "Mary Melissa Hall," brief biography in References in Mary Baker Eddy Papers—People (database), Mary Baker Eddy Papers (website), Mary Baker Eddy Library, Boston, MA, mbepapers.org; and see Bisbee, "Minnie B. Hall DeSoto,"; also see the link to Mildred N. Hall's biography in the text to the Caroline D. Noyes to Mary Baker Eddy letter of August 15, 1885.

[78] Stone, "Charles L. Hall," 4:211.

[79] Colorado Legislative Council Staff, Legislator History Database, s.v. "Charles L. Hall," https://leg.colorado.gov/agencies/legislative-council-staff/legislator-history-information.

[80] Simmons and Simmons, "Colorado Salt Works," sec. 8, 19.

[81] Charles A. Hall to Mary Hall and daughters, March 27, 1899, FF24, Charles L. Hall Family Papers, MSS 285.

[82] Charles A. Hall to Minnie Hall Perry, March 30, 1899, FF 24, Charles L. Hall Family Papers, MSS 285.

[83] Charles A. and Charles L. Hall to Mary Hall, May 21, 1899, FF 24, Charles L. Hall Family Papers, MSS 285.

[84] Mary Hall to Charles A. Hall, June 19, 1899, FF 23, Charles L. Hall Family Papers, MSS 285.

[85] Mary Hall to Charles A. Hall, July 6, 1899, FF 23, Charles L. Hall Family Papers, MSS 285.

[86] Stone, "Mrs. Mary Melissa Hall," in *History of Colorado*, 4:211; and see Find a Grave (database and images), s.v. "Mary Melissa *Hill* Hall," findagrave.com; also see Stone, "Charles L. Hall," in *History of Colorado*, 4:207.

[87] Simmons and Simmons, "Colorado Salt Works," sec. 8, 7.

88 Encyclopedia Staff, "Colorado Salt Works," *Colorado Encyclopedia* (website), last modified September 4, 2021, https://coloradoencyclopedia.org/article/colorado-salt-works; and see Simmons and Simmons, "Salt Works Ranch," sec. 7, 14; also see History Colorado (website), "Centennial Farms & Ranches Past Honorees," https://www.historycolorado.org/centennial-farms-ranches-past-honorees.

Figure 7.1. This 1857 map of the New Mexico Territory shows the upper right corner that was later made part of the Colorado Territory.

Courtesy of Denver Public Library Special Collections, Map-2017-1278

Maria Dolores Ballejos: Hispana Pioneer

Arrived in Colorado, circa 1849-1851

Maria Dolores Ballejos was one of the first pioneers to settle in Colorado's San Luis Valley, years before the Colorado gold rush began. She was born a citizen of Spain, living in Spain's northern New World territory. In 1821, when Spain acknowledged Mexico's independence, she became a Mexican citizen. After the Mexican-American War ended in 1848, Maria Dolores hadn't moved, but she now lived in the newly created Territory of New Mexico and was a citizen of the United States of America. None of these nationality changes impacted her life as much as when her home in the San Luis Valley became part of the Colorado Territory in 1861. The Colorado Territory established the 37th parallel as its southern border, separating Maria Dolores—along with approximately seven thousand Hispanos living in Southern Colorado—from the government, culture, and laws of the New Mexico Territory. Literally overnight, Maria Dolores was forced to obey a British legal tradition that stripped away many of the rights she, as a married woman, had been guaranteed under Spanish law. Maria Dolores now lived in an Anglo society that was largely unfamiliar, and often intimidating and hostile.[1]

Maria Dolores's ancestry can be traced back to Manuel Gonzales Vallejos, a blacksmith (*herrador*), who in 1693 answered the call for frontier settlers (*pobladores*) to colonize Spain's northern New World territory. As a member of the Velasco-Farfán Expedition, Vallejos traveled almost fifteen hundred miles with approximately 235 settlers from Mexico City into what would eventually become the United States state of New Mexico. During the long journey, his wife, María López de Arteaga, delivered the first baby of the expedition, but she died in childbirth.[2] Vallejos and his son settled in Villa Nueva de Santa Cruz, where he received a Spanish land grant. Five years later, he sold his land and moved to the Rio Abajo, in what is today Bernalillo County, with his new wife, Doña Mariana Hurtado, and her family.[3] Over the next hundred years, the spelling of Vallejos changed to Ballejos, and descendants moved northward into the Española Valley and eventually to Arroyo Hondo near Taos, New Mexico.[4]

Maria Dolores's parents, Juan Bautista Ballejos and Maria Gertrudis Martin, were living in Canoa, New Mexico, in the Española Valley, when Maria Dolores was born on January 27, 1804. She was baptized on February 2, 1804, in the mission at San Juan de Los Caballeros (now Ohkay Owingeh Pueblo).[5] She married Ricardo de Jesus Vigil at the San Juan Mission, and in 1823 or 1824, their first child, Maria Guadalupe Vigil, was born. Interestingly, Maria Dolores's sister, Maria Guadalupe Ballejos, married Maria Dolores's husband's brother, Juan Angel Vigil, making the ties between the two families very close.

Maria Dolores and her husband had eleven children, but fewer than half survived to adulthood. Those who lived were: Maria Guadalupe, their oldest daughter; Jose Tomas, the only son who lived to adulthood; Antonia Rosa; Maria Francisca; and Maria Micaela.[6] In the late 1840s or early 1850s, Maria

Dolores and her family, along with several of her siblings and their families, moved to the Precinct of Culebra in the San Luis Valley, an area that would later become part of the state of

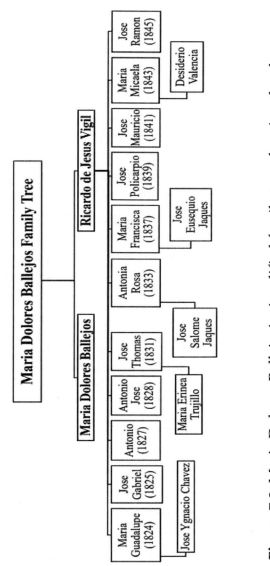

Figure 7.2. Maria Dolores Ballejos's simplified family tree showing the eleven children to whom she gave birth. Her adopted children are described later.

Colorado. The promise of owning their own lands lured the families into the untamed and dangerous wilderness.[7]

The San Luis Valley, or *El Valle de San Luis* as it was originally called by early Spanish explorers, is a high desert valley situated at seven-thousand-eight-hundred feet and surrounded by the Sangre de Cristo Mountains to the east and the San Juan Mountains to the west. Before Hispano settlements began, the valley was primarily the home of Ute Indians, although several Indigenous tribes hunted and raided there.

In 1598, nine years before the first permanent English settlement at Jamestown was established, Spain founded the town of *San Juan de los Caballeros* in New Spain, about eighty miles south of the current Colorado border.[8] That same year, the newly appointed governor of New Mexico, Don Juan de Oñate, claimed the San Luis Valley and surrounding area for New Spain. Over the next hundred years, numerous Spanish explorers visited the area, creating maps and leaving behind landmarks that still retain their Spanish names: the Sangre de Cristo Mountains, Culebra Creek, Rio Grande River, San Pedro Mesa, and La Veta Pass, to name a few. During this time, Spanish settlements in the San Luis Valley were attempted, but repelled by Native Americans protecting their homelands.

After the United States completed the Louisiana Purchase in 1803, explorers began investigating the United States' new territory. Along with the explorers came French and United States mountain men in search of better trapping and trading. These foreigners sometimes crossed the Arkansas River, the border between New Spain and the United States, and visited the San Luis Valley. In 1821, when Mexico won its independence from Spain, Mexico became alarmed by foreign encroachment on its northern lands. By enacting the colonization law of 1824, Mexico authorized the allocation of large land grants, up to eleven square leagues (around fifty thousand acres) to individual grantees. To keep the land grant, the recipients had to promote permanent settlement and cultivation on two-thirds of the grant. If the grantee was successful, the remaining one-third of the grant would become his or her personal property. If settlements were unsuccessful, the grant would become null and void and the grantee would lose all rights to the entire grant.[9]

One of the first Mexican land grant in the San Luis Valley was issued in 1833, giving the land around the Conejos River to a group of fifty families.[10] Utes, Navajos, and Jicarilla Apaches fought to retain their homeland, and they prevented these families from fulfilling their settlement obligations. In 1842, the heirs of these families petitioned for a revalidation of the Conejos Grant. Eighty-three families became grantees and again attempted to settle in the San Luis Valley. Exact locations of early settlements in the San Luis Valley vary in different historical resources, but between 1849 and 1851, successful settlements were made on the Costilla and Culebra Creeks in the area around San Acacio, in present-day San Luis, and along the Conejos River.[11]

The Conejos Land Grant was unusual in that it was issued to a group of settlers. Most other Mexican land grants transferred ownership of huge swaths of land to individuals. In 1841, Charles H. Beaubien (also called Carlos) and Guadalupe Miranda were granted more than 1.7 million acres that became known as the Sangre de Cristo Land Grant. Two years later, in 1843, Cornelio Vigil and Ceran St. Vrain received the Las Animas Grant,[12] encompassing more than four million acres. Within a few years, large portions of northern New Mexico and southern Colorado were owned by just a few families.

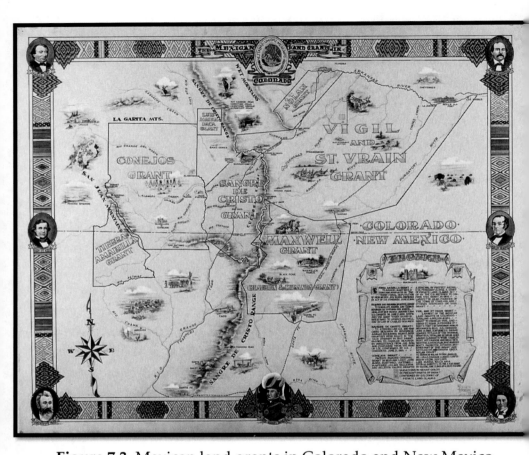

Figure 7.3. Mexican land grants in Colorado and New Mexico

Courtesy of History Colorado, Denver, Colorado, Accession #G4311.G465

Maria Dolores and her family settled on Charles Beaubien's Sangre de Cristo Land Grant. To fulfill his grant obligations, Beaubien encouraged settlement by offering free land to settlers. Land grant communities, like those formed by Maria Dolores and her extended family, were farm and ranch settlements. Beaubien assigned communal land (*ejido*) and offered individual ownership of land, an economic system typical in Mexican law, yet foreign to most Anglos who later settled in the San Luis Valley. Under this arrangement, a land grantee provided each community with property that was divided into three areas: agricultural land individually owned; communal land in the mountains for gathering timber and wild plants, and for hunting game; and communal pastureland for grazing domesticated cattle, sheep, goats, horses, and other livestock.

On January 14, 1850, Maria Dolores's daughter, Antonia Rosa, married Jose Salome Jáquez, and they listed their place of residence as San Acacio. Maria Dolores's other daughter, Maria Francisca, married Jose Salome's brother, Jose Eusequio Jáquez four years later in San Pedro de la Culebra. Sisters marrying another family's brothers, as happened in two generations of Maria Dolores's family, seems unusual today, but in the United States before the Industrial Revolution, people "didn't travel far to find a spouse, and the closer you were to home, the more likely it was you'd marry within your family."[13] Even marrying a first cousin was culturally acceptable in the 1800s. Charles Darwin's marriage to his first cousin Emma Wedgwood was not unusual.

The 1850 United States Census lists Maria Dolores and her extended family living in the Northern Division, Taos County, New Mexico Territory.[14] Maria Dolores and her husband also owned land in the San Luis bottomlands, considered part of Old San Acacio.[15] These facts, along with the family's oral history, provide strong evidence that Maria Dolores was one of the first Hispana pioneers to settle the San Luis Valley in what would later become the state of Colorado, perhaps arriving as early as 1849.[16]

Hispano settlers typically built their homes around a central plaza, usually rectangular or square in shape. Their homes became the walls around the community, and gates, usually one on each side of the plaza, were added to form a protected enclosure. Violence between Native Americans and settlers

Figure 7.4. A jacal of logs and adobe, built around 1885, Los Sauces, Colorado

©Robert Adams, courtesy of Fraenkel Gallery, San Francisco, CA

was common and often deadly; at night, after all livestock were driven inside the plaza, the gates were closed and watchmen were posted to protect livestock and people from attack.[17] Maria Dolores's brother-in-law, Juan Angel Vigil, was killed in one such attack in 1855.[18]

Settlers initially built *jacales* to surround their plazas. Only later, when the settlement thrived, were the *jacales* replaced by more sturdy adobe homes, made from large bricks of mud and straw. Unlike Anglo log cabins, *jacales* were built by setting posts upright in the ground and filling the spaces between the vertical posts with mud. The sturdier adobe buildings were made by using thick earthen bricks stacked on top of each other, held together with adobe mud, and topped with a flat, wooden roof. Adobe buildings were extremely robust, and the adobe bricks helped keep the home cool and comfortable in the summer and warm in the winter.[19]

Like most Hispano settlers, Maria Dolores and her husband made their living growing wheat, corn, beans, squash, and other hardy, drought-tolerant crops. The corn was preserved by steaming it in an adobe oven (*horno*) overnight and then drying it for later use. Wheat was grown to feed the household and as a cash crop.

In April 1852, Beaubien and Joe Pley recorded the location and amount of land given to individual settlers on the border of the San Pablo River. In this allocation, Maria Dolores's husband was allotted two hundred rods (around two acres), while the married men in her extended family—Jose Tomas Vigil (Maria Dolores's son), Jose Ausequinio Jaques (her daughter Maria Francisca Vigil's husband), Jose Salome Jaques (her daughter Antonia Rosa Vigil's husband), and Juan Angel Vigil (her sister's husband)—each received one hundred rods.[20] Each individual received land that fronted a watercourse for irrigation, and when a watercourse was unavailable, community *acequias* were dug.[21] In 1852, the town of San Luis de la Culebra built *la acequia de la gente*, or the People's Ditch establishing Colorado's earliest known water rights.[22]

Water rights in Colorado were as critical in the 1800s as they are today. Miners needed water for personal use, for placer mining, and to run the stamp mills that pulverized their ore. During the general assembly of 1859-1860, before Colorado became a territory, water laws were enacted to prevent the application of riparian rights in which water is owned only by landowners who border the water. The general assembly wanted to make sure that property owners whose land didn't border a stream could still divert water for their needs.[23]

English common law tended to stress individual rights, and these laws often conflicted with Mexican communal land grant laws. Early Hispano water rights, like Mexican land grant ownership, produced numerous legal conflicts for the Hispanos living in the San Luis Valley.

Day-to-day details about Maria Dolores's life, like those of other Hispana settlers of the San Luis Valley, are scarce. Most Hispana pioneers were poor and often illiterate, and few recorded their lives in personal journals or diaries. Deborah Mora-Espinosa is quoted in *La Gente: Hispano History and Life in Colorado* as stating, "Had it not been for the religious traditions that marked the milestones of their lives, any knowledge we might have of early frontier Spanish and Mexican women would be lost to all time."[24]

The 1860 United States Census, taken one year before Colorado became a territory, lists Maria Dolores Ballejos living in the Precinct of Culebra, Territory of New Mexico, in household #1972. The Culebra Precinct encompased several San Luis Valley villages, including San Luis, San Pedro y San Pablo, San Acacio, El Rito de Jose Gregorio, and Los Fuertes. Maria Dolores's son Jose Tomas Vigil and his family were the family enumerated next, #1973. Her daughter, Antonia Rosa Vigil, and family were listed next, #1974, and her other daughter, Maria Micaela Vigil, and her husband were in household #1975.[25] In this census, Maria Dolores's age is recorded as fifty-four (two years younger than her actual age, according to church records), and her husband Ricardo's age is recorded as sixty. They list their occupation as farmers with $1000 value in real estate and $1000 in personal property. In 2023 dollars, that is an equivalent purchasing power of approximately $73,000.[26]

Life for early Hispano settlers was challenging even before Anglo miners arrived. Then, as now, land in the San Luis Valley was arid and difficult to cultivate. Native Americans protected their homeland and often warred with the settlers.

Taos and El Pueblo, the closest trading posts, were several days' travel away. Settlers worked hard, and like their Anglo counterparts, Hispano men and women contributed typically through different roles. In addition to feeding her family, Maria Dolores and her daughters would have hauled water to their homes, washed clothes in the local stream, and spun wool from their sheep. They would have hand woven the wool into cloth for clothing, bedding, and rugs. To keep their homes tidy and clean, they would have whitewashed and plastered the interior walls and kept the dirt floors swept and clean. Still, the women's hardest chore was feeding their families.

Having enough food was often a challenge. Women grew gardens in courtyards near their homes.[27] In addition, they harvested wild plants such as wild spinach, purslane (*verdolagas*), wild onions, berries, wild plums, and wild oregano. Chile peppers were cultivated and strung into *ristras* and hung to dry until they could be ground into chile powder. Fresh meat came from both wild game and domesticated livestock. Meat, fruits, and vegetables needed to be dried or preserved by the women for use during the winter.

Maria Dolores's husband and sons were primarily farmers, tending their fields on the outskirts of the town and keeping track of their sheep, cattle, goats, burros, and other livestock. Some men, such as Maria Dolores's son Jose Tomas Vigil, left farming to become freighters, hauling goods from Taos, Santa Fe, and Bent's Fort back to their community.[28] As the settlements grew, more businesses were established. Dario Gallegos opened a store in San Luis in 1857 offering green coffee, unrefined sugar, cornmeal, dried fruit, salt, peas, chocolate, tobacco, matches, and yard goods.[29] Hispano men were also community guards on the lookout for unfriendly intruders.

The relationship between Hispano settlers and their Native American neighbors was complex. Open hostilities caused injury and death on both sides, but trade also existed, including human trade. Native Americans often raided enemy tribes, capturing women and children who would be sold in Hispano plazas. Native American slaves (*genízaros*) were purchased by Hispano settlers and used as domestic workers, shepherds, and general laborers.[30] Today in the San Luis Valley, many Hispanos are *Mestizos*, individuals of both Spanish and Native American heritage.

After living in the San Luis Valley for several years, Maria and her husband acquired two Navajo children, Jose Antonio Vigil, baptized in December 1860 in San Pedro de la Culebra,

Figure 7.5. Erinea (Trujillo) Vigil, second wife of Maria Dolores's son, Jose Tomas Vigil, and her grandchildren, circa 1918

Courtesy of the collection of Bertha Manzanarez

and Maria del Rosario Vigil, baptized in January 1861 in the same church. Both Navajo children are listed in genealogical records as Maria Dolores's children, each adopted at age four.[31] However, an 1865 survey of Native American captives living in Costilla County included Maria Dolores's two children: Jose Antonio, age nine, year acquired in 1858; and Maria del Rosario, age seven, year acquired 1859.[32] In this survey, Maria Dolores Vallejos also was listed as the owner of a forty-year-old Navajo woman named Maria, also acquired in 1859.[33] Maria is not listed in Maria Dolores's family genealogy records nor in United States census records.

Native American slavery, or debt peonage, as it became known after Mexico abolished slavery, played a huge role in Hispano culture, economy, and interethnic relations. It is estimated there were between forty thousand and ninety thousand Native Americans kept in bondage in North America (excluding Mexico) between 1851 and 1900.[34] Slavery in the West was practiced not only by Hispanos, but also by Native Americans and Anglos. There is strong evidence well-

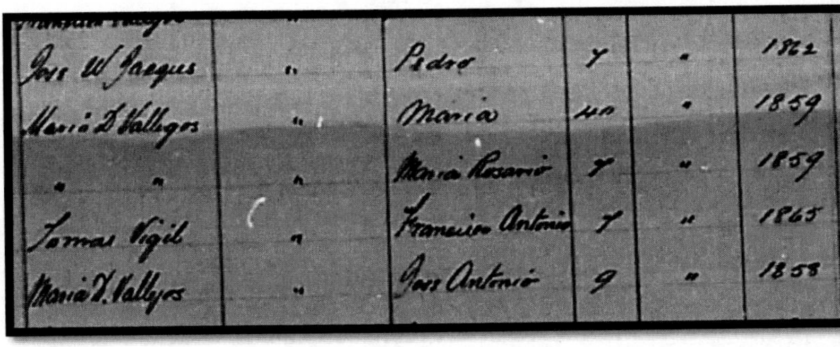

Jose W Jaques	"	Pedro	7	"	1862
Maria D Vallejos	"	Maria	40	"	1859
" "	"	Maria Rosario	7	"	1859
Tomas Vigil	"	Francisco Antonio	7	"	1865
Maria D. Vallejos	"	Jose Antonio	9	"	1858

Figure 7.6. A portion of Indian Agent Lafayette Head's 1865 Indigenous captive list, showing Maria D. Vallejos's ownership of two Native American children and one adult

Courtesy of the National Archives and Records Administration

known Indian Agent Lafayette Head—the man who created the 1865 report on Native American captives in Costilla County—owned at least one Native American child.[35] In his book, *The Other Slavery*, Andrés Reséndez writes:

> Any white person who wished to employ an Indian child could present himself before a justice of the peace accompanied by the "parents or friends" of the minor in question, and after showing that this was a voluntary transaction, the petitioner would get custody of the child and control "the earnings of such minor until he or she obtained the age of majority" (fifteen for girls and eighteen for boys).[36]

In January of 1860, New Mexico's territorial legislature amended its Mexican laws, in effect, legalizing the enslavement of Native Americans. As a result, many Navajo children were captured that year and taken into debt peonage.[37] After the United States' Thirteenth Amendment was signed into law, Hispano peons became a source of friction and conflict, and the United States Congress passed the Peonage Act of 1867, which abolished peonage. This law was aimed specifically at New Mexicans.[38]

Like most Hispano families, Maria Dolores and her family were Catholics, following the traditions of their church. Maria Dolores baptized her children and celebrated numerous Catholic holidays. Initially there were no priests or churches in the San Luis Valley, forcing Catholic families to either travel to Arroyo Hondo for weddings and baptisms or to wait until a visiting priest arrived in the Culebra villages. In 1855, Father Vicente Montano was assigned to Conejos Parish, establishing the first non-native place of worship in Colorado. A small *jacal* was built as a church, and in 1858 the community replaced the *jacal* with an adobe building dedicated to Our Lady of Guadalupe, the patron saint of the settlement. [39] This church, located near Antonito, Colorado, remains the state's oldest non-native place of worship.

Maria Dolores's yearly routines would have been dictated by her Catholic beliefs. On New Year's Eve, she and her family would have attended midnight mass, and when a village could afford it, there would have been community performances depicting Christ's life. Celebrated on January 6 was *Los Reyes Magos,* a depiction of the birth of Christ and the coming of the Magi with gifts, and in February, *El Niño Perdido,* the story of Jesus studying in the temple, might have been performed. [40] There were celebrations during Holy Week, religious songs, activities by the Society of Penitente Brothers (Hermanos Penitente) for the men, and numerous village feast days celebrated with horse races, community meals, and dances.

Catholic traditions were part of the Hispano lifestyle and culture, but like many aspects of Hispano lives, they were sometimes difficult for Anglos to understand and appreciate. The Hermanos Penitente community and their traditions were especially difficult for Anglos. Newspapers at the time described the Penitente community as "a 'secret' and 'strange mountain cult' enacted by 'swarty hot-eyed Mexicans and half-breeds.'" [41] Religious differences, along with language differences, water rights conflicts, and land ownership disputes, led to conflicts between the two cultures, especially after the San Luis Valley became part of the Colorado Territory.

The Mexican-American War (1846-1848) forced Mexico to cede more than half of its territory to the United States. The conditions of this massive land and population transfer were written into the Treaty of Guadalupe Hidalgo, which stated

that all Mexicans living on what was now United States soil
were guaranteed to be "incorporated into the Union of the
United States" and protected "of their liberty and property,
and secured in the free exercise of their religion without;
restriction."[42] The Treaty of Guadalupe Hidalgo promised
Hispanos living on United States soil full citizenship if they
wanted it, but the reality was far different.

Prejudices against Hispanos abounded in the second half of
the 1800s and were often expressed in vulgar, ugly language.
The following excerpt from the *Colorado Daily Chieftain* of
March 30, 1876, demonstrates the type of prejudices Maria
Dolores and other Hispano settlers would have experienced:

Figure 7.7. Map showing Mexican lands, more than half of which
were ceded to the United States in1848 at the end of the Mexican-
American War. Published by John Disturnell in 1847.

Courtesy of the Library of Congress, 2004627240.

A great many greasers, a mixed race of Spaniards and In-dians are found "making believe" farming in the valleys of Southern Colorado. They combine the slothfulness of the Hidalgos with the filth and shiftlessness of the Indians, and are a libel on the races represented by Cortez and Montezuma. They are just rapid enough for sheepherders, and take more to this than any other branch of hus-bandry.[43]

This article was reproduced in several Colorado newspapers in 1876. The writer, like many Anglos at that time, ignored the hard work and successes of the Hispanos living in the San Luis Valley. Allen Bradford, an associate justice of the Colorado territorial supreme court, visited the San Luis Valley in 1864 and wrote a letter to former Territorial Governor William Gilpin saying, "I learned that stock to the amount of 50,000 head were owned by people on the Sangre de Cristo Grant."[44] The book *History of Colorado* notes that the "finest 'freighting' oxen in the country were raised here, and when the railroad reached Alamosa in 1878 fully a thousand Mexicans started freighting in all directions with yokes of oxen, running as high as twenty-eight head for one wagon and trailer."[45] Despite reports such as this, racial prejudices continued. Vilma Ortiz and Edward Telles describe some of these issues in their article "Racial Identity and Racial Treatment of Mexican Americans":

Historically and legally, Mexicans have been treated as second-class citizens. Within a few short decades after their conquest in the mid-nineteenth century, Mexican Americans, although officially granted United States citizenship with full rights, lost much of their property and status and were relegated to low-status positions as laborers.[46]

Land grants and water rights were two areas in which a sec-
ond-class-citizen attitude harmed Hispano settlers. In 1860,
the United States Congress confirmed Charles Beaubien's
claim to the Sangre de Cristo grant, giving him ownership of
the land, and on May 11, 1863, Beaubien issued deeds to all
his settlers, legally giving individuals the rights to the land
they had cultivated. Unfortunately, communal land rights
were not transferred to individual towns and issues ensued.
Richard Garcia and Todd Howland described some of these
issues in their article, "Spanish Land Grants in Colorado:
Conflicting Values, Legal Pluralism, and Demystification of
the Sangre de Cristo/Rael Case," by writing: "While the
settlers obtained and exercised usufructuary rights over land
outside of the plots they obtained in fee simple for cultivation,
the title to this common land was apparently not transferred
to the town, as conditioned by the Grant and Mexican Law."[47]
These communal land disputes came about partially due to
the differences between Spanish and United States law.
Coloradan Hispanos had been raised with laws that enforced
Mexican land grant property allocations and defined land and
water rights. In addition, these Mexican laws gave married
Hispana women far more rights than married Anglo women
had. In the New Mexico Territory, these laws remained
mostly intact, but Hispanos living in southern Colorado were
suddenly subject to Colorado Territorial laws, none of which
were translated into Spanish, and many of which conflicted
with Spanish/Mexican laws. These laws caused hardships,
especially for Hispana women, and many families were
forced into legal battles just to remain on the land they had
cultivated and called home for years.

In 1860, trying to solve some of these issues, United States

Senator Stephen Douglas of Illinois proposed altering the borders of what would become the Colorado Territory to remove the New Mexico land. Senator Douglas pointed out that the Hispano land titles were governed by Mexican laws and usages "entirely incompatible with the laws that we are in the habit of making for our own people."[48] His legislation failed, and soon thereafter, Coloradan Hispano claimants were required to appear before the surveyor general to prove their land titles. Some land titles and Mexican land grants were confirmed, such as the Sangre de Cristo Land Grant, but many, including the Conejos Land Grant, were entirely rejected.[49]

The same year that Charles Beaubien issued deeds to his San Luis Valley settlers, he also sold the Sangre de Cristo grant to former Territorial Governor William Gilpin and a group of investors. These new landowners subdivided the land and attempted to evict the Hispano residents. The communal land ownership within the Sangre de Cristo grant has been disputed for a hundred and fifty years. In 2002, one of Maria Dolores's relatives, Shirley Romero Otero, and other land rights activists helped overturn years of legal decisions against Hispano communal lands, and they won back the rights of their forebearers. The Colorado Supreme Court ended one of the state's longest legal battles by announcing that the descendants of individuals who settled the Sangre de Cristo Land Grant in southern Colorado did indeed have the right to access the communal lands within the original grant, for wood, timber, and grazing.[50]

Hispana women such as Maria Dolores experienced unique hardships due to United States laws prejudiced against a married woman's right to own land in her own name. Spanish civil codes "recognized the legal right of women to own and control property independent of patriarchal relationships."[51]

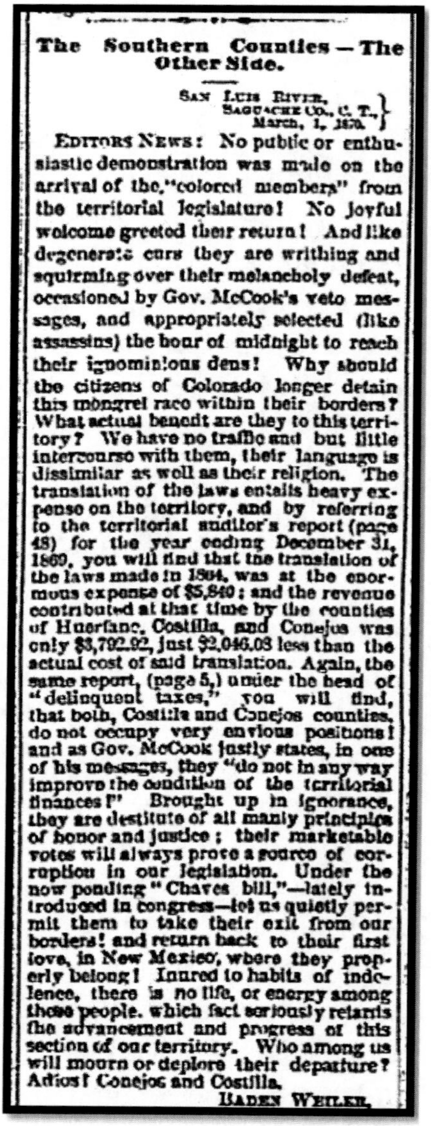

The Southern Counties — The Other Side.

SAN LUIS RIVER,
SAGUACHE CO., C. T.
March, 1, 1870.

EDITORS NEWS: No public or enthusiastic demonstration was made on the arrival of the "colored members" from the territorial legislature! No joyful welcome greeted their return! And like degenerate curs they are writhing and squirming over their melancholy defeat, occasioned by Gov. McCook's veto messages, and appropriately selected (like assassins) the hour of midnight to reach their ignominious dens! Why should the citizens of Colorado longer detain this mongrel race within their borders? What actual benefit are they to this territory? We have no traffic and but little intercourse with them, their language is dissimilar as well as their religion. The translation of the laws entails heavy expense on the territory, and by referring to the territorial auditor's report (page 48) for the year ending December 31, 1869, you will find that the translation of the laws made in 1864, was at the enormous expense of $5,840; and the revenue contributed at that time by the counties of Huerfano, Costilla, and Conejos was only $3,792.92, just $2,046.03 less than the actual cost of said translation. Again, the same report, (page 5,) under the head of "delinquent taxes," you will find, that both, Costilla and Conejos counties, do not occupy very envious positions! and as Gov. McCook justly states, in one of his messages, they "do not in any way improve the condition of the territorial finances!" Brought up in ignorance, they are destitute of all manly principles of honor and justice; their marketable votes will always prove a source of corruption in our legislation. Under the now pending "Chaves bill,"—lately introduced in congress—let us quietly permit them to take their exit from our borders! and return back to their first love, in New Mexico, where they properly belong! Inured to habits of indolence, there is no life, or energy among those people, which fact seriously retards the advancement and progress of this section of our territory. Who among us will mourn or deplore their departure? Adios! Conejos and Costilla.

BADEN WEILER.

Figure 7.8. *Rocky Mountain News* editorial of March 16, 1870, promoting Chaves's bill

Courtesy of Colorado Historic Newspapers Collection

Women owned their own property, often inherited from parents and grandparents, and sons and daughters shared in a system of partible or equal inheritance. In contrast, United States law at that time allowed a woman to legally "buy and sell property, enter into contracts, sue and be sued, and write a will" *until* she was married. Once she married, she became *fem covert*, literally "a covered woman," legally one with her husband."[52] She lost most of her legal rights and any property she owned became her husband's property. It wasn't until 1874 that Colorado passed the Married Women's Property Act, which gave married women the rights that Hispana women had always enjoyed.

By 1866, cultural differences, legal issues, and Anglo prejudices caused José Francisco Cháves, a

New Mexico Territory delegate to the United States House of Representatives, to again introduce legislation aimed at redrawing Colorado's southern border, from the 37th parallel to the 38th parallel, in an attempt to return the San Luis Valley and a swath of southern Colorado to New Mexico.[53] Cháves's bill forced public debate in Colorado's Hispano communities as they struggled to decide if they were Coloradans or New Mexicans. The bill eventually failed, yet as historian Jake Swisher wrote in his article about race and identity on the Colorado border, Coloradan Hispanos "could never fully claim an identity as citizens of Colorado on account of cultural differences that were increasingly hardening into racial distinctions."[54]

Although Hispanos in Southern Colorado had been given representation in the Colorado territorial government as early as 1861, all government discussions and deliberations were held in English. Despite the Treaty of Guadalupe Hidalgo, the United States Congress refused to allocate funds for translating laws into Spanish because, as Virginia Sánchez writes in *Pleas and Petitions: Hispano Culture and Legislative Conflict in Territorial Colorado*, it "considered the Hispanos alien and noncitizens."[55] Hispano representatives from southern Colorado, Sánchez writes, were not even allowed to choose their own interpreters: "In 1874 the House hired Salas Hawes to interpret for the Spanish-speaking representatives from Southern Colorado. Nine days into the session, Colorado Council member Juan Bautista Jáquez (Huerfano) sought to have Hawes replaced by Celestino Domínguez because Hawes was 'not competent in Spanish.'"[56]

Despite all these hardships, Maria Dolores and her extended family remained in the San Luis Valley, moving to the Cuchara Valley and to Conejos County sometime after the 1860 census. Of Maria Dolores's five surviving adult children, sadly three of her daughters died young. Maria Guadalupe Vigil married Jose Ygnacio Chavez in 1840 and died a few years later. Antonia Rosa Jáquez and Francisca Jáquez, who had married brothers, both died in childbirth between 1863 and 1871. Maria Dolores's only surviving daughter, Maria Micaela Vigil, married Desiderio Valencia and moved to Blanco, New Mexico.

Maria Dolores's son, Jose Tomas Vigil, married Guadalupe Pacheco in 1853, and after her death, he married Maria Erinea Trujillo in 1874. Throughout his life, he maintained ranches in both Culebra and Huerfano County. Four of his children from his first wife remained in Culebra and raised families there. Most of the children from his second marriage moved to Huerfano County.

Maria Dolores's husband, Ricardo de Jesus, died around 1870, but Maria Dolores lived well into her eighties, enjoying her many grandchildren and great-grandchildren. The last recorded event found for Maria Dolores occurred in 1884 when she became the godmother of her grandchild, Maria Benigna Vigil, the seventh child of her son, Jose Tomas Vigil. A burial record has not been found for Maria Dolores, but it is thought that she died before 1890, the year her son, Jose Tomas, died in a freighting accident.

Maria Dolores lived under three governments: Spanish, Mexican, and United States. She survived the transfer of her land and home into the Territory of Colorado, separating her from her people and her culture. She died in her early to mid-eighties, but her legacy lives on through the lives of her children's children. Her descendants are architects, doctors, lawyers, musicians, high ranking government employees, professors, teachers, and community activists. Many of her descendants have served in the military, earning Purple Hearts, Silver Stars, and Bronze Stars, and some gave their lives in the World Wars and the Vietnam War.[57]

Special Acknowledgment

Specific details about Maria Dolores's life are few, but one of her descendants, Maria Clara Martinez, has spent her lifetime researching her family's history.[58] Maria Martinez is the great granddaughter of Maria Dolores's son, Jose Tomas Vigil. Maria Martinez generously shared Maria Dolores's history, her own genealogy research, and family stories that have been passed down orally. It would have been impossible for the authors to include Maria Dolores's biography in this collection without the substantial contributions of Maria Clara Martinez.

---

[1] Virginia Sánchez, *Pleas and Petitions: Hispano Culture and Legislative Conflict in Territorial Colorado* (Louisville, CO: University Press of Colorado, 2020), 3.

[2] José Antonio Esquibel, *Early Settlers of Santa Cruz de la Cañada 1695-1715* (José Antonio Esquibel, Sierra Azul Monograph No. 1, privately published, 2015), 3, 11-13, 52, https://drive.google.com/file/d/1GcjQkbSd7YpHDq4zkBLR8QSlB0_-6Azh/view. See also José Antonio Esquibel and John B. Bolligan, *The Spanish Recolonization of New Mexico* (Albuquerque, NM: Hispanic Genealogical Research Center of New Mexico, 1999), 4, 10.

[3] Esquibel, *Early Settlers*, 3, 52; and see Fray Angélico Chávez, *New Mexico Roots, Ltd.: A Demographic Perspective from Genealogical, Historical, and Geographical Data Found in the Diligencias Matrimoniales or Pre-Nuptial Investigations (1678-1869) of the Archives of the Archdiocese of Santa Fe* (unpublished typescript, Santa Fe, NM: 1983), 2042, DM 1694, October 22 (no. 19). The manuscript, arranged in eleven digitized volumes, is online at https://digitalrepository.unm.edu/cswr_reference/5. The 1694 pre-nuptial

investigation is found in volume 11, page 2042, under the heading "Vallejo, Vallejos."

[4] Family genealogy provided to the authors by Maria Clara Martinez, San Luis Valley historian and genealogist, descendant of Maria Dolores Ballejos, 2020-2022.

[5] San Juan de los Caballeros Catholic Church, baptismal registers, 1726-1837, Book 42 (1799-1820), 39, birth and baptism of Maria Dolores, microfilm of original records, FamilySearch.org (website), Church Records, Rio Arriba County, San Juan, New Mexico, 1726-1956, Family History Library film 16981, film image 386.

[6] Family genealogy provided to authors by Maria Clara Martinez, December 12, 2020.

[7] Olibama López Tushar, *The People of El Valle: A History of the Spanish Colonials in the San Luis Valley* (Pueblo, CO: El Escritorio, 1992), 46-67.

[8] Robert Adams, *The Architecture and Art of Early Hispanic Colorado* (Boulder, CO: Colorado Associated University Press, 1974), 6.

[9] Richard Garcia and Todd Howland, "Determining the Legitimacy of Spanish Land Grants in Colorado: Conflicting Values, Legal Pluralism, and Demystification of the *Sangre De Cristo/Rael Case*," *Chicana/o Latina/o Law Review* 16, no.1, (1995): 42, https://doi.org/10.5070/C7161021057.

[10] Virginia McConnell Simmons, *The San Luis Valley: Land of the Six-Armed Cross* (Niwot, CO: University Press of Colorado, 1999), 78; and see Tushar, *The People of El Valle*, 32.

[11] Wilbur Fisk Stone, *History of Colorado* (Chicago, IL: S. J. Clarke, 1918), 2:528. Stone wrote, "The first attempt failed as the Indians resented the coming of the Mexicans. But in 1849 another settlement was made in Costilla and in 1854 in Conejos." Simmons, in *The San Luis Valley: Land of the Six-Armed Cross*, 84-85, writes, "During the next year, 1851, Costilla achieved the status of a village . . . " and "A second cluster of plazas was begun on the Sangre de Cristo grant at Culebra Creek in 1850."

12 Bonnie Clark, "Understanding Amache: The Archaeobiography of a Victorian-era Cheyenne Woman," *Colorado Heritage,* Autumn, 2006, 45.

13 Steph Yin, "When Did Americans Stop Marrying Their Cousins? Ask the World's Largest Family Tree," *The New York Times,* Mar. 1, 2018, accessed May 21, 2023, https://www.nytimes.com/2018/03/01/science/cousins-marriage-family-tree.html.

14 1850 US Census Northern Division, Taos County, New Mexico Territory, digital image s.v. "Maria Dolores Ballejos," Ancestry.com.

15 Family genealogy provided to the authors by Maria Clara Martinez.

16 Family genealogy provided to the authors by Maria Clara Martinez.

17 Meliton Velasquez, "Guadalupe Colony Was Founded 1854," *Colorado Magazine,* October 1957, 265.

18 Family genealogy provided to the authors by Maria Clara Martinez; and see Simmons, *The San Luis Valley: Land of the Six-Armed Cross,* 85-86. Simmons lists the year of Juan Angel Vigil's death as 1851, but since he was granted land by Carlos Beaubien in 1852, Martinez's date of Juan Angel Vigil's death in 1855 appears more accurate.

19 Natassia Paloma, "Borderland Treasures: Exploring the tenements of Segundo Barrio," updated January 24, 2022, KTSM.com (website), https://www.ktsm.com/local/el-paso-news/borderland-treasures-exploring-the-tenements-of-segundo-barrio/ https://www.ktsm.com/local/el-paso-news/borderland-treasures-exploring-the-tenements-of-segundo-barrio/.

20 "Raices," *La Sierra: Voice of Costilla County* (San Luis, CO), Feb. 26, 2021, 8. Article provided by Maria Clara Martinez.

21 Garcia and Howland, "Determining the Legitimacy of Spanish Land Grants in Colorado," 41.

22 Gregory A. Hicks and Devon G. Peña, "Community Acequias in Colorado's Rio Culebra Watershed: A Customary Commons in the Domain of Prior Appropriation," *University of Colorado Law Review* 74, no. 2 (2003): 374,

https://digitalcommons.law.uw.edu/faculty-articles/374.

[23] Gregory A. Hicks and Devon G. Peña, "Community Acequias," 399-400.

[24] Vincent C. De Baca, ed., *La Gente: Hispano History and Life in Colorado*, (Denver, CO: University Press of Colorado, 1998), 3.

[25] 1860 US Census, Culebra, Taos County, New Mexico Territory, digital image s.v. "Maria Dolores Ballejos," Ancestry.com.

[26] The equivalent purchasing power of $2,000 in 1860, as of June 20, 2023, was calculated to be $73,283 assuming a 2.3% inflation rate, Consumer Price Index (CPI) inflation calculator (webpage), https://www.officialdata.org/us/inflation/1860?amount=2000.

[27] Janet Lecompte, *Pueblo, Hardscrabble, Greenhorn: Society on the High Plains 1832-1856* (Norman, OK: University of Oklahoma Press, 1978), 66.

[28] Family genealogy provided to the authors by Maria Clara Martinez.

[29] Simmons, *The San Luis Valley: Land of the Six-Armed Cross*, 101-2.

[30] Andrés Reséndez, *The Other Slavery: The Uncovered Story of Indian Enslavement in America* (New York, NY: Mariner Books Houghton Mifflin Harcourt, 2016), 324.

[31] Family genealogy provided to the authors by Maria Clara Martinez.

[32] Cody White, archivist, "'The Most Barbarous and Inhumane Practice': The Elimination of Slavery in the Territories, as Seen in the Office of Indian Affairs Microfilm Series," *The Text Message, Blog of the Textual Records Division at the National Archives*, July 28, 2020, https://text-message.blogs.archives.gov/2020/07/28/the-most-barbarous-and-inhuman-practice-the-elimination-of-slavery-in-the-territories-as-seen-in-the-office-of-indian-affairs-microfilm-series/. Article includes images of Agent Head's Report, found in Record Group 75, Records of the Bureau of Indian Affairs, Series: Letters Received 1824-1880, file unit: M234 (microfilm),item: Colorado Superintendency, 1861-1880; 1865-1866, roll 198, frames 88-91, which record Maria Dolores's ownership of three Native American slaves.

33 Estevan Rael-Galvez, "Native American Captivity, Slavery & Identity," *News*, Colorado's Museum Trails (website), Museums of the San Luis Valley and Southern Colorado, October 24, 2018, https://www.museumtrail.org/native-american-captivity-slavery-identity. Rael-Galvez shows that in the July 1865 Lafayette Head lists in Costilla and Conejos Counties, in addition to the two Navajo children owned by Maria Dolores, there is a forty-year-old Navajo woman, Maria, who lived in Maria Dolores's household. His blog also shows Navajo children living in Maria Dolores's sister's home, and in the home of her son, Tomas.

34 Reséndez, *The Other Slavery*, 280-81.

35 Sánchez, *Pleas and Petitions*, 145-51. According to this reference, there is significant historical evidence that Lafayette Head engaged in buying, kidnapping, and selling enslaved Native Americans, although there was never any action taken against him.

36 Reséndez, *The Other Slavery*, 265.

37 Reséndez, *The Other Slavery*, 280-81.

38 Simon Romero, "Indian Slavery Once Thrived in New Mexico. Latinos Are Finding Family Ties to It," *New York Times*, Jan. 28, 2018, https://www.nytimes.com/2018/01/28/us/indian-slaves-genizaros.html.

39 Tushar, *The People of El Valle*, 17.

40 Tushar, *The People of El Valle* , 62-63.

41 Alberto Lopez Pulido, *The Sacred World of the Penitentes* (Washington, D.C.: Smithsonian Institution Press, 2000), 26.

42 Steven Mintz and Sara McNeil, "Treaty of Guadalupe Hidalgo, Article IX, 1848," (annotated), Digital History (website), University of Houston, accessed May 29, 2023, https://www.digitalhistory.uh.edu/disp_text-book.cfm?smtID=3&psid=1141#:~:text=The%20treaty%20explicitly%20guaranteed%20Mexican,and%20deleted%20Article%20X%2C%20which.

43 "Millions in it. A Flying Trip to San Juan County, A Great Many Greasers," *Colorado Daily Chieftain* (Pueblo, CO), Mar. 30,

1876, 3, Colorado Historic Newspapers Collection (website), Colorado State Library, coloradohistoricnewspapers.org.

[44] Stone, *History of Colorado,* 2:528.

[45] Stone, *History of Colorado,* 2:529.

[46] Vilma Ortiz and Edward Telles, "Racial Identity and Racial Treatment of Mexican Americans," *Race and Social Problems* 4, (April 2012): 41-56, https://www.ncbi.nlm.nih.gov/pmc/articles/PMC3846170/pdf/nihms470196.pdf.

[47] Garcia and Howland, "Determining the Legitimacy of Spanish Land Grants in Colorado," 46.

[48] Phillip B. Gonzales and Virginia Sánchez, "Displaced in Place: Nuevomexicanos on the Northern Side of the New Mexico-Colorado Boundary, 1850-1875," *New Mexico Historical Review* 93, no. 3 (Summer 2018): 270.

[49] Ricardo Simmonds, "Mexican Land Grants in Colorado," *Colorado Encyclopedia* (website), last modified November 23, 2022, https://coloradoencyclopedia.org/article/mexican-land-grants-colorado.

[50] Ryan Golten, "Lobato v. Taylor: How the Villages of the Rio Culebra, the Colorado Supreme Court, and the Restatement of Servitudes Bailed Out the Treaty of Guadalupe Hidalgo," *Natural Resources Journal* 45, no. 2, (Spring 2005): 457-94. http://www.jstor.org/stable/24888984.

[51] Carol Archer, "'*El Amparo de la Ley*': Hispanas' Use of Spanish Mexican and Anglo American Law in Northern New Mexico and Southern Colorado, 1848-1912" (PhD thesis, University of Calgary, Department of History, 2014), 11-12, https://prism.ucalgary.ca/bitstream/handle/11023/1986/ucalgary_2014_archer_carol.pdf;jsessionid=67E17B76372EE6F1C91C4BC07BE31235?sequence=2.

[52] Archer, "'*El Amparo de la Ley,*'" 99.

[53] Jake Swisher, "Were They Mexicans or Coloradans? Constructing Race and Identity at the Colorado-New Mexico Border," *Colorado Magazine,* History Colorado (website), February 20, 2020, https://www.historycolorado.org/story/2020/02/20/were-they-mexicans-or-coloradans-constructing-race-and-identity-colorado-new.

[54] Jake Swisher, "Were They Mexicans or Coloradans?"

[55] Virginia Sánchez, *Pleas and Petitions*, 5.

[56] Virginia Sánchez, *Pleas and Petitions*, 247.

[57] Family genealogy provided to the authors by Maria Clara Martinez.

[58] Family genealogy provided to the authors by Maria Clara Martinez.

Figure 8.1. Augusta Tabor, circa 1879-1882 (based on clothing and hair fashion)

Courtesy of Denver Public Library Special Collections, X-21992

Augusta Tabor:
Industrious Entrepreneur

Arrived in Colorado, June 1859

Augusta Tabor and her family trekked for six weeks by covered wagon from Pillsbury Crossing, Kansas, arriving in Denver in mid-June of 1859. Later she said:

> What I endured on this journey only the women who crossed the plains in '59 can realize. There was no station until we arrived within eighty miles of Denver via the Republican route; no road, and a good part of the way no fuel. We were obliged to gather buffalo chips, sometimes traveling miles to find enough to cook a meal with. This weary work fell to the women.[1]

For over two decades, she supported her husband's aspiration to strike it rich as they moved from one mining camp to another, but once her husband's dream was fulfilled, Augusta faced betrayal and national scandal and had to forge a new life on her own.

Louisa Augusta Pierce, the third of ten children, was born in Augusta, Maine, on March 29, 1833, to William B. and Lucy S. Pierce. Family and friends called her Augusta.[2] She and her siblings grew up in their home on fifty acres of land on Church Hill Road, where her father earned a living quarrying granite.[3]

In the early 1850s, Augusta and her older sister Melvina worked in the Atlantic Cotton Mills in Lawrence, Massachusetts, about one hundred fifty miles from their Maine home. Called mill girls or female operatives, they lived in the number ten block of the Atlantic Mills boarding house run by a keeper who enforced the curfew and moral standards set by the mills. Six days a week, the loud factory bell called them to a twelve-to-fourteen-hour workday for monthly wages of around $13.60 ($533 in 2023 dollars).[4] Augusta and Melvina may have worked to gain a little financial independence or, more likely, to help their family back home.

Figure 8.2. Augusta's childhood home, Augusta, Maine, built circa 1838

Courtesy of author Jan Gunia's collection

In 1853, Augusta's father hired Horace Tabor, a young stonecutter from Vermont. Augusta and Horace fell in love and became engaged, but they postponed their marriage until Horace fulfilled his ambition to be a landowner. To reach his goal, he joined the first regular spring party of the New England Emigrant Aid Company and set out for the Kansas Territory on March 13, 1855.[5] The mission of the company was

Figure 8.3. Horace Tabor, circa 1883-1890

Courtesy of Denver Public Library Special Collections, X-22028

to populate the Kansas Territory with men who would likely vote to make Kansas a free state and thwart the pro-slavery people who were pouring into the territory to make it a slave state. Horace established his homestead via the Preemption Act of 1841, which allowed settlers to purchase up to 160 acres of land from the federal government for $1.25 per acre. The act stipulated that a claimant had to be living on the land and actively improving it, but payment was not due until after the land was surveyed.[6]

Augusta remained with her family in Maine while Horace built a cabin and began farming part of his acreage at Pillsbury Crossing, Riley County, Kansas. After an absence of almost two years, Horace returned for Augusta. A Baptist minister, the Reverend John H. Ingraham, presided over their marriage in the parlor of Augusta's childhood home on January 31, 1857.[7]

After traveling for fifty-four days by train, Missouri river boat, and oxen-drawn wagon, Augusta arrived at her new home in Kansas. She thought herself prepared for a home far less civilized than the one she left behind, but her despair is evident in her recollection of seeing it for the first time: "The cabin stood solitary and alone upon an open prairie. It was built of black walnut logs, 12x16 feet; not a building, a stone or stick in sight."[8] The interior of the cabin did not improve her opinion: "The only furniture was a No. 7 cook stove, a dilapidated trunk, and a rough bedstead made of poles, on which was an old tick filled with prairie grass."[9]

Augusta set to work cleaning the cabin, covering the rough-hewn-log walls with old copies of the *New York Tribune*, and cooking dinner for Horace and the two male boarders who had traveled from Maine with them. She wanted to make the cabin into the best home possible since she was already several months pregnant.

Each day after she finished her work in the cabin, Augusta joined Horace to work in the cornfields, but drought took their first-year crops. They subsisted on the money from Augusta's boarders and her egg business. In the fall, Horace traveled to Fort Riley, where he resumed his work as a stonecutter. Alone and pregnant in the isolated cabin, Augusta feared the rattlesnakes that sought shade indoors and the Native Americans who came begging food. Horace was likely at Fort Riley, roughly twenty-five miles distant, when Augusta gave birth to their son, Nathaniel Maxcy, in October of 1857.[10]

The next year, the Tabors brought in a bumper crop of corn, as did other farmers, so prices were low. Augusta added but-ter-making to her projects to augment their income. Horace again worked at Fort Riley, leaving Augusta alone with their baby.

In early 1859, rumors ran rampant of plentiful gold for the taking in a region to the west near Pikes Peak. Horace caught gold fever and saw it as the answer to his financial problems. He thought to leave Augusta in Kansas, or if she preferred, she could return to Maine while he went west and collected enough gold to pay off the farm and buy a few head of cattle. Her two boarders had agreed to accompany him. Augusta wanted to keep her little family together, and she successfully argued that if she went along, she could continue to cook for their boarders. That income would sustain them on their journey.[11]

They packed their oxen-drawn wagon with the heavy canvas tent Augusta had sewn by hand, along with several months' supply of food, tools, and other necessities; tethered a milk cow to the back; and on the fifth of May 1859, headed west.[12] The journey proved especially difficult for Augusta, who suffered recurring bouts of ague that she, like some of

her neighbors, had contracted while living at Pillsbury
Crossing. Sweating, fever, and chills left her weak, but she
still had to do her chores and care for eighteen-month-old
Maxcy, who was fretful with teething. Augusta recalled,
"Every Sunday we rested, if rest it could be called. The men
went hunting, while I stayed to guard the camp, wash the
soiled linen and cook for the following week."[13]

They arrived in Denver in mid-June and camped beside the
South Platte River to allow the cattle's feet, raw from the
trail's alkaline soil, to heal. On the first of July, they followed
Clear Creek toward present-day Golden and camped. There
the men left Augusta and her toddler alone while they explored the best way to get the wagon up to Gregory's Diggings (near the boundary between present-day Central City
and Black Hawk), where gold was said to be plentiful. In a
later interview, Augusta described her ordeal:

> Twelve miles from a human soul save my babe. The only
> sound I heard was the lowing of the cattle. . . . Every morn-
> ing I had a 'round up' all to myself. There were no cow-
> boys for me to cut, slash and shoot, no disputing of brands
> or mavericks. Three long weary weeks I held the fort. At
> the expiration of that time they returned.[14]

By the time the men came back for Augusta, they had
decided to go beyond Gregory's Diggings to Payne's Bar
(present-day Idaho Springs). Theirs was the first wagon
through that precipitous and rocky terrain, and they often
had to widen the foot trail or cut a new road. When going
down steep inclines, they tied a full-grown pine tree to the
back of the wagon to slow it down. To ease the oxen's burden
on uphill climbs, they unloaded the wagon and pushed it
from behind.[15]

When the Tabor party descended into the camp at Payne's Bar, the tents of over two hundred miners lined the banks of Clear Creek and dotted the surrounding hills.[16] Augusta was the first White woman at Payne's Bar, and her arrival created a great deal of excitement. The miners welcomed her by building her a cabin of sorts—a log base topped with her own seven-by-nine-foot tent.

Horace began prospecting at Spanish Bar, several miles farther west. Augusta stayed at her cabin, where her knack for entrepreneurial pursuits blossomed. She not only served meals, but also sold milk from her cows, and pies and bread that she baked. Beyond her business endeavors, she served as nurse to one of her boarders, who suffered with mountain fever for weeks, and she tended the gunshot wound that pierced a miner's hand. During her six-week stay at Payne's Bar, she made more than enough money to pay for their Kansas land.[17]

After the first snowstorm in the fall, an old miner warned Horace that winter would bring avalanches and that Augusta and Maxcy would be safer in Denver. So the Tabors packed up and went to Denver, where they rented a room above Vasquez's store. Augusta cooked for a couple of boarders to pay for rent and food, which were exorbitantly expensive in the gold rush town. Horace returned to his claim only to find he had been duped—the old miner had jumped his claim.[18]

Augusta's earnings paid for the Kansas farm, fulfilling Horace's original reason for taking up prospecting, but his gold fever persisted. He set his sights on new discoveries near the Arkansas River to the southwest and, along with the two boarders from the Kansas farm, made plans to join a party headed that way.

Augusta suffered paroxysms of ague that made it impossible for them to leave with the party, but they made plans to meet up with the departing group later. Finally, on February 19, 1860, the Tabors and their two boarders left Denver, even though Augusta was so ill that she had to be lifted into the wagon.[19]

They headed south along Plum Creek and then Monument Creek. Supplies in the gold region were not only expensive but scarce, since they had to be transported from the East in freight wagons. In her diary, Augusta wrote of a breakfast of venison ham and "sasaphras tea, this I call a poor apology for coffee."[20] They no longer enjoyed the luxury of milk in their ersatz coffee, or for Maxcy to drink, because Horace had sold their remaining milk cow to finance this prospecting trip. To make matters worse, Maxcy had a cold and croupy cough. Despite the privations and difficulties, Augusta also wrote of her appreciation of the landscape: "We come near to the mountains and passed some natural [monuments?] some white as marble and standing thirty or forty feet high. We drove into a beautiful valley and halted for noon."[21]

A week later, they reached the area of present-day Manitou Springs, where they intended to head west into the mountains. Again, they had to cut their own wagon road where only a foot path existed. Two weeks of difficult travel over mountain passes brought them into South Park. Augusta later recalled their arrival:

> The sun was just setting. I can only describe it by saying it was one of Colorado's sunsets. Those who have seen them know how glorious they are. . . . The park looked like a cultivated field, with rivulets coursing through, and herds of antelope in the distance.[22]

After a harrowing crossing of the swift and icy waters of the Arkansas River, where they nearly lost all their supplies, the party proceeded up the west bank of the river in search of Cache Creek (near present-day Granite). Rumors told of large gold discoveries in the area, but they found only gold particles intermixed with iron-laden black sand. Augusta used a magnet to separate out the gold, but a day's effort yielded only a few pennyweights. (A pennyweight is one-twentieth of a troy ounce.) The group's supplies had run as low as their spirits, when a man came along from the party that had left Denver ahead of them. He gave them directions to his camp, where he said there were rich deposits.[23]

Again, the Tabors faced crossing the Arkansas River. With Augusta and Maxcy riding in the wagon, they found a shallow section and had crossed part way when they came into deep water. The wagon bed lifted from the wheels, floated downstream, and began filling with water. Quick-thinking Augusta grabbed willow branches at the shore's edge and clung to them, until the men rescued her.[24]

They arrived at California Gulch (near present-day Leadville) on May 8, 1860. Once more, Augusta was the first White woman in camp. The men built her a twelve-by-eighteen-foot

Figure 8.4. Nathaniel Maxcy Tabor, circa 1860-1865

Courtesy of Denver Public Library Special Collections, X-22009

cabin of green pine logs. The ground served as floor, poles covered in dirt and bark formed the roof. The cabin had no window nor door, only an opening for access, but Augusta said, "I entered the place feeling queenly."[25]

Forced by lack of food, as Augusta sadly watched, the men slaughtered and butchered the oxen that had brought them all the way from their Kansas farm. That night they shared the meat with the camp. Augusta took on seven boarders and, using their portion of the fresh meat, served them "poor beef and dried apples."[26]

Word of the California Gulch bonanza spread quickly, and men poured into the region. Before the summer ended, roughly ten thousand men mined the gulch. Augusta not only cooked and washed for her boarders but also weighed the gold for the miners in the upper gulch. Horace obtained the postmaster appointment and management of the express office, but Augusta ran both enterprises while he worked a claim he had staked on a waterfall. It turned out that most of the gold washed into the claim below, and its owners took in $80,000 that first summer. For their combined work, the Tabors took in about $5,000.[27]

In the autumn of 1860, Horace gave Augusta $1,000 and sent her, along with almost three-year-old Maxcy, to visit her family in Maine. She traveled with a mule train and paid her way by cooking for the teamsters. At Pillsbury Crossing, she purchased 160 acres of land adjacent to the land they already owned. In the spring, she returned to California Gulch, which by then was part of the newly-formed Colorado Territory. She brought a large supply of goods to stock the mercantile store that she and Horace opened in their cabin. Horace worked the mine while Augusta took on the additional responsibility of running the store.[28]

In August of 1861, news came to California Gulch of large

gold discoveries in the Mosquito Mountain Range, to the northeast, in a camp called Buckskin Joe. Horace, still dreaming of striking it rich, packed his family, their belongings, and the general store's stock on the backs of mules and ascended the mountain pass. Before they reached the peak, where they planned to stay overnight in the tollgate-keeper's cabin, a heavy blizzard forced them to stop and spend the night without the benefit of even a tent, rolled in blankets and protected only by a snow drift.[29]

When the Tabors arrived in Buckskin Joe, about six hundred people resided there, including about thirty women. The population soon grew to a thousand, and four stamp mills crushed ore day and night, filling the air with their loud thud-thumping.[30] At the height of the mining boom, the

Figure 8.5. A street in Buckskin Joe, Colorado, circa 1864

Courtesy of Denver Public Library Special Collections, X-11927

number of stamp mills and their racket increased three-fold. Although Buckskin Joe was a rough mining camp with a red-light district, saloons, billiard halls, and dance halls, by 1862, it also presented a more refined side that included four hotels, a bank, a theater, numerous stores, and Park County's first courthouse.[31]

The Tabors settled into their routine in a more sturdily built cabin than the one in California Gulch. Horace worked his claims while Augusta served food to boarders, washed their clothes, and ran the mercantile store and post office. Augusta may have found life in Buckskin Joe more satisfying because there were other families and, for a time, a school.[32]

Samuel Leach, a friend of the Tabors and postmaster of nearby Sterling, wrote letters to his brother George back East in which he described visits to the Tabor cabin. He listed some

Figure 8.6. Tabors' abandoned cabin and store in Buckskin Joe, Colorado, 1940

Courtesy of Denver Public Library Special Collections, X-63037

of the many chores Augusta performed, including mending, re-making worn clothing, sewing clothes for Maxcy, knitting socks, making her own soap, and churning butter. She collected eggs from her flock of one hundred chickens, milked her two cows, and kept a sow and a boar that had a litter of piglets in the spring of 1863. Leach described Augusta as a good cook and wrote that "the men [probably referring to Augusta's boarders] like her pretty well although she is a driver."[33]

In a later letter, Leach wrote of Augusta:

> You should see her place. Nothing slack or careless thereabouts, unless it is her husband. I cannot say that he does much himself . . . he does not do anything of his own accord. As he says, he has to be prodded just like the ox they drove across the plains.[34]

In the spring of 1863, Augusta planned a garden and ordered seed from Illinois—lettuce, carrots, onions, radishes, turnips, beets, and potatoes. The men scoffed at her and told her the growing season was too short at Buckskin's ten-thousand-foot elevation. She countered that she had read of vegetables being grown successfully in the Alps and Apennines. She ignored the men's warnings and started seed in boxes indoors. By May she had her garden planted, although Leach doesn't mention whether her vegetables made it to harvest.[35]

Augusta may have felt her own roots taking hold in Buckskin Joe because even after the boom was over, a community remained for a while. The town was the Park County seat, and Horace served as the county's superintendent of schools for a time.[36]

Mining prospects in Buckskin took a brief upswing in 1866, but by the spring of 1868, they were grim. There was no boom to attract Horace, but hard rock mining had replaced placer mining in California Gulch with some success. Consequently, the Tabors pulled up roots, trekked back across the mountains, and settled two miles farther up the gulch from where they had lived seven years earlier. The miners called the new camp Upper Oro to distinguish it from the original camp. The Tabors set up their store, Augusta took in boarders, and in November, Horace secured the postmaster appointment. To increase his chances of striking it rich, he engaged in a practice called grubstaking, which meant he outfitted some miners, at no cost to them, with the understanding that he would receive an interest in their discovery, should there be one.[37]

During the ensuing years, Augusta and Horace fared well in comparison to their neighbors. The 1870 United States Census shows Horace's combined real estate and personal estate value of $13,000 as the highest in Oro City. A physician ranked second at $9,000.[38] As mining in the area prospered, so did the Tabors' retail business. By the summer of 1870, they had added a store in Lower Oro.[39] Horace wanted thirteen-year-old Maxcy to work in the stores, but Augusta insisted on keeping the books for both stores so her son could attend school.[40]

By the mid-1870s, gold mining waned in California Gulch, but it turned out that the black mud Augusta had found so troublesome years before, when she had used a magnet to separate it from the gold, held high concentrations of lead carbonate and silver. A. B. Wood, a mining engineer and metallurgist, and William H. Stevens, a promoter with some mining experience, suspected that the black mud hampering their hydraulic gold mining operation might be composed of lead carbonate. An assay proved them correct. They went in search of the source, and Wood discovered outcroppings of the ore on the sides of California Gulch on April 30, 1874. The two men kept their secret while they bought property up and down California Gulch, and they did not announce their discovery until the spring of 1876.

After a promising local assay, August Meyer, an assayer and agent for Saint Louis Smelting and Refining Company, sent a load of the Stevens and Wood ore to the home company for processing. The exorbitant cost of transportation proved the exercise unprofitable, but in the spring of 1877, Edwin Harrison, president of Saint Louis Smelting and Refining Company, came to survey the area. Finding the prospects promising, he decided to build a smelter and to improve the roads to haul ore from the mines. The furnace at Harrison Reduction Works blazed into operation on October 11, 1877, and paved the way for the silver rush.[41]

During that same month, the Tabors packed up their household goods, consolidated the two stores' stock, and moved into a one-and-one-half-story, four-room log cabin at what would become the southwest corner of Harrison Avenue and Chestnut Street in Leadville.[42] The town, incorporated as Leadville in an election on February 4, 1878, elected Horace its first mayor. He also secured the postmaster appointment the same month.[43]

In 1878, twenty-one years after her wedding, Augusta finally moved into a home not built of rough-hewn logs. The white, two-story frame house boasted a large bay window and sawtooth bargeboard trim.[44] A side porch led to the entrance. The first floor contained a spacious parlor, a small dining room, and a kitchen; the second floor housed three bedrooms.

Not content with the profits from the store's burgeoning business, Horace, always hoping for the big strike, reinvested much of those profits in grubstaking miners. In mid-April 1878, he grubstaked a pair of German shoemakers, August

Figure 8.7. Tabors' home, Leadville, Colorado, 1955

Courtesy of Denver Public Library Special Collections, X-21996

Rische and George Hook. Even though many in the town scoffed at his chances, Horace financed the pair twice more while they continued to work the claim they named the Little Pittsburg (without the *h*). On May 15th, they struck ore that assayed at an astounding two hundred ounces of silver per ton.[45] Augusta's recollection of receiving news of the discovery is evidence that she had sided with the doubters: "I was coming downstairs, and Rische rushed into the room with his hands full of specimens, shouting, 'We've struck it! We've struck it!' I said to him, rather frigidly I expect, 'Rische, when you bring me money instead of rocks, then I'll believe you.'"[46]

Horace hired a team of men to work the Little Pittsburg, and by the end of July, the mine brought in an incredible $8,000 per week.[47] News of the Little Pittsburg and other large discoveries brought an influx of Eastern capitalists, mechanics, miners, and laborers. Heading the pack, came the gamblers, prostitutes, and confidence men. Crime skyrocketed. Even though the ring of hammers and the grating of saws filled the air day and night, construction of shelters could not meet the demand. Men paid a dollar (about twenty-seven dollars in 2023) to sleep on a dirty mattress, whether in a boarding house or a tent, and slightly less for a space on a saloon's sawdust floor.[48] The latter half of 1878 and all of 1879 saw the boom grow and Leadville become a city.

Horace's good fortune continued with his purchase of interests in other mines, most notably, the Chrysolite in 1878

Figure 8.8. Reproduction of lithographic rendering of Leadville's Chestnut Street, spring 1880.

Courtesy of Denver Public Library Special Collections, X-11476

Figure 8.9. Tabors' residence on Broadway, Denver, Colorado, circa 1900-1920

Courtesy of Denver Public Library Special Collections, X-22040

and the Matchless in 1879.[49] His wealth and generous nature made him a sought-after figure. The Republican Party courted his help with the election of 1878 and nominated him to run for lieutenant governor. The opposition suggested in newspaper articles that Horace was a bigamist, and although untrue at the time, the accusation would prove eerily prophetic.[50]

Horace won the election, which meant he would need to spend lengthy periods of time in Denver performing his duties as lieutenant governor. Late in January of 1879, he whisked Augusta off to Denver and surprised her with a twenty-room mansion situated on a large plot of land between Broadway and Lincoln Street, and Sixteenth and Seventeenth Avenues. She looked up at the pressed-brick home with its white marble trim and large verandas, from which one could enjoy mountain views, then turned and reportedly said, "I will never go up these steps, Tabor, if you think I'll ever have to go down them."[51]

Horace had purchased the home already lavishly furnished with Brussels carpets, mirrors, and elegant chandeliers. Still, his announcement that he intended for them to host a reception for the entire legislature and their spouses within weeks of her arrival presented Augusta with a daunting task. She met the challenge, decorating her new home with flowers and flowering plants, despite the fact it was winter. She planned a lavish menu with a caterer and hired an orchestra to provide music for dancing. On the evening of the party, she wore a black silk and velvet gown piped with canary yellow silk and accessorized it with diamond jewelry. She warmly greeted her guests, who included some of the Tabors' friends outside of the legislature. According to the newspaper accounts, the affair was a grand success.[52]

After the Tabors attained great wealth, many people and organizations, including churches, sought their support. Augusta told the ladies at a meeting at Denver's Unity Church that she chose to join that denomination because, unlike the others, Unity Church did not seek the Tabors' money.[53] In an interview, she quipped, "I suppose Mr. Tabor's and my souls are of more value now than they were a year ago."[54]

Possibly to fill the spare time Augusta enjoyed, since she no longer ran the mercantile store and post office, she began submitting correspondence to Eastern newspapers about life in the West. In July of 1879, she represented the *Boston Investigator* at the annual meeting of the Colorado Press Association in Colorado Springs.[55]

In 1879, the Tabors split their time between Denver and Leadville. Horace invested in improvements for both cities, including construction of the luxurious Tabor Opera House in Leadville. When the theater opened in November, it was

Figure 8.10. Tabor Opera House, Leadville, Colorado,
circa 1879-1880

*Courtesy of History Colorado, Denver, Colorado,
Accession #2000.129.169*

declared "the most perfect place of amusement between Chicago or St. Louis and San Francisco."[56]

Newspaper accounts in 1879 and 1880 show Augusta and
Horace enjoying their new-found wealth and prestige
together. She accompanied him on an autumn business trip
back East. In Chicago they stayed at the Palmer House and in
New York at the Fifth Avenue Hotel.[57] Back home they were
feted like royalty at balls and receptions hosted by
organizations Horace sponsored, such as Tabor Hose
Company No. 5 in Denver and the Tabor Light Cavalry in
Leadville.[58] The Tabors even entertained General Ulysses S.
Grant and his party when they toured Leadville.[59] Early in
1880, Horace gave Augusta $100,000 to do with as she
wished.[60]

By the late summer of 1880, Horace seldom stayed at the
Broadway mansion, and by January of 1881, Horace had
deserted Augusta and ceased financial support.[61] He

continued to split his time between Leadville and Denver, residing at the Tabor Opera House in Leadville and boarding at the Windsor Hotel in Denver.[62] Coinciding with Horace's long absences from home, the young, blonde Elizabeth (McCourt) Doe, called "Baby Doe" by the miners, had moved from Central City into a house directly across Fifth Street from the Tabors' Leadville house.[63]

Horace asked Augusta for a divorce. She refused and continued to do so until mid-April 1882, when she received a letter from the La Plata County clerk's office in southwestern Colorado. A new clerk had found two pages glued together in the record book, and those pages recorded the divorce of the Tabors on March 24, 1882. That came as a shock to Augusta, because she knew nothing about it and had not been served papers. It turned out that Horace had sworn falsely that he was a resident of La Plata County, and he had accused Augusta of, in her words, "every crime in the calendar except

Figure 8.11. Baby Doe Tabor, circa 1883

Courtesy of Denver Public Library Special Collections, Z-231

drunkenness."[64] Even his lawyer, Lewis Rockwell, said, "I told Mr. Tabor that it was not worth the paper it was written upon, and I advised him to secure another."[65]

The fraudulent La Plata County divorce was probably the impetus for Augusta's hiring Amos Steck as her lawyer and filing suit for separate maintenance, basically asking for alimony without a divorce. Perhaps she still loved Horace and didn't want to give up on their marriage, but she also likely wanted to avoid the stigma of divorce attached to a woman in the Victorian era who sought a divorce. In *Framing American Divorce*, author Norma Basch writes:

> In a culture that increasing [*sic*] invested middle-class women with a powerful moral influence over their husbands, that valorized the role of women in the domestic sphere, and that indeed imbued women with an idealized autonomy in marriage, to succeed in divorce was tantamount to a more fundamental failure. A true woman was expected to exert her moral influence to prevent her husband from roving—or at the very least, to do nothing that would encourage him to cast about for a new companion.[66]

Horace's lawyers filed a demurrer arguing, among other things, that there could be no alimony without a divorce. The court battle continued the rest of 1882.[67]

In September of that same year, Horace married Baby Doe in a secret civil ceremony in Saint Louis, Missouri, hence becoming a bigamist. Baby Doe, at twenty-seven, was just three years senior to the Tabors' son, Maxcy.[68]

In December the court struck down Horace's demurrer against Augusta's suit for maintenance.[69] Since he had no grounds for divorce, Horace repeatedly sent his agent, William Bush, to badger Augusta into filing for divorce. He even threatened to leave her homeless if she didn't comply.[70] Augusta later told a reporter she agreed to obtain the divorce because she "was inveigled into it by my attorney and Mr. Tabor's attorneys. I had no rest day or night." Her lawyer had told her that paid witnesses would testify falsely against her if she did not acquiesce.[71]

In an after-hours courtroom, on January 2, 1883, Augusta sued Horace for divorce on the grounds of desertion. He chose not to be present and appointed his lawyer to represent him. The settlement had been agreed upon prior to the proceedings. In exchange for the divorce, Augusta received title to her home and a high-end apartment complex in Denver called La Veta Place. Before the judge ruled the divorce final, Augusta asked, "Judge, I wish to enter upon the record, 'Not willingly asked for.'" She broke down. "Oh, God! Not willingly, not willingly."[72]

Speaking to a reporter on the evening of the divorce, Augusta estimated the value of the property she received in the divorce settlement at $250,000 and stated, "He is worth $3,000,000 dollars, and that is all I get. I should have half."[73] She later assessed her own contribution to Horace's success in an interview with author Alice Polk Hill:

> I feel that in those years of self-sacrifice, hard labor, and economy, I laid the foundation to Mr. Tabor's immense wealth; for had I not staid with him and worked by his side, he would have been discouraged, returned to his trade, and so lost the opportunity which has since enriched him.[74]

After the divorce, Horace told a reporter that he valued the properties Augusta received in the settlement at $300,000. He gloated that if the settlement had been arranged by the court, instead of prior to the proceeding, she would have received one-quarter of his assets—over $1 million.[75]

Late in January of 1883, Horace won a thirty-day seat in the United States Senate to fill a vacancy. While in Washington, DC, he again wed Baby Doe, this time in an extravagant affair held in the parlors of the Willard Hotel. President Arthur and Colorado's officials attended, but their wives refused to participate due to their disgust with Horace's behavior during his separation and divorce from Augusta.[76]

After the divorce, Augusta wintered in California. Upon her return to Denver, two hundred of her friends and family surprised her with a welcome-home reception that included musical performances and refreshments. One newspaper reporter called the attendees the "crème de la crème" of Denver society.[77] Maxcy stood by her side while she greeted her guests and received their well wishes.[78]

Even with that strong support, Augusta apparently grieved the loss of Horace for the remainder of 1883. An absence of social notes in the newspapers the rest of that year suggests her withdrawal. Some accounts say she

Figure 8.12. Nathaniel Maxcy Tabor, circa 1880-1890

Courtesy of Denver Public Library Special Collections, X-22291

never recovered from the divorce, but her actions indicate that by 1884 she squared her shoulders and took on life as an independent woman.

In January of 1884, Augusta attended Maxcy and Luella Babcock's wedding and gave them a home on California Street in Denver.[79] After the ceremony, she embarked on an extended trip to New Orleans, Cuba, Florida, and the northeastern United States. A New Orleans reporter who interviewed her wrote that "Mrs. Tabor is a pleasant, intelligent lady and chatted knowingly on a number of subjects." She spoke about mining, her pride in Denver, and

Figure 8.13. Augusta Tabor, circa 1889-1892 (based on clothing and hair fashion)

Courtesy of Denver Public Library Special Collections, X-21985

her interest in horses. She said she especially liked watching Maxcy's pair of trotters race on land near her home that was used for "speeding horses."[80] She continued to enjoy travel, and in 1889, she toured Rome, Naples, Sicily, and Spain.[81]

Augusta chose to manage her own finances, and she invested in Denver real estate, banks, and Leadville mines. She grew her wealth to $3 million, and—even after the Panic of 1893 left many previously wealthy Coloradans destitute and contributed to Horace's downfall—at her death, she still left an estate of $1.5 million. The *Denver Republican* called her "a woman of remarkable business capacity."[82] She used that wealth to help institutions and individuals in her community.

As an active member of Denver's Unity Church, Augusta supported it financially; hosted fundraisers, such as elaborate lawn and strawberry festivals, on the grounds of her mansion; and organized other money-making projects.[83] Her roles as a member of the Ladies' Relief Society included offering her home for meetings and working on a committee to solicit linen donations for the Ladies' Relief Hospital.[84] She also proudly served as a charter member and four-time officer of the Pioneer Ladies' Aid Society—a group that helped less fortunate pioneers and founded a home for the homeless in 1893.[85]

During the final three years of her life, Augusta suffered lung problems and a condition that caused intermittent paralysis. Her doctor recommended that she seek a lower altitude, but she refused to go until after she cast her ballot in November 1894 in the first election held after the women of Colorado had won the right to vote.[86] After voting, Augusta traveled to Pasadena, California, where her health seemed to be improving, but late in January, Maxcy received a telegram that his mother had taken a turn for the worse. He boarded a train but arrived too late to be at her side. She passed away on January

30, 1895, two months short of her sixty-second birthday.[87] The *Denver Republican,* in the sub-head to her obituary, called her "An Illustrious Example of the Plucky Pioneer Women Who Helped Their Husbands Make Colorado."[88]

On February 8, 1895, the Pioneer Ladies' Aid Society marched en masse from Augusta's home to her funeral at the Unity Church. Attendees overflowed the church's seating and stood in the hallways.[89] At Denver's Riverside Cemetery, her simple, flat grave marker reflects her modest ways, but it is marred by her birth year's being incorrectly inscribed as 1835 instead of 1833. Augusta left half of her estate to Maxcy and the rest to be divided equally among her siblings.[90]

Horace followed Augusta to the grave four years later, dying from appendicitis on April 10, 1899. After the divorce, Horace over-invested indiscriminately in ventures that, along with the Panic of 1893, led to his ruin. The Leadville *Herald Democrat* summarized his financial life in the sub-head to his obituary: "A Sudden Rise to the Glittering Pinnacle of Wealth, and Then the Millions

Figure 8.14. Augusta Tabor's new gravestone and historical marker, Riverside Cemetery, Denver, Colorado, erected in 1995

Courtesy of Dr. Thomas J. Noel Collection, Auraria Library Special & Digital Collections.

Are Swept Away."[91]

Honors bestowed on Augusta since her death include her induction in 1991 into both the National Mining Hall of Fame and the Colorado Women's Hall of Fame. She would be especially proud of the inscription on the back of the historical marker that the Colorado State Society of the Daughters of the American Revolution erected at her gravesite in 1995:

> She came where there were no roads and left a path for us to follow. She came to a wilderness and made it a place of settlement. She fed the hungry and healed the sick, giving generously of those motherly gifts which gentled rough mining camps. She came searching for gold and left behind the treasure of civilization. She was, above all, the epitome of a pioneer.[92]

---

[1] Alice Polk Hill, *Tales of the Colorado Pioneers* (Glorieta, NM: Rio Grande, 1976), 221.

[2] "Maine Births and Christenings, 1739-1900," 127, database FamilySearch (https://familysearch.org/ark:/61903/1:1/F4HN-C21: 14 January 2020), Louisa Augusta Pierce, 1833.

[3] Deed Book 0111, page 0133, Kennebec County Registry of Deeds, Augusta, ME; and see "William Pierce House," Maine Historic Preservation Commission, Historic Building/Structure Preservation Form #021-1708, Augusta Survey Phase VI, Charlton Hudson, surveyor, 1996, Church Hill Road file, Collection of Maine Historic Preservation Commission, Augusta, ME. The survey describes William Pierce as mason, quarry owner, and supplier of stone for the insane hospital and estimates the date of construction of the home as 1838.

[4] 1850 US Census, Lawrence, Essex County, MA, digital image s.v. "Augusta Pierce," Ancestry.com; and see Charles S. Newell, *The Lawrence Almanac, Directory, and Business Advertiser* (Lawrence, MA: Franklin Grant, 1851), 86-87, in the Lawrence History Center

(Lawrence, MA) City Directory Collection, object ID: 1984.049.001; and see "The Mill Girls of Lowell" (webpage), Lowell National Historical Park, https://www.nps.gov/lowe/learn/historyculture/the-mill-girls-of-lowell.htm. See also Judith A. Ranta, "Researching the Lives of 19th Century New England Mill Workers," *American Ancestors,* winter 2013, 18. For wages see J. D. B. De Bow, superintendent of the United States Census, *Statistical View of the United States, Embracing the Territory, Population [. . .]* (Washington, DC: Beverly Tucker, Senate Printer, 1854), 180, babel.hathitrust.org. See also "How Much Is a Dollar from the Past Worth Today?" MeasuringWorth *2022,* www.measuringworth.com/dollarvaluetoday/.

⁵ Riley County Genealogical Society, *Pioneers of Riley County, KS: 1853-1860* (Manhattan, KS: Riley County Genealogical Society, 2004), 128.

⁶ Thomas H. Webb, *Information for Kanzas Immigrants,* 12th ed. (Boston: Alfred Mudge & Son, 1857), 16-18; and see Eli Thayer, *The Kansas Crusade: Its Friends and Foes* (New York: Harper and Bros., 1889), 22-24, https://archive.org/details/ahistorykansasc01halegoog/page/n52/mode/2up; also see Kansapedia, s.v. "New England Emigrant Aid Company sign," last modified: December 2014, https://www.kshs.org/kansapedia/new-england-emigrant-aid-company-sign/1023. See also "The Preemption Act of 1841" in *Land Acts,* https://www.archives.gov/files/calendar/genealogy-fair/2014/handouts/session-11-handout-5of5-martinez-land-other-land-acts.pdf?_ga=2.47832679.1171976476.1689090367-1310073644.1689090367.

⁷ "Maine Marriages, 1771-1907," page 56, database, FamilySearch (https://familysearch.org/ark:/61903/1:1:F4DB-PNY: 14 January 2020), Augusta L. Pierce in entry for Horace A. M. Taber, 1857. Also see James W. North, *The History of Augusta Maine* (Somersworth, NH: New England History Press, 1981), 886.

⁸ Hill, *Colorado Pioneers,* 219.

⁹ Hill, *Colorado Pioneers,* 219.

[10] Augusta Tabor, "Reminiscenses [*sic*, henceforth "Reminiscences"] of Mrs. Augusta Tabor." In Betty Moynihan, *Augusta Tabor: A Pioneering Woman* (Evergreen, CO: Cordillera Press, 1988), 118.

[11] Hill, *Colorado Pioneers,* 221.

[12] Hill, *Colorado Pioneers,* 221. Augusta gives the departure date as April 5, but she also says Horace worked at Fort Riley through March and April. In Tabor, "Reminiscences," Moynihan, *A Pioneering Woman,* 119, Augusta says they left on May 5. This is more likely the correct date.

[13] Hill, *Colorado Pioneers,* 221-22.

[14] Hill, *Colorado Pioneers,* 222.

[15] Hill, *Colorado Pioneers,* 222-23.

[16] Beth Simmons, *A Quick History of Idaho Springs* (Lake City, CO: Western Reflections, 2004), 7.

[17] Hill, *Colorado Pioneers,* 223.

[18] Tabor, "Reminiscences," in Moynihan, *A Pioneering Woman,* 120-21.

[19] Hill, *Colorado Pioneers,* 224.

[20] Augusta Tabor diary page, MSS 1705, Augusta Tabor Collection, History Colorado, Denver, CO.

[21] Augusta Tabor diary.

[22] Hill, *Colorado Pioneers,* 224.

[23] Hill, *Colorado Pioneers,* 226-27.

[24] Hill, *Colorado Pioneers,* 227.

[25] Tabor, "Reminiscences," in Moynihan, *A Pioneering Woman,* 124.

[26] Hill, *Colorado Pioneers,* 227.

[27] Hill, *Colorado Pioneers,* 227-28.

[28] Hill, *Colorado Pioneers* 228; and see Duane Smith, *Horace Tabor: His Life and the Legend* (Niwot, CO: University Press of Colorado, 1989), 24.

[29] Tabor, "Reminiscences," in Moynihan, *A Pioneering Woman,* 127.

[30] Nolie Mumey, *The History and Proceedings of Buckskin Joe, C.T. 1859-1862* (Boulder, CO: Johnson, 1961), 4-5; and see Robert L.

Brown, *Ghost Towns of the Colorado Rockies* (Caldwell, ID: The Caxton Printers, Ltd., 2006), 69.

31 Mumey, *Buckskin Joe*, 5-7; and see Brown, *Ghost Towns*, 70-71.

32 Brown, *Ghost Towns*, 70; and see Samuel Leach, "Mosquito Mining District 1862," *The Trail: A Magazine for Colorado* March 1926, 10; also see Samuel Leach, "Mosquito Mining District 1862," *The Trail: A Magazine for Colorado*, May1926, 8.

33 Leach, *The Trail*, March 1926, 10; and see Leach, *The Trail*, May 1926, 8-9.

34 Leach, *The Trail*, May 1926, 10.

35 Leach, *The Trail*, May 1926, 8-9, 10.

36 Colorado State Teachers' Association, *Education in Colorado: 1861-1885, a brief history of the early educational interests of Colorado [. . .] and short sketches of private and denominational institutions* (Denver, CO: News Printing Co., 1885), 23, https://www.loc.gov/item/e09001336/. This shows the appointment in 1867 of Louis F. Valiton as superintendent of Park County Schools to fill the vacancy left by H.A.W. Tabor's resignation.

37 Mrs. H.A.W. Tabor, "Cabin Life in Colorado," *Colorado Magazine*, March 1927, 73; and see Smith, *Horace Tabor*, 35.

38 1870 US Census, Lake County, Colorado Territory, digital image s.v. "Augusta Tabor," Ancestry.com.

39 Don L. Griswold and Jean Harvey Griswold, *History of Leadville and Lake County, Colorado: From Mountain Solitude to Metropolis* (Boulder, CO: Colorado Historical Society in cooperation with the University Press of Colorado, 1996), 1:83.

40 Tabor, "Cabin Life," 75.

41 Edward Blair, *Leadville, Colorado's Magic City* (Boulder, CO: Pruett, 1980), 20-22; and see Griswold and Griswold, *Leadville*, 1:136, 139-40, 144.

42 Griswold and Griswold, *Leadville*, 1:145; and see "Ancient Homes: The Old Landmarks in California Gulch," unidentified clipping, Tabor Scrapbooks, 2:7, WH475, Western History Collection, Denver Public Library.

43 Griswold and Griswold, *Leadville*, 1:145, 148.

[44] Griswold and Griswold, *Leadville*, 1:296. This cites the *Leadville Chronicle*, Aug. 1, 1879, which states the home was painted white.

[45] Blair, *Leadville*, 46-48.

[46] Flora Ellice Stevens, "A Rich Man's Wife - Sketch of a Colorado Millionairess," unidentified clipping, Tabor Scrapbooks, 3:5, WH475, Western History Collection, Denver Public Library.

[47] Don L. Griswold and Jean Harvey Griswold, *The Carbonate Camp Called Leadville* (Denver, CO: University Press of Denver, 1951), 37.

[48] Griswold and Griswold, *Carbonate Camp*, 74; and see R. G. Dill, "History of Lake County," in *History of the Arkansas Valley, Colorado* (Chicago, IL: O.L. Baskin, 1881), 224-225.

[49] Smith, *Horace Tabor*, 76, 122.

[50] Griswold and Griswold, *Leadville*, 1:171-72.

[51] "The Home of One of Our Millionaires," unidentified clipping, Tabor Scrapbooks, 2:19, WH475, Western History Collection, Denver Public Library; and see Stevens, "A Rich Man's Wife."

[52] "Wealth and Honor: Brilliant Reception at Governor Tabor's Last Night," *Rocky Mountain News* (Denver), Feb. 8, 1879, 4, Colorado Historic Newspapers Collection (website), Colorado State Library, coloradohistoricnewspapers.org.

[53] "Augusta Tabor," *Girard Daily Press* (Girard, KS), Aug. 15, 1895, 1, online at Newspapers.com.

[54] Stevens, "A Rich Man's Wife," 3:6.

[55] Stevens, "A Rich Man's Wife," 3:6; and see "The State Press Association," *Daily Gazette* (Colorado Springs, CO), July 10, 1879, 4, Penrose Library, Colorado Springs, CO; also see "Pilgrims of the Press," *Rocky Mountain News* (Denver, CO), July 9, 1879, 5, Colorado Historic Newspapers Collection (website), Colorado State Library, coloradohistoricnewspapers.org.

[56] Griswold and Griswold, *Leadville*, 1:399. The book quotes *Leadville Chronicle* of Nov. 18, 1879.

[57] "A Talk with Tabor," *Rocky Mountain News* (Denver, CO), Nov. 6, 1879, 8, in Tabor Scrapbooks, 2:36-37, WH475, Western History Collection, Denver Public Library.

58 "The Tabor's Tribute," *Rocky Mountain News* (Denver, CO), Jan. 16, 1880, 8, Colorado Historic Newspapers Collection (website), Colorado State Library, coloradohistoricnewspapers.org; and see "The Tabor Light Cavalry Ball," unidentified clipping, Tabor Scrapbooks, 2:64, WH475, Western History Collection, Denver Public Library; also see "Soldier's Soiree," *Chronicle* (Leadville, CO), Tabor Scrapbooks, 2:55; and see "The Light Guards," *Democrat* (Leadville, CO), unidentified clipping, Tabor Scrapbooks, 2:54.

59 Unidentified newspaper clippings in Tabor Scrapbooks, 2:58, 61, WH475, Western History Collection, Denver Public Library.

60 "The Tabor Troubles," *Denver Republican*, Jan. 3, 1883, 8, Western History and Genealogy, Denver Public Library.

61 "Troubles," 8.

62 Denver, Colorado, City Directory, 1881, in U.S. City Directories, 1822-1895, digital image s.v. "Horace A. W. Tabor," Ancestry.com. This lists Horace as still living at their Denver mansion, even though both Horace and Augusta testified he was not. The exact date the information was collected for the 1881 directory is not known. See also *Corbett and Ballenger's Second Annual Leadville City Directory, 1881,* in U.S. City Directories, 1822-1895, digital image s.v. "Horace A. W. Tabor," Ancestry.com, which lists him as residing at the Leadville opera house. The date the information was collected is not known. See Denver, Colorado, City Directory, 1882, and Denver, Colorado, City Directory, 1883, in U.S. City Directories, 1822-1895, digital images s.v. "Horace A. W. Tabor," Ancestry.com, which list Horace as boarding at the Windsor Hotel.

63 1880 US Census, Leadville, Lake County, Colorado, digital image s.v. "Lizzie Doe," Ancestry.com.

64 "Still Tabor's Wife," *Denver Republican*, Oct. 31, 1883, 8, Western History and Genealogy, Denver Public Library; and see "Troubles," 8.

65 "Troubles," 8.

66 Norma Basch, *Framing American Divorce: From the Revolutionary Generation to the Victorians* (Berkeley and Los Angeles, CA: University of California Press, 1999), 117.

[67] "Suit for Separate Maintenance," and "Governor Tabor Demurs," Tabor Scrapbooks, 3:3, WH475, Western History Collection, Denver Public Library; and see unidentified newspaper clipping and "Tabor vs Tabor," Tabor Scrapbooks, 3:4.

[68] "The La Plata Divorce," *Denver Republican*, Mar. 12, 1883, 1, Western History and Genealogy, Denver Public Library.

[69] "Tabor vs Tabor," and unidentified newspaper clipping in Tabor Scrapbooks, 3:4, WH475, Western History Collection, Denver Public Library.

[70] "Counter Claims," *Tribune* (Denver, CO), Oct. 31, 1883, 6 and "The Tabor-Bush Trial," *Denver Republican*, Oct. 31, 1883, 5, Western History and Genealogy, Denver Public Library; also see "Still Tabor's Wife," 8.

[71] "Still Tabor's Wife," 8.

[72] "Troubles," 8.

[73] "Troubles," 8.

[74] Hill, *Colorado Pioneers*, 228.

[75] "Troubles," 8.

[76] Griswold and Griswold, *Leadville*, 1:1104.

[77] Unidentified newspaper clipping, Tabor Scrapbooks, 3:30, WH475, Western History Collection, Denver Public Library.

[78] "A Sweet Surprise," and an unidentified newspaper clipping, Tabor Scrapbooks, 3:30, WH475, Western History Collection, Denver Public Library.

[79] Griswold and Griswold, *Leadville*, 1:1375.

[80] "A Colorado Lady," *The Times-Picayune* (New Orleans, LA), Jan. 30, 1884, online at newspapers.com.

[81] "Personal Mention," *Denver Republican*, Feb. 17, 1889, 13, Western History and Genealogy, Denver Public Library.

[82] "Mrs. Augusta Tabor Dead," *Denver Republican*, Feb. 2, 1895, 1, Western History and Genealogy, Denver Public Library.

[83] "Royally Received," *Rocky Mountain News* (Denver, CO), June 18, 1886, 8, Colorado Historic Newspaper Collection (website), Colorado State Library, coloradohistoricnewspapers.org; and see "Received Royally," *Rocky Mountain News* (Denver, CO), June 19,

1885, 8, Colorado Historic Newspaper Collection (website), Colorado State Library, coloradohistoricnewspapers.org; also see Jade Martin, "Augusta Tabor," *Colorado Encyclopedia* (website), last modified Nov. 2, 2022, https//coloradoencyclopedia.org.

[84] "Providing for Poverty," *Rocky Mountain News* (Denver, CO), Mar. 29, 1882, 8, Colorado Historic Newspaper Collection (website), Colorado State Library, coloradohistoricnewspapers.org.

[85] "In Memoriam," *Rocky Mountain News* (Denver, CO), Feb. 10, 1895, 8; and see "Augusta L. Tabor," *Rocky Mountain News* (Denver, CO), Feb. 2, 1895, 1, both at Colorado Historic Newspaper Collection, Colorado State Library, coloradohistoricnewspapers.org; also see Frank Hall, *History of the State of Colorado* (Chicago, IL : Blakely Printing, 1895), 4:57-58.

[86] "Augusta Tabor Dead," 1; also see "Augusta L. Tabor," 1.

[87] Photocopy of Augusta Tabor death certificate in Augusta Tabor Estate Papers, M87, Western History Collection, Denver Public Library.

[88] "Augusta Tabor Dead," 1.

[89] "Pioneers Wept," *Rocky Mountain News* (Denver, CO), Feb. 9, 1895, 5, Western History and Genealogy, Denver Public Library.

[90] Typed transcript of Augusta Tabor's will, Augusta Tabor Estate Papers, M87, Western History Collection, Denver Public Library.

[91] "Early Day Bonanza King Gone to His Last Home," *Herald Democrat* (Leadville, CO), Apr. 11, 1899, 1, Colorado Historic Newspapers Collection (website), Colorado State Library, coloradohistoricnewspapers.org.

[92] National Mining Hall of Fame & Museum, s.v. "Augusta Louise Tabor," https://www.mininghalloffame.org/alphabet/t; and see Colorado Women's Hall of Fame, s.v. "Augusta Tabor," https://www.cogreatwomen.org/project/augusta-pierce-tabor/; also see Find a Grave, (database and images) s.v. "Augusta Louise Tabor," Findagrave.com.

Figure 9.1. Elizabeth Byers, circa 1860-1865

Courtesy of Denver Public Library Special Collections, Z-2318

Elizabeth Byers:
Denver Philanthropist

Arrived in Colorado, August 7, 1859

Elizabeth Byers, or "Libby" as she was called by friends, arrived in Colorado's Cherry Creek settlements (later the city of Denver) on August 7, 1859. She lived in Colorado for the next sixty years, becoming an active member of the Denver community as it changed from a rough settlement to a boom-and-bust mining town and finally to the capital of a thriving state. Although relatively well-off compared with many of the women who came west during the Pikes Peak Gold Rush, Elizabeth was burned out of one home, flooded out of another, and of her four children, she lost the two who were born in Colorado. She once reflected, "Had I known the hardships and experiences which lay before me in this pioneer country, all the gold in the mountains could not have induced me to come."[1]

Elizabeth Minerva (Sumner) Byers was the third oldest of the nine children born to Horatio Nelson Sumner and Minerva (Lucas) Sumner. Her grandfather, Robert Lucas, was the governor of Ohio at the time of her birth on August 31, 1834, in Chillicothe, Ohio. Her grandmother, Friendly Ashley (Sumner) Lucas, was her father's older sister.[2] In 1838, when Elizabeth was four years old, her grandfather was appointed the first governor of the Territory of Iowa, which had been established on July 4, 1838. Elizabeth's family decided to move with her grandparents. They bought a farm near Muscatine, Iowa, and her father became a farmer and cattle merchant.[3]

Elizabeth's first childhood memory was of their journey to Iowa when she was four years old. Her family had to cross the Mississippi River by ferry boat on a windy day. Ferry boats at that time were usually large, flat-bottomed boats — called mud scows — that were often propelled by oars or poles. They were notoriously unstable, especially in poor weather. Elizabeth described this river crossing by saying, "I was frightened almost to death, and nothing but my Father's threats to throw me into the river saved me from convulsions. When the boat finally touched the frontier bank of the Mississippi, I was the first one ashore."[4] This was only the first of several dangerous river crossings that she would experience in her adventurous life.

Elizabeth grew up on her family's farm outside Blooming-ton in Muscatine County, Iowa. Like many girls at that time, she would have been expected to help her mother with chores and the raising of her younger siblings, but she was a spirited girl, writing later in her life: "There was nothing my five brothers did that I could not do."[5] She was a good shot and she rode a horse well, skills that served her well later in her life. As she grew to adulthood, William Newton Byers, who had lived on a nearby farm, began courting her.[6]

William's courtship included writing and reciting "verbal bouquets," a common tradition at that time. One verse he liked to recite (altered slightly to modern English) had been written by the Scottish poet Robert Burns, in his poem "It Is Na, Jean, Thy Bonie Face":

> *Something in every part of thee*
> *To praise, to love, to find;*
> *But dear as thy form to me,*
> *Still dearer is thy mind.*[7]

On November 16, 1854, Elizabeth and William married. At the time of their marriage, William Byers was an engineer and surveyor living in the Territory of Nebraska. He had been born in Ohio, like Elizabeth, and in 1850, the United States Census recorded his family also living in Bloomington. As a young man, he had left his home and become a government surveyor, working in the western part of Iowa and spending the winter of 1853-1854 traveling to California. Later he was appointed the first county surveyor of the Territory of Nebraska.[8] In this position he drew the first official plat of the town of Omaha.[9]

After their marriage, the couple set out with a covered wagon for their new home in Omaha, Nebraska's territorial capital. They reached Council Bluffs and attempted to cross the Missouri River, but the weather was so poor and the boat so unstable that they were forced to leave their team of oxen behind. They crossed the river, and upon reaching the far side, William left Elizabeth alone with their belongings while he walked to Omaha in search of a new team. Remembering this experience years later, Elizabeth wrote, "to say I was frightened as I sat there in the dark on the west bank of the

Williams & McDonald Denver City, C. T.

Figure 9.2. William Byers, circa 1867-1868

Courtesy of Denver Public Library Special Collections, Z-2351

Missouri River would be putting it mildly."[10]

Elizabeth and William began their lives together in a small cabin near Omaha where their son Frank was born in 1855 and their daughter Mary Eva, or "Molly," was born in 1857. William worked as a surveyor until the Panic of 1857, the first world-wide financial crisis.[11] This crisis, caused in part by the sinking of the *SS Central America*, which was carrying tons of California gold to the East Coast, caused banks and businesses to fail.[12] Numerous men, like William Byers, lost their jobs and their income.

A year later, like many out-of-work Americans, the Byerses became interested as rumors of gold discoveries in the Rocky Mountains circulated in newspapers. Financial desperation was a huge factor in driving so many people to the Pikes Peak region during the Colorado Gold Rush. As details of gold discoveries solidified, Elizabeth and William decided to move to the Cherry Creek settlements of Auraria and Denver City, not to seek their fortune searching for gold, but instead to start the first newspaper in the region.

Elizabeth's father helped finance their newspaper venture, and several of Elizabeth's brothers traveled with William on his initial journey to Colorado to start the newspaper.[13] Another financier of the venture was Dr. A. F. Peck, who contributed three hundred dollars—money he'd found on the body of a lynched horse thief. He'd obtained the man's body for examine in order to improve his anatomy knowledge.[14] Before William Byers and his partners left Omaha, they contemplated several names for their fledgling newspaper. Chauncey Thomas, William's nephew, later reported in the *Rocky Mountain News* that after they considered the *Cherry Creek Express* and the *Pikes Peak Herald*, Elizabeth suggested the *Rocky Mountain News,* and the name was settled.[15]

Leaving Elizabeth and her younger brother, Charles

ROCKY MOUNTAIN NEWS.

THE MINES AND MINERS OF KANSAS AND NEBRASKA.

VOL. 1. CHERRY CREEK, K. T., SATURDAY, APRIL 23, 1859. NO. 1.

Cherry Creek Pioneer.

VOL. 1. DENVER CITY, KANSAS, APRIL 23, 1859. NO. 1.

Figure 9.3. Mastheads of the inaugural issues of the *Rocky Mountain News* (Cherry Creek) and the *Cherry Creek Pioneer* (Denver City)

Courtesy of Denver Public Library

Sumner, alone with the children in their Omaha cabin, William and his partners loaded two wagons with a printing press and newspaper supplies and headed toward the Rocky Mountains. The group reached the Cherry Creek settlements on April 17, 1859, and soon found that another man, John Merrick, was already hard at work on a newspaper. William Byers and John Merrick each wanted to publish the first newspaper in the young settlements, and a race ensued. William and his partners set up their press in the attic of "Uncle Dick" Wootton's store, saloon, and meeting hall. After several days of frantic work, William and his partners published the first edition of the *Rocky Mountain News* on April 23, 1859, beating out Merrick's publication of the *Cherry Creek Pioneer* by just twenty minutes.[16]

During this publication race, William learned about the rivalry between the two Cherry Creek settlements. Denver City, founded by General William Larimer Jr. and his supporters, was located on the east side of Cherry Creek, while Auraria, founded by William Green Russell and his party of Georgians, was on the west side of the creek. Each community vied for new settlers. William had published his newspaper in Auraria, and he tried to remain neutral by identifying his paper's location as Cherry Creek, K. T. (Kansas Territory). Eventually, after moving the *News* from Wootten's saloon to a rough cabin in Auraria, he built a new *News* office on the banks of Cherry Creek, the dividing feature between the two towns, trying to appease both communities.[17]

This rivalry between the two communities was influenced by the North-South antagonism facing the United States in 1859, but it was also due to worries about the viability of either town. Until George Jackson and John Gregory announced their gold discoveries, the prospects of both towns appeared questionable. Initial gold discoveries earlier in the spring were minimal, and many argonauts who arrived at the Cherry Creek settlements stayed only a few days before turning back. These "go-backers," as they were called, claimed the gold rush was a hoax.

After gold discoveries in Gregory's Gulch and Idaho Springs, William became confident that his newspaper, and the Cherry Creek settlements, would survive. He returned to Omaha for Elizabeth and the children, leaving the *Rocky Mountain News* management to his partners. In Omaha, he and Elizabeth hired a man to take them and their belongings across the Great Plains in a prairie schooner, one of the standard covered wagons of the day. The Byerses chose to follow the Overland Trail, the northern route along the Platte River.[18]

Later in her life, Elizabeth wrote a short, hand-typed memoir titled *The Experiences of One Pioneer Woman.*[19] In it, she described her life during those difficult early years. One of the first adventures she writes about during their travels west was another unpleasant river crossing, this time on the Platte River:

> When we came to the Platte River, of which there were at least three channels at Fort Kearny, I drove the team, the men plunging into the water from two to three feet deep. The quick sand was so bad in many places that a wheel would go down and the wagon careen, threatening to upset; perhaps a horse would be down and by the time the men could get them up the sand would be solid under their feet, and that is the way we worked across the first stream. The children were very badly frightened, clinging to me so I hardly knew I was driving, and you can imagine my consternation when I found there was another stream to cross that was equally as bad.[20]

They paused at Fort Kearny, located in the Territory of Nebraska, and Elizabeth and William met an agent from the new Overland Stage Company. This gentleman was engaged in setting up a stagecoach route to the Rocky Mountains, and the Byerses convinced him to take them to the Cherry Creek settlements. They left their hired man to bring their wagon and belongings. At that time, the Overland Stage Company had set up stations and horses, but their stagecoaches had not yet arrived. Undeterred, Elizabeth, William, and their two children, both under the age of five, traveled 365 miles in a buckboard wagon. In her memoir, Elizabeth described this experience by writing, "You can imagine how cramped we were in a vehicle of that kind, traveling day and night, stopping of course every ten miles. We had our meals at the stations, and came through without accident, or very great discomfort."[21]

They reached the Cherry Creek settlements on August 7,

1859, and one can only imagine Elizabeth's reaction to her new home. Unfortunately, she didn't describe the condition of the settlements in her memoir, but Lavinia Porter, who traveled through Denver in 1860, described the Cherry Creek settlements as "consisting of numerous tents and numbers of rude and illy constructed cabins, with nearly as many rum shops and low saloons as cabins. Horses, cows, and hogs roamed at will over the greater part of the village."[22]

Elizabeth may not have described Denver City and Auraria, but she did have clear memories of the Vasquez House where they stayed until their belongings arrived. She described their lodging as "a crude frame building" where their "room" was the front room of the building. The so-called hotel, run by a Captain Sopres and his partner named Slaughter, "had no bedsteads" and "mattresses were placed on the floor."[23] Harsh living conditions were not the only difficulty Elizabeth and her family faced. The rough settlement had very few women and children. Elizabeth believed she was the eighth White woman to settle there.

In October, the wagon with their belongings finally arrived, and they moved into a one-room log cabin with a board roof and a dirt floor. Despite the crudeness of the structure, Elizabeth wrote that she felt fortunate to have a wooden roof over her head instead of the more common mud roof, which dripped mud onto anything inside when it rained. Unlike most of her neighbors, Elizabeth had one of the few cook stoves in the settlement. Despite these advantages, Elizabeth wrote, "In this one room house I had many laughable experiences some, however, were pretty hard to bear. There is much that is pathetic in a pioneer's life, and much that is awfully funny. We often laughed through tears."[24]

William and his partners moved the *Rocky Mountain News* from Wootton's saloon to a cabin on the Auraria side of

Cherry Creek. Elizabeth soon complained that the *News* office was nicer than her one room cabin, so William moved the family into the two back rooms of the *News* building. During those days, it was said, "Elizabeth fed the printers along with her family of four."[25]

One of the more interesting experiences Elizabeth wrote about while living in the back of the *News* office was a dinner party with early Colorado pathfinders. Her husband had

Figure 9.4. The first *Rocky Mountain News* office was located in Auraria, an early settlement of Denver, Colorado.

Courtesy of Denver Public Library Special Collections, X-28846

invited Colonel Ceran St. Vrain, Jim Baker, Kit Carson, and Jim Beckwourth, or Beckwith. Elizabeth described this dinner, showing a remarkably flexible attitude, considering that the meal took place before the Civil War:

> When our guests arrived and I found that one of them, Jim Beckwith, was a colored man, my aristocratic Virginia blood rather boiled, because I hadn't been used to sitting at a table with a colored man, and I hardly knew what to do, but almost instantly decided that there was but one thing to do and that was to ignore it altogether and treat them all alike, which I did.[26]

The cold winter of 1859-1860 caused many miners to leave their claims high in the Rocky Mountains and return to Denver City and Auraria. Many of these men had found little gold and were destitute. The Legislative Council for the Cherry Creek settlements appointed three men, one of them William Byers, as "overseers of the poor."[27] It is assumed that he encouraged Elizabeth to take over this duty since in January of 1860, Elizabeth and several other women met in Elizabeth's home and formed the Ladies' Union Aid Society, Colorado's first charitable organization. [28] Later in 1874 reorganized into the Ladies' Relief Society. The women made the organization non-denominational with the goal to "give aid and comfort to those in need."[29] Elizabeth was elected the first president of the Ladies' Union Aid Society, and during their initial meeting, sixty dollars was raised. The group started with a soup kitchen, and they later provided medical services, sewed underwear and warm nightshirts, and buried those miners who didn't survive the winter.[30]

In the summer of 1860, Elizabeth and her family moved to a new, two-story "frame building, lined with muslin."[31] The couple's third child was born in this house. It was during this time that William experienced some of his worst trouble at the *News* office. Newspaper publishers often developed enemies due to the articles they published. In fact, some publishers, including William, were challenged to duels over their newspaper content. On November 24, 1859, William published an

Figure 9.5. Elizabeth Byers with daughter Molly, circa 1860-1862

Courtesy of Denver Public Library Special Collections, Z-2338

answer to one such challenge by writing, "To anyone who may feel like calling us out, we have only one remark, that you are wasting your time in sending us challenges or other belligerent epistles. You may murder us, but never on the so-called field of honor, under the significant name of a duel."[32] Still, the summer of 1860 brought an escalation of violence that almost cost William his life.

Just like in the rest of the United States, tensions in 1860 between pro-slavery Southerners and anti-slavery Northerners were running high. In Denver, Charley Harrison, a Southern sympathizer and a professional gambler, shot and killed "Professor" Charles Stark, a well-liked blacksmith and former slave.[33] The killing was determined a bar fight, however, and nothing was done to punish Harrison. Still, Stark's death infuriated William. A week after the event, the *Rocky Mountain News* published an article calling the killing "wanton and unprovoked; in short a cold blooded murder."[34]

On the same day, another article remonstrated against Denver's lawless elements: "The rowdies, ruffians, shoulder-hitters and bullies generally, that infest our city had better be warned in time, and at once desist from their outrages upon the people."[35] These lawless men, nicknamed "Bummers" by the *News*, took offense and kidnapped William Byers from his office, forcing him at gunpoint to go to Charley Harrison's gambling saloon, the Criterion. Fortunately, Harrison helped William escape, but the Bummers chased after him and a gunfight ensued outside the *News* office. Elizabeth wrote of these times by saying, "My husband never came from the office at night without wearing a disguise, and many a time I have seen men hiding in an old building waiting and watching for his return to attack him."[36]

To add to these difficulties, in October 1860, Elizabeth's two-story home burned to the ground. Homes at this time were built of wood and lighting was from candles and oil lamps, making fire a constant danger. In Elizabeth's house-fire, the family lost all their "worldly possessions" that had been brought across the plains, but her baby was rescued from the flames and her other two young children survived.[37]

In the spring of 1861, Elizabeth's eighteen-year-old brother, Charles Sumner, arrived. The young man had hoped to become a Pony Express rider, but within a month, he became ill with what was assumed to be mountain fever, an illness attributed to both altitude sickness and tick fever. Elizabeth called a doctor, but the medication prescribed only seemed to make Charles sicker. After the doctor recommended a second, larger dose of medicine, Charles went into a coma and died. Only later did Elizabeth learn there had been a mistake, and her brother had been given morphine instead of quinine.[38]

A few months after her brother's death, Elizabeth's third child, the baby who'd been rescued from the burning house, died. Elizabeth described these times by writing: "In relating these incidents of my pioneer life, I only touch the high places, leaving you to read between the lines the many dishearten[ing], discouraging, hopeless things that could happen at a time like that."[39]

Despite her own difficulties, Elizabeth continued to work with other women to provide charity for Denver's most destitute inhabitants and to raise her children. Frank and Molly were growing older and would soon be in need of formal schooling. On October 3, 1859, Owen J. Goldrick opened the first school in the Cherry Creek area, housing it in a sod-roofed log cabin at 12th and Market Streets.[40] "Professor" Goldrick, as he was called, had arrived in Denver driving a team of two oxen and dressed in "a neatly pressed

Figure 9.6. Charles Sumner, Elizabeth's brother,
circa 1859-1861

Courtesy of Denver Public Library Special Collections, Z-2341

Prince Albert coat over spotless white linen which in turn tucked into fashionable tight, striped trousers."[41] His arrival caused quite the stir, but he is mainly remembered for his school and the articles he wrote for the *Rocky Mountain News*. Frank Byers attended Goldrick's school.[42]

By the summer of 1861, Elizabeth and her family had

moved into a new country home in Valverde, an area south-west of downtown Denver. Their new home lay on the edge of the South Platte River, and Elizabeth described the area as a place with "luxuriant foliage" where the "grass and fresh water were so unusual that our friends almost lived with us that summer."[43] The family had a large garden where William liked to grow watermelon, and when guests visited, he proudly served watermelon juice to them. On February 15, 1864, Elizabeth gave birth to her fourth and final child, James Henry. Just as her family was growing, the community

Figure 9.7. The Byers family at their home in Valverde, Colorado, circa 1861-1862

Courtesy of Denver Public Library Special Collections, Z-9980

around them was also expanding and changing. Denver City and Auraria had merged into one town on April 5, 1860, and the Territory of Colorado had been established on February 28, 1861.

In 1863, a fire broke out at the Cherokee House in Denver, and overnight a third of the city went up in flames. Denver residents rebuilt their homes and businesses, and they enacted a new "brick ordinance" to make the town more fire resistant.[44] Elizabeth and her family were fortunate that the fire didn't directly affect their home or the *News* office, but in 1864 they weren't so lucky.

Before Auraria and Denver City had merged into a single city, William Byers had built a new *Rocky Mountain News* office on stilts on the banks of Cherry Creek. His location was an attempt to show the *News'* impartiality to the two competing towns. When he built this new building, he'd been warned by the Arapaho Indians that Cherry Creek sometimes flooded, but until 1864, no one had ever seen the small creek as anything but a gentle brook. Unusually high rainfall in the spring of 1864 caused Denver streets to become muddy, and more concerning, Cherry Creek and the Platte River swelled to alarmingly high levels.

On the evening of May 19, 1964, a flash flood down Cherry Creek sent several giant waves through Denver, destroying bridges and buildings as water overflowed the stream's banks. At dawn on May 20, a third of Denver was under water, and the *News* office was swept away, along with a three-thousand-pound printing press, type, machinery, and other supplies. Byers and Company sustained estimated losses of $19,200,[45] about $372,000 in 2023 dollars.[46] Professor Goldrick wrote about this flood in the May 25, 1864, *Commonwealth*, published in Denver, describing the flood's destruction:

Figure 9.8. The *Rocky Mountain News* office location in Denver, Colorado, before the 1864 flood.

Courtesy of Denver Public Library Special Collections, RH-233

The first object selected by the element, was the Methodist Episcopal Church, at Larimer street bridge, which, together with the bridge, was hurled from its fastenings down the furious stream, with a velocity worthy of Niagara, either above or below the falls. The blacksmith-shop near the Church immediately followed, and then a succession of fearful noises, of buildings continually falling, waves surging high in the air, the sight of which, by the pale clouded light of the moon, was so awfully grand, that the imminent danger was forgotten.[47]

The Byerses were living in their Valverde home when the flood struck. The home was on the east side of the South Platte River, but when the flooding began, the river formed a new

Figure 9.9. Denver, Colorado, after the 1864 flood, which washed away several buildings including the *Rocky Mountain News* office.

Courtesy of Denver Public Library Special Collections, X-19363

channel, marooning the family in their home. They watched the water rise until it flowed over their doorway. In her memoir, Elizabeth makes light of the experience by writing that they "sat on the table telling funny stories. My husband wrote a note in which he stated his wife and babies were clinging to the tree tops, in danger of flood and starvation, and asked immediate aid, which he sealed up in a bottle and we sent it afloat."[48]

Fortunately, Elizabeth and her family were well-known Denver residents, and aid soon came. Soldiers from Camp Weld arrived and "constructed a skiff in a military wagon" to rescue the family.[49] Colonel John Chivington took part in the rescue, and this cemented his friendship with William Byers.

Later, this relationship was probably one of the reasons the *Rocky Mountain News* had such favorable reporting toward Colonel Chivington and his involvement in the November 1864 Sand Creek Massacre.

Chivington was a Methodist minister turned soldier. Following the 1862 battle at Glorieta Pass, in the New Mexico Territory, where Colorado Union troops engaged Confederate soldiers, Chivington earned accolades and a new nickname, the "Fighting Parson." By 1864, Chivington had become the commanding officer at Camp Weld, the military camp near Denver, and in November, he rose to notoriety when he led the Third Colorado Volunteer Cavalry and massacred hundreds of peaceful Arapaho and Cheyenne Indians camping on their reservation at Sand Creek.

Utes, Arapaho, Cheyenne, and many other Native American tribes had called the Rocky Mountains and Eastern Plains of Colorado their home long before the Anglos arrived. In 1851, the Arapaho, Cheyenne, and other Great Plains Indian nations signed the Treaty of Fort Laramie. Article 5 of this treaty granted the Cheyenne and Arapaho sovereignty over the territory that spanned from "the Red Bute, or the place where the road leaves the north fork of the Platte River; thence up the north fork of the Platte River to its source; thence along the main range of the Rocky Mountains to the head-waters of the Arkansas River; thence down the Arkansas River to the crossing of the Santa Fé road; thence in a northwesterly direction to the forks of the Platte River, and thence up the Platte River to the place of beginning."[50] Basically, this encompassed the entire Front Range and Eastern Plains of Colorado. Article 3 of the treaty stated the "United States bind themselves to protect the aforesaid Indian nations against the commission of all depredations by the people of the said United States."[51]

Throughout its history, the United States ratified more than 370 treaties with different Native American nations and, as with the 1851 Treaty of Fort Laramie, almost all of these treaties were broken by the United States.[52] When gold was discovered in Colorado in 1858, miners invaded the Cheyenne and Arapaho territory, killed wildlife, and completely ignored the Native Americans' rights to the land. The United States did nothing, and issues between Native Americans and Colorado pioneers increased with each passing year. Finally, conflict flared into the Indian Wars of the mid-1860s.

The conflict with the Native Americans affected Elizabeth and her family in numerous ways, especially as tensions with the Cheyenne and Arapaho tribes worsened. The Great Plains separated Colorado settlers from the rest of the United States, leaving many feeling isolated and alone. In addition, settlers knew they were encroaching on Native American lands. In October 11, 1860, Golden's newspaper, *The Western Mountaineer*, published an article complaining that "nothing was done effectually to extinguish the Indian title to the lands we are occupying."[53] By 1864, an article in Black Hawk's newspaper, *The Daily Mining Journal*, called for an all-out war, stating, "the Indians want to be killed off—that's certain; our new Maj. Generals and Brigadiers want to distinguish themselves. . . . Only get the thing well started, and it will win by a decided majority."[54]

After the Denver flood made their Valverde home unsafe to live in, Elizabeth and her family moved into the Colorado Seminary building on the corner of Fourteenth and Arapahoe. While they were living there, Denver experienced the "great Indian scare" in which it was believed that Arapaho and Cheyenne Indians were attacking Denver. Elizabeth writes of this scare with probably more bravado than she felt at the time:

While in the Seminary building we had the great Indian scare. Col. Fillmore was in charge of the troops at that time. He seemed the most frightened man in the village. He rushed the women and children to the old Mint building, where they were huddled in like sheep; a good many came to the Seminary building where I was. Col. Filmore rushed to me in a frenzy and said: "My God, woman, take your children and get down to the Mint." I said: "Colonel I am as safe here as at the Mint. If the Indians want my scalp they can take it right here."[55]

Ultimately, on November 29, 1864, Colonel Chivington attacked friendly Cheyenne and Arapaho Indians who were peacefully camped on Sand Creek, about 180 miles southeast of Denver and thirty miles north of Fort Lyon. Earlier that summer, Territorial Governor John Evans had instructed these same Indians to camp near Fort Lyon so they would be safe.

Over two hundred Cheyenne and Arapaho were massacred by Chivington and his soldiers, and since most of the Indian men were out hunting buffalo, the deaths were primarily the elderly, women, and children. Captain Silas Soule, a respected Union officer who refused to participate in the massacre, later wrote brutally explicit descriptions of what he had witnessed:

> . . . it was hard to see little children on their knees have their brains beat out by men professing to be civilized. One squaw was wounded and a fellow took a hatchet to finish her, she held her arms up to defend her, and he cut one arm off, and held the other with one hand and dashed the hatchet through her brain. One squaw with her two children, were on their knees begging for their lives of a

dozen soldiers, within ten feet of them all, firing—when one succeeded in hitting the squaw in the thigh, when she took a knife and cut the throats of both children, and then killed herself.[56]

Native American retribution for the Sand Creek Massacre was both bloody and tragic. In the years after the Sand Creek Massacre, Native Americans attacked ranches, wagon trains, and stagecoaches across the Eastern Plains, further isolating Denver. These attacks hardened settlers' attitudes and led to almost all of Colorado's Native American tribes being forced onto reservations outside of Colorado.

Despite the Native American unrest surrounding Denver, Elizabeth Byers and her children decided to travel by stagecoach across the Great Plains in 1865. She wanted to visit her family in Iowa, but their travels were halted when a stagecoach on their line was attacked and burned. Elizabeth and her children spent several tense days at a stagecoach stop, finally crossing the Great Plains with a military escort. Although they arrived safely in Muscatine, that winter, while visiting her parents, her youngest son, James, contracted pneumonia and died.

By the spring of 1869, Elizabeth and the rest of the nation were engrossed in news articles about Major John Wesley Powell as he and his crew began their famous voyage down the Colorado River through the Grand Canyon. Elizabeth must have been especially worried since her younger brother, John "Jack" Colton Sumner, was Powell's guide and lead boatman. At the same time, Elizabeth was busy raising two growing children while William, along with other influential men, continued their fight for Colorado statehood.

There had been numerous attempts to organize the Colorado Territory into a state over the years. State constitutions were framed and voted on in both 1865 and 1867. Bills for Colorado statehood were ratified by Congress only to be vetoed twice by President Andrew Johnson.[57] Finally, by 1875, it appeared Colorado would finally become a state, and William hoped to become the state's first govenor. Unfortunately, his own follies would lead to the destructon of this dream.

In the early 1870s, William had begun an affair with Hattie Sancomb, a widow who had moved to Denver from Lawrence, Kansas.[58] If Elizabeth knew of this affair, she didn't mention it in her memoir. Nonetheless, perhaps because of his aspirations to become Colorado's first governor, William had broken off his relationship with Hattie in 1875. As a spurned and furious woman, she promised to "dedicate the rest of my life to your misery. . . . You are only dear to me as an object of revenge."[59]

Her revenge became more than words on April 5, 1876, although what truly happened is dependent on which historical source is read. In one version, Hattie climbed into the horsecar William normally rode home in from his *Rocky Mountain News* office. They argued, and when William tried to escape on foot, she followed him and pulled out a pistol. Elizabeth, waiting to go to lunch with her husband, watched from her parlor window as Hattie struggled with William. Hurrying to her buggy, Elizabeth climbed inside and drove down to rescue William. He scrambled into the buggy and Hattie fired her pistol. The bullet struck the buggy, fortunately injuring no one, but in the chaos that followed, Elizabeth lost control of the horses, and they turned around and headed back toward home. As they passed Hattie, she didn't fire her weapon, but instead followed them to the Byers' house. Their son Frank, armed and waiting at the door, turned her away. A few blocks from their home, Hattie was arrested for disturbing the peace.[60]

Hattie's version of this incident, printed on the front page of the April 15, 1876, *Golden Globe*—a competitor of the *Rocky Mountain News*—presents a very different version of the event. In her version, William was an "Abelard," a "Corsair and Assassin Upon Female Virtue," and in her story, it was Elizabeth who fired the pistol.[61]

Regardless of what the truth might have been, the *Globe* not only published Hattie's side of the story, but the newspaper also blasted William's reputation and published several of his love letters to Hattie. The incident damaged his reputation enough that a few months later, John Long Routt was voted in as Colorado's first governor.

Elizabeth had to have been mortified by the event, but her complaints, if there were any, were private. Later in life, she described her husband as "a queer old chap" and complained only about his financial incompetence. Once she said of William, "he has never been out of debt since I have known him . . . and there has been no excuse for it."[62] Although they lived a good life compared with most Denver residents, with trips to Europe, a Caribbean cruise, and homes in Denver and California, by the time William died on March 25, 1903, Elizabeth and her children inherited an estate worth only around $7000 (over $241,000 in 2023 dollars).[63]

The affair and scandal did not appear to hurt Elizabeth's reputation, and she remained in Denver until her death more than forty-three years later. Throughout this time, she continued actively contributing to numerous charities and remained active in her Methodist Church. In 1893 Elizabeth established the Working Boy's Home and School for homeless boys, which was later renamed The Elizabeth M. Byers Home for Boys.[64]

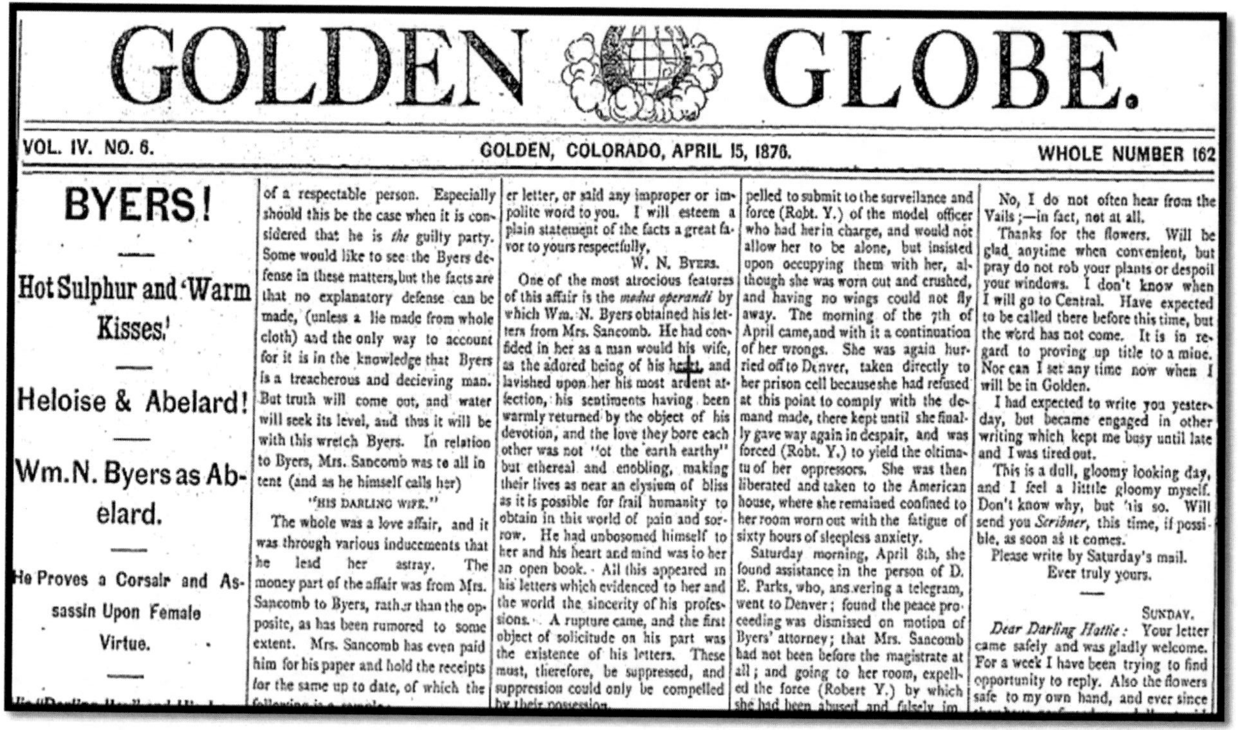

GOLDEN GLOBE.

VOL. IV. NO. 6.   GOLDEN, COLORADO, APRIL 15, 1876.   WHOLE NUMBER 162

BYERS!

Hot Sulphur and Warm Kisses!

Heloise & Abelard.

Wm. N. Byers as Abelard.

He Proves a Corsair and Assassin Upon Female Virtue.

of a respectable person. Especially should this be the case when it is considered that he is *the* guilty party. Some would like to see the Byers defense in these matters, but the facts are that no explanatory defense can be made, (unless a lie made from whole cloth) and the only way to account for it is in the knowledge that Byers is a treacherous and decieving man. But truth will come out, and water will seek its level, and thus it will be with this wretch Byers. In relation to Byers, Mrs. Sancomb was to all intent (and as he himself calls her)

"HIS DARLING WIFE."

The whole was a love affair, and it was through various inducements that he lead her astray. The money part of the affair was from Mrs. Sancomb to Byers, rather than the opposite, as has been rumored to some extent. Mrs. Sancomb has even paid him for his paper and hold the receipts for the same up to date, of which the

er letter, or said any improper or impolite word to you. I will esteem a plain statement of the facts a great favor to yours respectfully,

W. N. BYERS.

One of the most atrocious features of this affair is the *manha etervnall* by which Wm. N. Byers obtained his letters from Mrs. Sancomb. He had confided in her as a man would his wife, as the adored being of his heart, and lavished upon her his most ardent affection, his sentiments having been warmly returned by the object of his devotion, and the love they bore each other was not "of the earth earthly" but ethereal and ennobling, making their lives as near an elysium of bliss as it is possible for frail humanity to obtain in this world of pain and sorrow. He had unbosomed himself to her and his heart and mind was to her an open book. All this appeared in his letters which evidenced to her and the world the sincerity of his professions. A rupture came, and the first object of solicitude on his part was that these letters must, therefore, be suppressed, and the suppression could only be compelled by their possion

pelled to submit to the surveillance and force (Robt. Y.) of the model officer who had her in charge, and would not allow her to be alone, but insisted upon occupying them with her, although she was worn out and crushed, and having no wings could not fly away. The morning of the 7th of April came, and with it a continuation of her wrongs. She was again hurried off to Denver, taken directly to her prison cell because she had refused at this point to comply with the demand made, there kept until she finally gave way again in despair, and was forced (Robt. Y.) to yield the ultimatu of her oppressors. She was then liberated and taken to the American house, where she remained confined to her room worn out with the fatigue of sixty hours of sleepless anxiety.

Saturday morning, April 8th, she found assistance in the person of D. E. Parks, who, answering a telegram, went to Denver; found the peace proceeding was dismissed on motion of Byers' attorney, that Mrs. Sancomb had not been before the magistrate at all; and going to her room, expelled the force (Robert Y.) by which she had been abused and falsely im

No, I do not often hear from the Vails;—in fact, not at all.

Thanks for the flowers. Will be glad anytime when convenient, but pray do not rob your plants or despoil your windows. I don't know when I will go to Central. Have expected to be called there before this time, but the word has not come. It is in regard to proving up title to a mine. Nor can I set any time now when I will be in Golden.

I had expected to write you yesterday, but became engaged in other writing which kept me busy until late and I was tired out.

This is a dull, gloomy looking day, and I feel a little gloomy myself. Don't know why, but 'tis so. Will send you *Scribner*, this time, if possible, as soon as it comes.

Please write by Saturday's mail.

Ever truly yours.

SUNDAY.

Dear Darling Hattie: Your letter came safely and was gladly welcome. For a week I have been trying to find opportunity to reply. Also the flowers safe to my own hand, and ever since

Figure 9.10. The Byers scandal headlined the front page of the *Golden Globe's* (Golden, CO), April 15, 1876.

Courtesy of Colorado Historic Newspapers Collection

When Colorado's State Capitol Building was built in the early 1900s, the builders decided to create a Hall of Fame in the building's dome. Fifteen men—including William Byers—were memorialized with stained glass windows, but the committee decided the sixteenth spot should go to a woman. Elizabeth's tireless contributions to charity organizations caused the Ladies' Relief Society to nominate her, but after seeing the nomination, Elizabeth refused:

> Please don't, because I see I was not named for any merit of my own, but as the 'wife of the editor of the first newspaper in Denver.' While I gladly accord my husband every honor he is entitled to, and rejoice that he is so honored and appreciated by his fellow-citizens, I remember that he and I stood shoulder to shoulder through all the trials and hardships of pioneer life and I feel I ought not to stand wholly in the light of reflected glory.[65]

Elizabeth Byers passed away on January 6, 1920, almost seventeen years after her husband's death. She was buried beside her husband in their family plot at Fairmount Cemetery. Her life was long and rich, although perhaps only a few now remember it. Dr. Thomas Noel, a well-known Colorado historian, wrote in his book, *Colorado Givers: A History of Philanthropic Heroes*, "Although William Byers remains prominent as Colorado's greatest booster and the founder of the *Rocky Mountain News*, his wife's role as a pioneer philanthropist is largely forgotten."[66]

The history of Colorado's pioneering women is often over-looked, and Elizabeth Byers' remarkable life is no exception. Elizabeth, like so many women of her day, spent her years

Figure 9.11. Elizabeth Byers on her eightieth birthday, 1914

Courtesy of Denver Public Library Special Collections,
Z-2311

determined to build a good life for herself and her family while also contributing in significant ways to shaping the fledgling State of Colorado. She helped establish Colorado's first charitable organization, founded a home for orphan boys, and she spent her life making civic contributions that improved Denver and Colorado. Her influence in Colorado was real, meaningful, and worthy of being remembered.

---

[1] Thomas J. Noel, Stephen J. Leonard, and Kevin E. Rucker, *Colorado Givers: A History of Philanthropic Heroes* (Niwot, CO: University Press of Colorado, 1998), 8.

[2] Betty Porter Hall, *Governor Robert Lucas: his Ancestors and Descendants* (La Verne, CA: University of La Verne Press, 1989), 66.

[3] Mrs. William N. Byers, "The Experiences of One Pioneer Woman," unpublished manuscript circa 1900-1920, Box 3, FF 43, William N. Byers and Family Papers, WH55, Denver Public Library Western History and Genealogy Repository, 1.

[4] Byers, "Experiences," 1.

[5] Byers, "Experiences," 1.

[6] 1850 US Census, Bloomington Township, Muscatine County, Iowa, digital image s.v. "William N. Byers" and digital image s.v. "Elizabeth Sumner," Ancestry.com.

[7] Noel, Leonard, and Rucker, *Colorado Givers*, 8.

[8] Eugene Parsons, "William Newton Byers," *The Mining American*, March 10, 1917, 8, online at Hathitrust.org.

[9] *Portrait and Biographical Record of Denver And Vicinity, Colorado: Containing Portraits and Biographies of many well known Citizens of the Past and Present [. . .]* (Chicago, IL: Chapman Publishing Co., 1898), 145-47, online at Hathitrust.org.

[10] Byers, "Experiences," 2.

[11] Karl Marx and Frederick Engels, preface to *Marx & Engels Collected Works, Vol. 28: Marx: 1857-1861* (London: Lawrence & Wishart, 1986), xii, https://muse.jhu.edu/book/34847.

[12] Diane McLaughlin, "This Month in History: When a Shipwreck Sank the Economy," *Banker & Tradesman,* , August 28, 2022, Banker & Tradesman (website), https://bankerandtradesman.com/this-month-in-history-when-a-shipwreck-sank-the-economy/.

[13] Robert L. Perkin, *An Informal History of Denver and The Rocky Mountain News: The First Hundred Years*, (New York, NY: Doubleday & Company, 1959), 84-85.

[14] Perkin, *Informal History*, 57.

[15] Perkin, *Informal History*, 83-84.

[16] James Melvin Lee, *History of American Journalism* (New York, NY: Houghton Mifflin Company, 1917), 251.

[17] Perkin., *Informal History*, 194-195.

[18] Byers, "Experiences," 2.

[19] Byers, "Experiences," 2.

[20] Byers, "Experiences," 2-3.

[21] Byers, "Experiences," 3.

[22] Lavinia Honeyman Porter, *By Ox Team to California: A Narrative of Crossing the Plains in 1860* (Oakland, CA: Oakland Enquirer, 1910), 54, https://archive.org/details/byoxteamtocalifo00port/page/54/mode/2up.

[23] Byers, "Experiences," 3.

[24] Byers, "Experiences," 4.

[25] Clé Cervi, Nancy M. Peterson, et al., *The Women Who Made the Headlines: Denver Woman's Press Club, the First Hundred Years,* (Lakewood, CO: Western Guideways, 1998), 7.

[26] Byers, "Experiences," 5.

[27] McKenna Solomon, "The Advanced Guard of Civilization," *Colorado Heritage Magazine*, November/December 2015, 16-19.

[28] Noel, Leonard, and Rucker, *Colorado Givers*, 9-10.

[29] Solomon, "The Advanced Guard," 18.

[30] Gail Marjorie Beaton, "Making Visible the Invisible: Herstory in Colorado's Queen City" (M.A. thesis, University of Denver, 2002), 16.

[31] Byers, "Experiences," 5.

[32] William N. Byers, "Our Late Challenge," *Rocky Mountain News* (Denver), Nov. 24, 1859, 2, Colorado Historic Newspapers Collection (website), Colorado State Library, coloradohistoricnewspapers.org.

[33] Stanley W. Zamonski and Teddy Keller, *The Fifty-Niners: A Denver Diary* (Denver, CO: Sage Books, 1961), 128.

[34] "Death of Stark," *Rocky Mountain News* (Denver), July 25, 1860, 2, Colorado Historic Newspapers Collection (website), Colorado State Library, coloradohistoricnewspapers.org.

[35] "Words of Caution," *Rocky Mountain News* (Denver), July 25, 1860, 3, Colorado Historic Newspapers Collection (website), Colorado State Library, coloradohistoricnewspapers.org.

[36] Byers, "Experiences," 6.

[37] Byers, "Experiences," 6.

38 Byers, "Experiences," 7.

39 Byers, "Experiences," 7.

40 Thomas J. Noel, "Goldrick Colorado's first professor," *Denver Post*, Aug. 14, 2015, online at Denverpost.com.

41 Zamonski and Keller, *The Fifty-Niners*, 57.

42 Emma Shepard Hill, compiler, *Foundation Stones*, (Denver, CO: Bradford-Robinson Printing Co, 1928), 109, https://history.denverlibrary.org/sites/history/files/Foundation-Stones.pdf.

43 Byers, "Experiences," 7.

44 William N. Byers, *Encyclopedia of Biography of Colorado: History of Colorado* (Chicago, IL: Century, 1901), 80-81.

45 Perkin, *Informal History*, 220.

46 The equivalent purchasing power of $19,200 in 1864, as of June 29, 2023, was calculated to be $371,926 assuming a 1.88% inflation rate, Consumer Price Index (CPI) inflation calculator (webpage), https://www.officialdata.org/us/inflation/1864?amount=19200.

47 "Great Flood in Denver. Several Lives Lost! Great Destruction of Property, West Denver Inundated. The *News Office* a Total Loss," *Weekly Commonwealth* (Denver), May 25, 1864, 3, Colorado Historic Newspapers Collection (website), Colorado State Library, coloradohistoricnewspapers.org.

48 Byers, "Experiences," 9.

49 Perkin, *Informal History*, 221.

50 Charles J. Kappler, compiler, "Treaty of Fort Laramie With Sioux, Etc. 1851," *Indian Affairs: Laws and Treaties, Vol. II*, (Washington, D.C.: Government Printing Office, 1904), 2:595, https://americanindian.si.edu/static/nationtonation/pdf/Horse-Creek-Treaty-1851.pdf.

51 Kappler, *Indian Affairs*, 595.

52 Hansi Lo Wang, "Broken Promises On Display at Native American Treaties Exhibit," *Code Switch* podcast, National Public Radio, January 18, 2015, https://www.npr.org/sections/codeswitch/2015/01/18/368559990/broken-promises-on-display-at-native-american-treaties-exhibit.

53 "Indian Matters," *The Western Mountaineer* (Golden, CO), Oct. 11, 1860, 4, Colorado Historic Newspapers Collection (website), Colorado State Library, coloradohistoricnewspapers.org.

54 *The Daily Mining Journal* (Black Hawk, CO), Mar. 19, 1864, 3, Colorado Historic Newspapers Collection (website), Colorado State Library, coloradohistoricnewspapers.org.

55 Byers, "Experiences," 9.

56 Silas Soule to Maj. Edward Wynkoop, Fort Lyon, Colorado Territory, Dec. 14, 1864, transcribed in "The Life of Silas Soule," (webpage), Sand Creek Massacre National Historic Site Colorado (website), National Park Service, last updated November 14, 2019, https://www.nps.gov/sand/learn/historyculture/the-life-of-silas-soule.htm.

57 Jerry Kopel, "How Colorado Became a State" (webpage), Jerry Kopel (website), accessed April 12, 2021, http://jerryko-pel.com/b/Colorado-statehood-struggle.htm. Also see "11 things you don't know about Colorado's path to statehood," July 20, 2018, (blog post), *Story* (blog), History Colorado (website), https://www.historycolorado.org/story/collections-library/2018/07/20/11-things-you-didnt-know-about-colorados-path-statehood.

58 Perkin, *Informal History*, 314-19.

59 Phil Goodstein, introduction in *The Seamy Side of Denver*, (Denver, CO: New Social, 1993).

60 Goodstein, introduction in *Seamy Side*.

61 "Byers!," *Golden Globe* (Golden, CO), Apr. 15, 1876, 1.

62 David Fridtjof Halaas, "William Byers and Family" (unpublished manuscript, undated), Envelope B, Box 11, Colorado Subject Collection Biographical Files, Stephen H. Hart Research Center, History Colorado, Denver, CO.

63 The equivalent purchasing power of $7,000 in 1903, as of May 17, 2023, was calculated to be $241,311 assuming a 2.99% inflation rate, Consumer Price Index (CPI) inflation calculator (webpage), https://www.officialdata.org/us/inflation/1903?amount=7000.

64 Noel, Leonard, and Rucker, *Colorado Givers*, 12.

[65] Halaas, "William Byers and Family"; and see Noel, *Colorado Givers*, 12.

[66] Noel, Leonard, and Rucker, *Colorado Givers*, 13.

Figure 10.1. Tsashin wearing a buckskin dress with fringe and quill work, bracelets, necklaces, a belt, beads, and a shawl, circa 1880-1900

Courtesy of Denver Public Library Special Collections, X-30460

Tsashin:
Forgotten Ute

Born in Colorado around 1850

Known by many names—She-towitch by her descendants,
Shasheen, Shashien, Shosheen, and Susan in newspapers, and
Cutshutchous and Tsashin within her Ute family—this
remarkable woman was the half-sister of Chief Ouray. At a
young age she was kidnapped by Arapaho, rescued by White
soldiers, and returned to her tribe as a gesture of goodwill.[1]
Later in her life, she and her family were involved in the
Meeker Incident and Tsashin won Colorado citizens'
admiration by speaking out to save the Anglo women and
children taken hostage.[2] Her heroics earned her a new Anglo
name, one she was known by for the rest of her life: "God
Bless Susan." Despite being a friend to settlers, Tsashin, like
all Northern Utes, was forced from her Colorado homeland
and placed on a reservation in Utah. She spent the rest of her
life forgotten by the Anglos who had praised her and
displaced to the arid land in Utah, far from her home in her
people's Shining Mountains, today's Colorado Rocky
Mountains.[3]

For centuries before Colorado's 1859 gold rush, Ute Indians had inhabited the Colorado Plateau, an area consisting of much of present-day Colorado and Utah, along with the northern edge of New Mexico, a corner of Arizona, and the southern edge of Wyoming. Calling themselves Nünt'z, meaning "the People," they shared a common language, Shoshonean, along with common social and political traditions.

Historians have divided the Ute into twelve or thirteen bands, based on their hunting grounds.[4] Today these bands have been regrouped into the Southern Ute Tribe centered around Ignacio, Colorado, and consisting mostly of Mouache and Caputa; the Ute Mountain Utes centered around Towaoc, Colorado, and consisting mostly of Weenuchiu; and the Northern Utes centered around Fort Duchesne, Utah, and consisting of mostly the Tabeguache, Grand, Yampa, and Uintah.[5]

Before Anglos arrived, each Ute band was organized into small, extended family groups, living nomadically during the summer in the high Rocky Mountains and wintering in lower, warmer valleys. Ute men traditionally hunted larger animals—buffalo, elk, deer, and antelope—while the women trapped smaller game and gathered edible plants. Wild onion, rice grass, various berries, roots, and other wild foods were important Ute food sources.[6]

Ute medicine men were experts at medicinal herbs, gathering and drying roots, plant greens, and bark to make teas and other healing mixtures. Several times a year, family groups joined together for trading and ceremonies. The Ute had no single leader, making it impossible for one person, or even a group of chiefs, to speak for the entire tribe. [7]

Tsashin, the daughter of Bird Track, is believed to have been born in 1850. She was raised in the Tabeguache (Uncom-pahgre) band and spent much of her childhood in the village where her father, Guera Murah, was chief.[8] Guera Murah, called Salvador by Spaniards, was believed to be a Jicarilla Apache, but he was raised as a Ute from a very young age.[9] He had two sons from his first marriage, Ouray and Quenche, and after his first wife's death, he returned to his tribe and married Bird Track. His two sons remained in Abiquiú, New Mexico, near where they had been raised, but they joined their father soon after Tsashin was born. When Tsashin was still quite young, her half-brother, Ouray, married Black Mare, Tukukavapiapi, and had a son, Queshegut (also called Paron, Pahlone, and later Coatan). His wife died soon after the child's birth and a young woman, Chipeta, just a few years older than Tsashin, took over childcare and eventually be-came Ouray's second wife.

Tsashin, around nine or ten years old at the time of Ouray's second marriage, spent time with the young couple. In the late

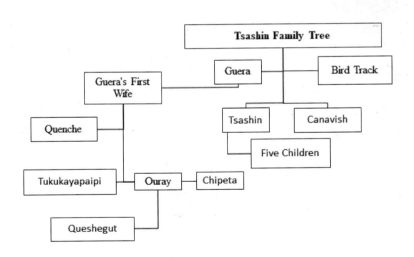

Figure 10.2. Tsashin's simplified family tree

Traditional Ute Bands	
Ute Band Names	**Traditional Hunting Areas**
Pahvant	Utah—Western Wasatch Range, desert area in the Sevier Lake region
Moanunts / Moanumts	Utah—Upper Sanpete Valley, central Utah
Sanpits (San Pitch) / Sahpeech	Utah—Sanpete and Sevier River Valleys
Timonogots / Timpanogots Núuchi / Toompahnahwach	Utah—Wasatch Range, Uinta Basin, southern and eastern area of Utah Lake
Uintah/ Uintah Núuchi / Yoowetuh	Utah—Utah Lake to the Uinta Basin
Sheberetch / Seuvarits Núuchi / Shebedteech	Utah—Moab area
Yamparika / 'Iya-paa Núuchi / Yampa / Yahpudttka	Colorado – Yampa River Valley, considered White River Utes
Pariyu Núuchi / Parianuche / Pahoteeahnooch / Nupartca	Utah and Colorado—Colorado River Valley, considered White River Utes
Saguaguana/Akanaquint	Colorado—Western and central mountains
Uncompahgre / Tavi'wachi Núuchi / Tabeguache / Taveewach	Colorado—Gunnison and Uncompahgre River Valleys
Weenuchiu/ Wugama Núuchi / Weeminuche / Weemeenooch	Utah and Colorado—San Juan Mountains and San Juan River Valley
Kapuuta Núuchi / Capote / Kahpota	Colorado—Sangre de Cristo Mountains, San Luis Valley
Mouache / Moghwachi Núuchi / Muache / Mooach	Colorado--Eastern slopes of the Rockies from Denver south to Las Vegas, New Mexico

Figure 10.3. Traditional Ute bands compiled from multiple sources. Spellings of band names vary depending on source, as does the identification of the twelve bands. Some sources list the Comumba/Weber as the twelfth band, but others cite the Saguaguana/Akanaquint. The authors have chosen to match the map in Figure 10.4.

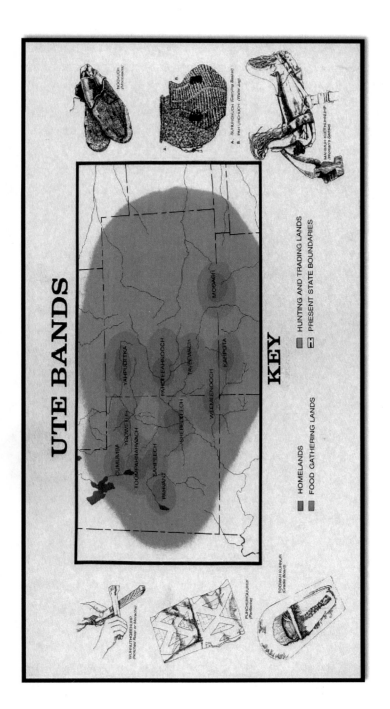

Figure 10.4. Homelands and food gathering areas of traditional Ute bands

J. Willard Marriott Library, University of Utah

summer of 1861, when she was about eleven years old, Tsashin was captured by members of the Arapaho tribe.[10] As a hostage, she was perhaps traded to other Arapaho bands as they traveled to Colorado's Front Range, taking her far away from her tribe and homeland.[11] Capturing children and adopting them was a common practice in many Indigenous tribes. For example, a year later, in 1862, Ouray's son disappeared, was assumed kidnapped, and later was raised by Lakota. Even Chipeta is believed to have been a Kiowa-Apache, brought to the Tabeguache Utes at a young age.[12]

Little is known about Tsashin's time in captivity, but in 1863, the Arapaho band holding her approached J. N. Hollowell, one of the Big Thompson's first pioneers. The Arapaho tried to swap the girl for trinkets, an experience Mr. Hollowell later described:

I was lying asleep in my cabin, a mile and a half southeast of the present city of Loveland. Being suddenly aroused from my slumbers by an unusual noise, I looked up and discovered that my cabin was full of Indians. They were painted and feathered up in regular war style. After I had dressed myself, the spokesman of the party said 'swap,' pointing at the hat I had on and at a looking glass hanging on the wall. He then pointed up the Big Thompson River as an invitation to go with them. My first thought was they wanted to 'swap' a pony for my hat and looking glass, so I took the glass and went with them to their camp, about a half mile distant. When we reached the camp I found about a half a dozen tepees which I supposed were for the use of the chiefs or headmen. One of my guides opened the entrance to one of the tepees and soon came out with a young squaw whom he pushed against me, saying 'swap,' pointing to my hat and my glass. I sized them up the best I could under the circumstances and replied 'no swap.' The squaw, judging by her dress, was about 13 years of age. There were some 200 or 300 Indians in the band, altogether, and when I refused to 'swap,' they set up such a yell as I shall probably never hear again.[13]

Shortly after Hollowell's experience, Sergeant William C. Carroll from Captain D. L. Hardy's Company M of the First Colorado Cavalry was ordered to "go to the southeast where they had heard was trouble between the settlers and Indians."[14] At the time, Carroll was stationed at Camp Collins (later Fort Collins).

Accounts written about Carroll's encounter with the Arapaho that day vary. In one version, the *Greeley Tribune* wrote that Carroll and his soldiers "rode to a hill, probably near Inspiration Point, and saw an Indian camp on the opposite side of the river. A young squaw was tied to a tree and fagots were piled around her preparatory to burning her."[15] Another version, published in the *Colorado Transcript,* claimed Carroll found "a fence post erected in the centre of the camp, and a quantity of wood around it ready to be ignited," but Tsashin was found "in one of the lodges, concealed under a lot of buffalo robes."[16] A third version, published in the *Weekly Courier* stated "she had already been tied to the stake and the fire lighted" before her rescue.[17]

No matter which version is accurate, Carroll rescued Tsashin, at the time speculating the girl had been a prisoner for a year or two and was about to be sacrificed in retaliation for a battle in May of 1863 in which the Arapaho lost several men. The *Colorado Transcript* article stated that, unable to trade the girl to Mr. Hollowell, the Arapaho returned "to their village, which was then located on the Platte near the mouth of the Cache-a-la-Poudre," and "proposed to take the revenge out of poor Susan [Tsashin]."[18] Carroll brought the rescued girl home to his wife, who welcomed Tsashin into their home and named her Susan.

Details and time frames conflict for Tsashin's rescue. Mr. Hollowell believed his encounter with the Arapaho took place in the latter part of June 1863, while Sergeant Carroll stated he rescued Tsashin in early May. The exact timeline may never be known, but on the Fourth of July 1863, "Sergeant Carroll and his wife went down the creek some miles to attend a dance, leaving Susan in the quarters, and on their return found she had 'lit out,' taking with her all the clothes that had been made for her by Mrs. Carroll, a piece of meat and a butcher-knife, but molesting nothing belonging to Mrs. Carroll."[19]

The Carrolls worried Tsashin had been recaptured by Arapaho but later heard the girl had been found by soldiers of Company D, who were stationed in Middle Park.[20] At some point during Tsashin's rescue and residence at the Carrolls, it was learned she was the half-sister of Ouray, who was becoming an important leader in Ute-Anglo relations. Trying to curry favor with the Ute leader, Territorial Governor John Evans sent a messenger to Major Simeon Whiteley, the Ute Indian agent, who at that time was on his way to Hot Sulphur Springs in Middle Park. Tsashin was brought to Whiteley, and he eventually returned her to her tribe.[21]

While Tsashin survived her kidnapping and grew into adulthood, her half-brother Ouray became one of the most powerful Ute voices in negotiations with Anglo settlers. During the early years of the Colorado gold rush, settlers came in contact mostly with the Plains Indians—the Arapaho and the Cheyenne—who roamed the Front Range. The Cheyenne maintained a close relationship with Bent's Fort,

Figure 10.5. Ute women and children, circa 1894

Courtesy of Denver Public Library Special Collections, P-179

and the Arapaho often camped at the junction of the South
Platte River and Cherry Creek, continuing to do so even after
pioneers established Denver in the same location. The Utes,
however, were more reclusive, living throughout the Rocky
Mountains. Only as miners penetrated farther and farther into
the mountains, did Anglos have contact and conflict with the
Utes.[22]

Southern Utes had interacted with Spaniards as early as the
sixteenth century, when Spaniards began exploring and
colonizing the region that later became New Mexico.[23] The
horses brought by Spaniards helped improve the Utes' way
of life, but smallpox and other foreign diseases were deadly,
often decimating entire Ute villages. Despite these issues,
Utes and Spaniards lived in relative harmony—becoming
trading partners, although Utes continued to defend their
territory as Spaniards encroached deeper into it. The
Mexican-American War resulted in both Mexican and Ute
territory being ceded to the United States. In December 1849,

Ute leaders, mostly from the Capote and Muache bands, met United States diplomats and signed the Treaty of Abiquiú (also called the Calhoun Treaty). This treaty established "peace and amity" between the United States and the Ute Nation while also providing "free passage" for Anglos through Ute lands.[24]

As more Americans headed west, conflicts with the Utes increased until October 1863, just months after Tsashin returned to her people, when Ouray and several other Ute leaders signed a new treaty, although members of the Weenuche, Capote, and Muache bands refused to attend these talks. The 1863 Conejos Treaty reduced the Ute Nation significantly, granting the United States the mineral rights in the San Luis Valley and the ownership of all land east of the Continental Divide, including Middle Park.[25] Unfortunately, as with other treaties between Native Americans and the United States, the Ute bands who didn't sign the treaty didn't recognize it. In addition, the United States promised the Utes annuities, which were often late or never paid. Worse, as years passed and the number of settlers increased, the treaties were often ignored, and settlers mined and settled on Ute lands.

Tsashin, with her close ties to Ouray and Chipeta, had to be aware of the negotiations between her people and the Anglos, but as a young woman, she moved on with her life. She married Canávish (also called Canalla or Johnson), an important White River medicine man from the Nupartca band.[26] Canávish was six feet tall, unusual for a Ute, muscular, and known as a good council listener. He was also well known for carrying a .50-caliber Sharps buffalo rifle and being an excellent marksman.[27] Over the next several years, Tsashin and Canávish had five children.[28]

In 1868, the United States asked the Utes to sign a new treaty. Ouray and nine other Ute chiefs, along with their

Figure 10.6. Ute medicine man Canávish (Johnson),
circa 1870-1880. Canávish holds a pistol and a
staff adorned with two human scalps.

Courtesy of Denver Public Library Special Collections, X-19253

advisor, Kit Carson, and Colorado Territorial Governor
Alexander Hunt, went to Washington, DC, to meet with
President Andrew Johnson.[29] The new treaty negotiated in

Washington moved the Utes onto their own reservation, reducing their territory by two-thirds—from around fifty-six million to eighteen million acres. As a nomadic people who survived by hunting and gathering, the loss of land was difficult, but on their reservation, the treaty guaranteed the Ute reservation land would be "set apart for the absolute and undisturbed use and occupation of the Indians."[30] In addition, the treaty created two Indian agencies: the White River Indian Agency in northern Colorado near present-day Meeker and the Los Piños Indian Agency near present-day Saguache. The Los Piños Agency was moved in 1875 to a location near present-day Montrose.[31]

After the Civil War, more Americans came west. The increased Anglo population put pressure on the federal government to solve what settlers considered the "Indian problem." White settlers coveted Ute lands, for both their mineral content and their rich farming potential. Despite the 1868 treaty and Chief Ouray's steadfast work for peace, many pioneers' attitudes reflected the mindset expressed in an 1870 *Boulder County News* article titled "Extermination the only Remedy":

> The result cannot be doubtful. It will not stop short of the complete overthrow, if not extermination, of the leading tribes now and always plotting mischief. Perhaps the sooner the present uncertainty culminates in the bloody dead-lock which must come before there can be any permanent peace, the better for every body involved—not excepting the savages themselves. For the latter, there is no cure but cavalry and bayonets. For them there is no balm but bullets. They will never sleep until they have taken a final draught of *lead poison* and crossed to their happy hunting grounds in the land of the Here-after![32]

Encroachment on the Ute reservation and the discovery of valuable mineral deposits in the San Juan Mountains motivated the United States government to again approach the Utes, this time to buy part of the Ute reservation. The Utes refused to negotiate and asked that the mining settlements, already established on Ute land, be removed. Ouray is reported as saying:

> We do not want to sell a foot of our land—this is the opinion of all. The government is obligated by its treaty

Figure 10.7. Tsashin (Susan) stands in the back row, second from the left, her husband, Canávish (Johnson), to her right. Ouray and his wife Chipeta sit in the front, center.

Courtesy of Denver Public Library Special Collections, X-19251

[1868] to [protect] our people, and that is what we want. For some time we have seen whites coming in on our lands; we have not done anything ourselves [to stop the inflow], but we have waited for the government to fulfill its treaty.[33]

Chairman of the Board of Indian Commissioners, Felix Brunot, attended these discussions and put pressure on the Utes to change their stance. Finally, in 1873, the Brunot Agreement was reached, removing a quarter of the Ute's former reservation. The Utes were offered a $25,000 per annum payment, but this money would be dispersed "at the discretion of the President, or as he may direct, for the use and benefit of the Ute Indians annually forever."[34] In addition, the government gave Ouray a salary of $1,000 dollars annually and told the Ute people they would be allowed to hunt on their former lands.

Throughout these turbulent years, Tsashin visited Chipeta and Ouray, but no doubt, she was busy raising her family. By 1878, she and her family lived near the White River Indian Agency and had probably learned first-hand the unreliability of Anglo promises and their treaties. Edward Danforth, the White River Indian Agent from 1874 to 1878, wrote in his 1877 report, "None of their annuity goods (and but part of their supplies) have reached this agency during the year. . . . No clothing, blanket, tent, implement, or utensil of any kind has been issued at this agency for nearly two years."[35] Danforth had lost the Ute's trust, but in 1878, the newly appointed Indian agent, Nathan Meeker, would prove to be much, much worse.

Nathan Meeker, an idealistic dreamer, had worked for Horace Greeley, the editor of the *New York Tribune*, and he shared Greeley's utopian society vision. In 1869, Meeker headed to Colorado to help establish and run Greeley's Union Colony.[36] By 1878, the colony was faltering and Meeker was in debt. He requested and obtained appointment as the White River Indian Agent. At age sixty-one, Meeker had failed in several enterprises, yet he saw his new appointment as a chance to prove his personal beliefs and to civilize the Utes. In April of 1878, he wrote:

> Perhaps the greatest obstacle at present in regard to civilizing any people, whether in America, Africa or Asia, arises first, from want of a strong, wise government, and second, from a defect in the character of the teachers or missionaries; for such have but imperfect knowledge of rural industries and but a faint idea of their great importance. The first step in getting the savage to be receptive of ideas is to teach him to work and have a fixed and comfortable home, for upon this basis he comes to attach a right to the work of his hands.[37]

Soon after his arrival at the White River Agency, Meeker moved the agency headquarters twelve miles downstream to Powell's Valley, a site with expansive meadows and a milder climate. Tsashin and her family lived in Powell's Valley, and her husband supported the agency's move. The couple's proximity meant they had significant contact with Nathan Meeker. He considered Tsashin and her family "good Indians." Meeker wrote several articles for the *Greeley Tribune,* including the following which described Tsashin and her husband:

> Some of them [Utes] planted potatoes last spring, and the one who is making the most of them is Johnson [Canávish], a considerable chief, and one who takes the lead in progress and enterprise. He is not given to politics at all—

by the way, they have parties as well as anybody but there is neither space nor desire to tell about them—and he devotes his energies to improving his domestic affairs. He has three cows from which he has milk, butter, and cheese; and poultry and goats. A table has been made for him at which he and his eat; he has crockery, dishes, and if he had a house he would probably make things shine. Susan [Tsashin], Johnson's wife, is a good genius. She is a large, handsome woman, reminding one of that Boston lady, Louise Chandler Moulton; she has dignity and good sense, and she makes her husband do as she bids. Her dress is of the finest buckskin ornamented with elaborate fringes and bead-work, costing fully as much as a good silk dress.

Johnson is one of those men who lead from the savage to the barbaric life on the way to civilization. He is not quite as far advanced as Cedric the Saxon, master of Garth, in Scott's Ivanhoe, but he is probably equal to the best among the British chiefs.[38]

Meeker eventually built Tsashin and her family a home near the agency headquarters. In his first report to the Commissioner of Indian Affairs, he describes the Utes in his care in glowing terms:

These Ute Indians are peacable, respecters of the right of property, and with few exceptions amiable and prepossessing in appearance. There are no quarrelsome outbreaks, no robberies, and perhaps not half a dozen who pilfer, and these are well known. The marriage relation is strictly observed, at least for the time it continues, and polygamy is practiced to but a limited extent. On the whole, this agent is impressed with the idea that if the proper methods can be hit upon they can be made to develop many useful and manly qualities and be elevated to a state of absolute independence.[39]

Nathan Meeker wrote this report in July 1878, but he obviously didn't find the "proper methods" to work with the Utes. Scarcely a year later, on September 29, 1879, Utes killed Meeker and ten other men working at the agency. At the same time, they took five hostages: Meeker's wife, Arvilla; his

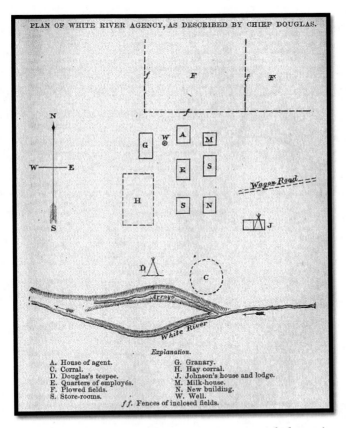

Figure 10.8. The White River Agency with locations of buildings, including Tsashin's agency home identified as J, circa 1879.

Chart from the White River Ute Commission Investigation

twenty-two-year-old daughter, Josephine; Mrs. Price, the wife of one of the agency employees; and the Price's two young children. Previously known as the Meeker Massacre, many historians now favor calling it the Meeker Incident in recognition of the part that Meeker's cultural insensitivity, the settlers' and miners' illegal encroachment on Ute lands, and the United States troops' entering Ute reservation land played in inciting this brutal encounter.

During the year between Meeker's glowing report and the Meeker Incident, Meeker's frustration increased as the Utes refused to farm and acclimate to his definition of "civilized." Meeker began illegally threatening the Utes, writing that they "had better be making up their minds pretty quick whether they are going to work or whether they propose to continue to be paupers. . . . In a year or so if I stay as long, I shall pro- pose to cut every Indian to bare starvation point if he will not work."[40]

Tensions worsened, partially due to Meeker's posturing, but also due to attitudes of that time. On July 5, 1879, Colo- rado Governor Frederick W. Pitkin sent a dispatch to the Commission of Indian Affairs in Washington, DC, that con- cluded with the statement: "These savages should be re- moved to the Indian Territory or New Mexico."[41] Pitkin, like many Colorado settlers, wanted the Utes to leave Colorado, and more importantly, the settlers wanted the Ute reservation land.

The relationship between the Utes and Meeker continued to deteriorate when the agent decided the only way to "control the Utes" was to "take away their horses; then give the word that if they would not work they should have no rations."[42] Despite strong opposition from local Utes, Meeker decided to get rid of the horses—along with the horse racing the Utes loved—by plowing up the pasture that the Utes used for horse racing, located near Tsashin's agency house. When an agency man began plowing the field, a shot was fired over his head, causing him to flee. Tsashin's son, Tatit'z, probably fired the shot, yet despite this warning, two days later the plowing continued.[43]

Tsashin's husband confronted Meeker, and in the angry words that followed, Meeker threatened Canávish with prison. After that point, accounts differ. Canávish claimed he took Meeker's shoulder and told him it was better he should go.[44] Meeker wrote an entirely different account of the September 10, 1879 incident, stating:

> I have been assaulted by a leading chief, Johnson, forced out of my own house, and injured badly, but was rescued by employes. It is now revealed that Johnson originated all the trouble stated in letter September 8th. His son shot at the plowman, and the opposition to the plowing is wide. Plowing stops. Life of self, family, and employes not safe; want protection immediately; have asked Governor Pitkin to confer with General Pope.[45]

As tensions rose, Major Thomas Thornburgh, stationed at Fort Fred Steele in Wyoming, received orders to go to the White River Agency to protect Meeker and the other agency personnel. Major Thornburgh was career military, a West Point graduate, and, at age thirty-two, the youngest major on active duty. After requesting more men, Thornburgh headed toward the White River Agency on September 21, 1879. Accompanying him were 175 cavalry troops and infantrymen, plus twenty-five or so civilian teamsters.[46]

The Utes learned of Major Thornburgh's advance, and on September 27, 1879, Thornburgh received a letter from Meeker stating, "The Indians seem to consider the advance of

troops as a declaration of real war."[47] Despite this dire
warning, Thornburgh continued to advance toward the Ute
reservation. As he traveled through Wyoming and Colorado,
Thornburgh encountered Captain Jack and Colorow, two Ute
chiefs. Thornburgh had to have realized the Utes knew he was
coming. He also should have realized the Utes feared trouble,
since he was also told that almost all Ute women and children
had left the White River Agency area. Despite these warning
signs, Thornburgh didn't send a message to his commanding
officer, presumably because he didn't expect trouble.[48]

As the troops approached Milk Creek, the border of the Ute
reservation, Meeker assured Chief Douglas, a chief of the
White River Utes, that the troops would not cross into the
reservation. Unfortunately, he apparently never informed
Thornburgh of this promise. Due to several factors, including
poor communication, Major Thornburgh and his troops
crossed Milk Creek on September twenty-ninth and began
marching through the Ute reservation toward the White River
Agency. From the Ute standpoint, the army had invaded their
reservation and the fear of violence similar to the 1864 Sand
Creek Massacre was high.

Thornburgh's troops entered a narrow canyon, and the Utes
attacked. The Battle of Milk Creek, as the battle became
known, lasted five days, with many lives lost on both sides.
Four hours after the Milk Creek battle began, Utes attacked
the White River Agency, killing Meeker and his men and taking the Anglo women and children captive. By evening, all
agency buildings, except for Tsashin's log home, had been pil-
laged and burned.

Meeker's letter of September 10, 1879, accused Tsashin's
husband of being the main Ute troublemaker, yet after the
Meeker Incident, Canávish testified at the White River Ute
Commission Investigation that he had moved his band two

days' walk from the agency and was not there during the attack.[49] Despite this testimony, Canávish's brother was killed at the White River Agency, and it is believed Tsashin's son Tatit'z, was killed in the Battle of Milk Creek. Soldiers who survived Milk Creek also identified an excellent Ute marksman whom they called Red Shirt. It is likely Red Shirt was Canávish.[50]

The Utes held Mrs. Meeker, her daughter Josephine, Mrs. Price, and her children as captives for twenty-three days, sometimes together and at other times in separate camps. The women were brutalized and raped, although only in the relative privacy of the White River Ute Commission Investigation did the women acknowledge the rapes, or "outrages" as the act was called at that time.[51] During her testimony, Mrs. Price identified Tsashin's husband as one of the men who raped her, although all three women had nothing but praise for Tsashin. Mrs. Meeker later wrote ". . . I shall never cease to respect her and to bless the goodness of her heart."[52]

All three women detailed their captivity in the book, *The Ute massacre! Brave Miss Meeker's Captivity!* The women repeatedly mention Tsashin and her kindness, including describing how she helped save their lives.[53] According to their accounts in the book, in late October, General Adams, Captain Cline, and several other Anglo men arrived at the Ute camp where the women were being held. [54] The men were trying to negotiate the release of the women, but were not having much success until Tsashin intervened, as Mrs. Meeker later wrote:

> The council was a stormy one. Various opinions prevailed. The war party wanted us held until peace should be made between the Indians and the Government. They wanted to set us against the guilty murderers, so as to save them

through us. After a few hours of violent speeches Mrs. Johnson [Tsashin] burst into the lodge in a magnificent wrap and demanded that the captives be set free, war or no war. Her brother Ouray had so ordered, and she took the assembly by storm. She told the pathetic story of the captives, and advised the Indians to do as Ouray requested and trust to the mercy of the government. General Adams said he must have a decision at once or he would have to leave. That settled it and we were set free.[55]

For the next few weeks, newspapers reported details of the release and gave Tsashin her final name, God Bless Susan.[56] Sadly, even though Tsashin had earned the respect and the gratitude of citizens throughout Colorado, her life, along with those of all Utes, was about to change forever.

After the Meeker Incident, Tsashin's family moved to the Los Piños Indian Agency, both to be closer to Ouray and Chipeta's farm and to allow Canávish to testify at the White River Ute Commission Investigation. Ouray died on August 24, 1880. On June 25, 1881, the *Colorado Miner* reported that "God Bless Susan will attend the graduating exercise at White River. G. B. Susan has a very handsome daughter who will shortly be emancipated from thraldom of school life."[57]

Soon after the graduation of Tsashin's daughter, as Sean Clason wrote in his master's thesis, the "backlash against the White River bands from newspapers and government authorities resulted in the complete removal of all Northern Utes from Colorado's Western Slope."[58] In 1881, the United States Army force-marched all Northern Utes out of Colorado and onto a small reservation in Utah. Their removal gave Anglos access to almost twelve million acres of arable lands, along with their respective mineral rights. Mining boomtowns such as Aspen, Ouray, and Telluride, located on

Figure 10.9. Advertisement in the *Denver Tribune*,
January 1, 1880

Courtesy of Colorado Historic Newspapers Collection

former tribal lands, extracted millions of tons of valuable minerals. In his book, *The Utes Must Go!*, Peter Decker wrote about the Meeker Incident saying, "Mostly this is the story of countless hateful, dishonest, and corrupt men and their insensitive and often brutal actions against an Indian tribe that wanted only to be left alone. But they were not to be left alone. Americans wanted their land and took it."[59]

Tsashin and her family were forced onto a new reservation in northeast Utah. They, along with most of her tribe, didn't know the plants and herbs of the dry Utah landscape, which obliged them to rely even more heavily on government annuities. Like Chipeta, Tsashin spent the rest of her life mostly forgotten by the Anglos who now occupied her homeland, and she eventually died in obscurity.

In 1935, Greeley's chapter of the Daughters of the American Revolution erected a stone monument to Tsashin's memory on the north side of Greeley where Tsashin was purportedly tied before her rescue from the Arapaho.[60]

In July 2008, the Smoking River Pow Wow was organized as a reconciliation event, and descendants of both Nathan Meeker and the Northern Utes were invited. Jonas Grant, Tsashin's great-great grandson attended.

"I had mixed feelings," Grant said afterwards. "The gesture from the town was very good. It was time to make amends. . . . it was a good beginning."[61]

The Utes were invited to attend the dedication ceremony for the Milk Creek Battlefield Park in September 2015. Ernest House Jr., Executive Director of the Colorado Commission of Indian Affairs, addressed the attendees and said, "The more you teach and tell the true stories, the more it will benefit future generations . . . as Native people all we want is the truth. . . . The stories of the Utes are still in the air and the mountains."[62]

Another speaker at the event, Southern Ute Chairman Clement J. Frost said, "The land doesn't belong to the Indians; the Indians belong to the land . . . we take pride in our culture we honor the land everyday. I feel drawn to this place, I feel this land is apart of all the Utes."[63]

Slowly, with time, Tsashin's life story, along with the Utes' history, is being remembered and honored. She was a remarkable woman who lived and persevered during a difficult time. Her children's children carry on her legacy and memory. The Utes, although forced from their homeland, continue to thrive and to renew their relationship with their traditional homeland in their Shining Mountains.

[1] "Grateful Susan: The Romance of the Squaw's Action on Behalf of the Meekers," *Chicago Daily Tribune,* Oct 30, 1879, 2, ProQuest.

[2] Encyclopedia Staff, "Meeker Incident," *Colorado Encyclopedia* (website), last modified August 27, 2022, https://coloradoencyclopedia.org/article/meeker-incident.

[3] Sean Clason, "Ghosts of the Meeker Massacre: Nathan Meeker, Thomas Thornburgh, and Josephine Meeker, 1842-1881" (unpublished master's thesis, University of Northern Colorado, Greeley, Colorado, 2016), 2.

[4] "Early History, Southern Ute Indian Tribe History" (webpage), Southern Ute Indian Tribe (website), https://www.southernute-nsn.gov/history/.

[5] James M. Potter, "Ute History and the Ute Mountain Ute Tribe," *Colorado Encyclopedia* (website), last modified January 25, 2023, https://coloradoencyclopedia.org/article/ute-history-and-ute-mountain-ute-tribe.

[6] "Early History, Southern Ute Indian Tribe History."

[7] "Early History, Southern Ute Indian Tribe History."

[8] Cynthia S. Becker and David Smith, *Chipeta, Queen of the Utes: A Biography* (Lake City, CO: Western Reflections Publishing Company, 2003) 17, endnote 10.

[9] P. David Smith, *Ouray, Chief of the Utes* (Ridgway, CO: Wayfinder Press, 1986) 34-35. See also "The Ute King. Interesting Biographical Sketch of Head Chief Ouray, Prepared at his Own Dictation," the *Denver Tribune,* Jan. 1, 1880, 9, Colorado Historic Newspapers Collection (website), Colorado State Library, coloradohistoricnewspapers.org. Ouray's parentage varies depending on reference. The latter reference and others say his mother was Apache and his father Ute.

[10] Becker and Smith, *Chipeta,* 23.

[11] "Details of Ute Susan Episode Are Requested," *Greeley Tribune,* Dec. 21 1933, 1. This article claims she was captured by Chief Left Hand, but other articles claim it was Chief Friday's band.

There is a good chance she was captured by one band and traded to another.

¹² Becker and Smith, *Chipeta*, 2.

¹³ Ansel Watrous, *History of Larimer County Colorado: Collated and Compiled from Historical Authorities, Public Reports, Official Records and other Reliable Sources—Stories of Indian Troubles and of the Pioneer Days* (Fort Collins, CO: The Courier Printing & Publishing Co., 1911), 108.

¹⁴ "Details of Ute Susan," 1.

¹⁵ "Details of Ute Susan," 1; and see "Squaw Susan's Send-off," *Colorado Transcript* (Golden, CO), Dec. 17, 1879, 3, Colorado Historic Newspapers Collection (website), Colorado State Library, coloradohistoricnewspapers.org. In the latter article, Tsashin was not tied to a tree, but the report instead states that when the soldiers "rode in among the tepees no captive was to be seen, but the preparations had been undisturbed, as they found a fence post erected in the centre of the camp, and a quantity of wood around it ready to be ignited."

¹⁶ "Squaw Susan's Send-off," 3.

¹⁷ "Indian Tales as Told in History: More Interesting Lore of the Early Days," *Weekly Courier* (Fort Collins, CO), Oct. 20, 1910, 16, Colorado Historic Newspapers Collection (website), Colorado State Library, coloradohistoricnewspapers.org.

¹⁸ "Squaw Susan's Send-off," 3.

¹⁹ "Squaw Susan's Send-off," 3.

²⁰ "Grateful Susan," 2.

²¹ "Grateful Susan," 2.

²² William N. Byers, "History of the Ute Nation!" *Dolores News* (Rico, CO), May 15, 1880, 1, Colorado Historic Newspapers Collection (website), Colorado State Library, coloradohistoricnewspapers.org.

²³ "Early History, Southern Ute Indian Tribe History."

²⁴ *Printed copy of the Treaty Between the United States and the Utah Tribe of Indians, Concluded December 30, 1849, Ratified September 24, 1850*; Ratified Indian Treaty 256: Utah – Abiquiu, New Mexico Territory, December 30, 1849; Indian Treaties 1789-1869; Ratified

Indian Treaties, 1722-1869 (National Archives Microfilm Publication M668, Roll 10); General Records of the United States Government 1778-2006, Record Group 11; National Archives, Washington, DC. Also available through the Archival Research Catalog, ARC identifier 175192405, https://catalog.archives.gov/id/175192405.

25 *Treaty with the Utah—Tabeguache Band, 1863, Concluded October 7, 1863, Ratified March 25, 1864*; Ratified Indian Treaty 328: Utah (Tabeguache) – Tabeguache Agency, Conejos, Colorado Territory; and see Indian Treaties 1789-1869; Ratified Indian Treaties 1722-1869 (National Archives Microfilm Publication M668, Roll 13); General Records of the United States Government 1778-2006, Record Group 11, National Archives, Washington, DC. Also available at https://collections.lib.utah.edu/ark:/87278/s6zp72n3/363520.

26 US House of Representatives, *White River Ute Commission Investigation (Executive Document 83), Letter from the Secretary of the Interior, transmitting copy of evidence taken before White River Ute Commission, Appendix B: Testimony of Johnson, Chief of the White River Utes, November 14, 1879*, 7, text in: University of Oklahoma College of Law Digital Commons, American Indians and Alaskan Native Documents in the Congressional Serial Set: 1817-1899 (database), House of Representatives Executive Document Submissions from 1881, *White River Ute Commission Investigation*, https://digitalcommons.law.ou.edu/cgi/viewcontent.cgi?article=6987&context=indianserialset.

27 Peter R. Decker, *"The Utes Must Go!" American Expansion and the Removal of a People* (Golden, CO: Fulcrum Publishing, 2004), 101.

28 "Families disagree on new burial site" *Vernal Express* (Vernal, UT), Oct. 6, 2004, A10.

29 Decker, *"The Utes Must Go!,"* 37.

30 *Treaty with the Ute Indians, March 2, 1868*, Ratified Indian Treaty 367: Ute (Tabaquache [Tabeguache], Moache, Capote, Wiminuche, Yampa, Grand River, and Uinta) – Washington, DC, March 2, 1868; and see Indian Treaties 1789-1869, Ratified Indian Treaties, 1722-1869 (National Archives Microfilm Publication

M688, Roll 16), General Records of the United States Government 1778-2006, Record Group 11, National Archives, Washington, DC, 619, https://catalog.archives.gov/id/179033894. Also available at https://collections.lib.utah.edu/ark:/87278/s6d826zs/361661.

[31] Steven G. Baker, "Los Piños Indian Agency," *Colorado Encyclopedia* (website), last modified November 12, 2022, https://coloradoencyclopedia.org/article/los-piños-indian-agency.

[32] "Extermination the only Remedy," *Boulder County News* (Boulder, CO), June 8, 1870, 2, Colorado Historic Newspapers Collection (website), Colorado State Library, coloradohistoricnewspapers.org.

[33] Decker, *"The Utes Must Go!,"* 53.

[34] *1874 Brunot Agreement with the Ute Nation*, (transcription), 1, https://ocs.fortlewis.edu/forestPlan/roundtable/brunotAgreement.pdf. See Article 3.

[35] E. H. Danforth, "Reports of Agents: Colorado," *Annual Report of the Commissioner of Indian Affairs for the year 1877* (Washington, DC: Government Printing Office, 1877), 46, http://digital.library.wisc.edu/1711.dl/History.AnnRep77.

[36] Clason, "Ghosts of the Meeker Massacre," 24.

[37] Nathan Meeker, "The Utes of Colorado," *American Antiquarian* 1, no. 4 (April 1878): 226.

[38] Robert Emmitt, *The Last War Trail: the Utes and the Settlement of Colorado* (Boulder, CO: University Press of Colorado, 2000), 123-24.

[39] N. C. Meeker, "Reports of Agents: Colorado," *Annual Report of the Commissioner of Indian Affairs for the year 1878* (Washington, DC: Government Printing Office, 1878), 19, http://digital.library.wisc.edu/1711.dl/History.AnnRep78.

[40] Emmitt, *The Last War Trail*, 73-74.

[41] "Governor Pitkin on the Indian Question," *Colorado Weekly Chieftain* (Pueblo, CO), July 10, 1879, 3, Colorado Historic Newspapers Collection (website), Colorado State Library, coloradohistoricnewspapers.org.

[42] N. C. Meeker, "Reports of Agents: Colorado," *Annual Report of the Commissioner of Indian Affairs for the year 1879* (Washington, DC:

Government Printing Office, 1879), 19, http://digital.library.wisc.edu/1711.dl/History.AnnRep79.

[43] Emmitt, *The Last War Trail*, 131.

[44] *White River Ute Commission Investigation, Testimony of Johnson,* 7.

[45] Nathan Meeker to E. A. Hayt , September 10, 1879, "Excerpts, Ute Indians in Colorado," transcription, Civil Works Administration Pioneer Interviews Collection, Object ID PAM.342.4, 4, History Colorado Online Collection.

[46] Decker, *"The Utes Must Go!,"* 128; and see Mark Miller, *Hollow Victory: The White River Expedition of 1879 and the Battle of Milk Creek* (Niwot, CO: University Press of Colorado, 1997) 25. Exact number of troops varies depending on reference. Miller estimated 216 men based on the muster roll.

[47] Miller, *Hollow Victory*, 43-44.

[48] Decker, *"The Utes Must Go!,"* 134.

[49] *White River Ute Commission Investigation, Testimony of Johnson,* 8.

[50] Miller, *Hollow Victory*, 98.

[51] *White River Ute Commission Investigation, Testimony of Johnson,* 17, 18, 26, 44.

[52] Josephine Meeker, *The Ute Massacre!: Brave Miss Meeker's Captivity! Her Own Account of It. Also, the Narratives of Her Mother And Mrs. Price* (Philadelphia, PA: Old Franklin publishing house, 1879), 30.

[53] Meeker, *The Ute Massacre*, 30, 46.

[54] Meeker, *The Ute Massacre, 18, 38.*

[55] Meeker, *The Ute Massacre*, 30.

[56] "The Noblest Indian Name," *Silver World* (Lake City, CO), Aug. 19, 1882, 1, Colorado Historic Newspapers Collection (website), Colorado State Library, coloradohistoricnewspapers.org.

[57] "Los Pinos Society Dots," *Colorado Miner* (Georgetown, CO), June 25, 1881, 1, Colorado Historic Newspapers Collection (website), Colorado State Library, coloradohistoricnewspapers.org.

[58] Clason, "Ghosts of the Meeker Massacre," 2.

⁵⁹ Decker, *"The Utes Must Go!,"* xvi.

⁶⁰ "Ute Indian Girl Who Saved Women to Have Marker,"
Steamboat Pilot (Steamboat Springs, CO), Dec. 25, 1935, 3, Colorado
Historic Newspapers Collection (website), Colorado State Library,
coloradohistoricnewspapers.org.

⁶¹ Jeff Burkhead, "Powwow offers chance for 'both sides' to
come together," *Rio Blanco Herald Times* (Meeker, CO), Sept. 26,
2009, 38, https://www.theheraldtimes.com/powwow-offers-
chance-for-%E2%80%98both-sides%E2%80%99-to-come-to-
gether/rio-blanco-county/.

⁶² Sacha Smith, "Remembering the Milk Creek Battle," *The
Southern Ute Drum* (Ignacio, CO), Oct. 2, 2015, 1, https://www.sud-
rum.com/eEditions/DrumPDF/2015/SUDrum-20151002.pdf.

⁶³ Sacha Smith, "Milk Creek Battle," 3.

Acknowledgments

The authors spent years researching and writing these biographies. During this time, we were assisted by numerous research librarians, museum curators, newspaper archivists, university professors, authors, and readers who provided critiques. When Covid caused the closure of many repositories, we couldn't have continued our research without the many professionals who answered our extensive email queries and, especially, those who gave access to closed museums and sent archived material to us. In the following paragraphs, we have tried to thank as many of these people as possible by name, but for anyone we missed, we apologize. Without the help and support of this extended community, these biographies would not have been possible. Any errors are ours alone.

First and foremost, we thank our husbands, Earl and John. They've taken road trips to distant libraries and historical sites with us, hiked through graveyards infested with bloodthirsty gnats, helped with computer issues and formatting, and put up with our spending our waking hours at a computer or lost in a library searching for nuggets of information. We are grateful for their patience, love, support, and understanding.

The staffs of Denver Public Library's Western History Collection and History Colorado's Stephen H. Hart Research Center provided essential assistance during our numerous visits and emails. They helped us find unpublished manuscripts, pictures, newspaper articles, census documentation, and other information. We thank all the research librarians from both institutions and add a special thank you to the following individuals who spent extra time with us at the Denver Public Library: Sarah Ganderup, Special Collections, for much appreciated online assistance; Laura Ruttum Senturia, Western History & Genealogy; Jamie Seemiller, Acquisitions Archivist; Liam Gray, Reference Librarian; and Cody Robinson, Collections Access Coordinator who helped find images and their copyrights. At the Stephen H. Hart Research Center at History Colorado we thank Tamar McKee, Manager; Jori Johnson, Collections Access Coordinator; Bethany Williams, Collections Access Coordinator; Ann Sneesby Koch, Assistant Curator, and Keegan Martin, Digital Imaging Assistant.

We have referenced numerous books and articles in this work and would like to thank all the men and women who took the time to research and produce quality historical nonfiction books. There are several who deserve special mention, because we relied heavily on their research and recording of pioneers' recollections. Roger Baker's excellent book, *Clara: An Ex-Slave in Gold Rush Colorado*, was important for the Clara Brown chapter. Likewise, Mayme G. Sturm's article in the *Colorado Magazine*, "Mary York (Cozens), Pioneer Woman in Gregory Diggings," and *Fraser Haps and Mishaps: The Diary of Mary E. Cozens*, edited by Alice Reich and Thomas J. Steele, S.J., paved the way for further research into the life of Mary York Cozens. Alice Polk Hill's *Tales of the Colorado Pioneers* and Betty Moynihan's inclusion of a version of Augusta Tabor's memoirs, "Reminiscenses [*sic*] of Mrs. Augusta Tabor" in *Augusta Tabor: A Pioneering Woman* gave us accounts of Augusta Tabor's early years in her own words.

Julie would like to thank the many people who answered emails and phone calls, and those who emailed newspaper articles and other important research, including: Margaret Langley, the High Plains Library District; Josh B. Mabe, Newspaper Librarian, Chicago Public Library; Gayle

Martinson, Wisconsin Historical Society; Auburn Nelson, the Schomburg Center for Research in Black Culture; Charleszine "Terry" Nelson, the Blair-Caldwell African American Research Library; Daphne Rice-Allen and Terri Gentry, the Black American West Museum & Heritage Center; Dr. Sarah Michaels, University of Nebraska-Lincoln; Robin Smith, Archivist, Kentucky Department for Libraries and Archives; Megan Friedel and David Hays, University Libraries, University of Colorado, Boulder; Dr. Nicolas Rügge of the Niedersächsisches Landesarchiv; Claudia Falk, Stadt Baden-Baden; Claudia Krink, Badische Landesbibliothek; Ilse Filser for German translations; Jacke Barnes, genealogist; Mary Walsh, MLS, the Nielsen Library, Adams State University; Dr. Estevan Rael-Gálvez, Creative Strategies 360°; Stephanie McClinton, Kansas City Public Library; Barbara Romero, Taos Public Library; Tabitha Davis, Pueblo City-County Library; John Hopper, Amache Preservation Society; Anita Pointon, Boggsville Historical Site; Wayne "Kovaahe" Leman, Chief Dull Knife College, who has put together an amazing Cheyenne language website; Dr. Bonnie Clark, University of Denver; Eleise Clark, Historian, Denver Shorter AME Church; Roger Davis, Director, Palmer Lake Vaile Museum, who opened the museum during Covid to allow Julie to research Katrina Murat; Kara Duggan, Business Manager, University of Denver; Clare Fanning of the Antoinette Perry Estate, and Albert Sieber, Louisville Public Library.

Special thanks go to Dana EchoHawk, Debra Faulkner, Rhonda Beck, Maria Clara Martinez, Dr. Bonnie Clark, and Marilyn Martorano. All of these women provided their personal expertise and research articles.

Jan's nearly life-long interest in Augusta Tabor led her to make two research visits to Augusta's childhood home in Augusta, Maine, and several treks to Pillsbury Crossing,

Kansas, where the Tabors first lived following their wedding. Jan thanks Bonnie Dwyer, Reference Librarian, Maine State Library; Anthony Douin, volunteer, Kennebec Historical Society; and Jeffrey E. Brown, Reference Services, Maine State Archives; for answering a plethora of questions, pointing out sources, providing requested documents, and sharing their wealth of knowledge about the area and its history. She's also grateful to Colette Bonte, Administrative Assistant, Unitarian Universalist Community Church, Augusta, Maine, and Patricia L. Edwards, Historian, Penney Memorial United Baptist Church, Augusta, Maine, for researching and answering trip follow-up questions via correspondence. Jeanne C. Mithen, Librarian/Archivist at the Riley County Historical Society and Museum in Manhattan, Kansas, provided Jan with priceless assistance in researching Augusta's Kansas years.

Jan also extends her thanks to all those who generously gave of their time via email: David Forsyth, PhD, Executive Director and Curator, Gilpin Historical Society, for researching and answering a long list of questions regarding Mary Cozens; Shanna Ganne, Executive Director, Grand County Historical Association, for culling their files for documents related to the Cozens family, hauling those files to Denver, and lending the treasure trove to Jan during the Covid lockdown; Grand County Historical Association Archivist, Patty Madison, for searching photos and answering questions; Susan Jones, Treasurer, LaPlata County Historical Society, for her help in locating and copying a rare newspaper article and researching and answering questions in regard to the Baker Expedition; and Collections Manager and Research Coordinator Amita Kiley and Head Researcher Kathleen S. Flynn at the Lawrence History Center, Lawrence, MA, for going above and beyond to confirm Augusta Tabor was a textile worker and for providing related materials.

For photo assistance and obtaining image reprint rights, we would like to thank Dot Donovan, Special and Digital Collections Program Lead, Auraria Library; Rebecca Robertson from the Fraenkel Gallery; Case Carroll, Director of Archives at the San Juan County Historical Society; Ashley Yager, Collections Manager at the Loveland Museum; Dot Donovan and Sommer Browning of the Auraria Library; Kellen Cutsforth of Denver Public Library; Teri Jobe, Acting Lead Interpretation Ranger at the Sand Creek Massacre National Historic Site; Lesley Struc, Curator of the Archive at the Fort Collins Museum of Discovery; and Deb Wold from the Longyear Christian Science Museum.

We are indebted to those who critiqued all or part of the book. First, we extend our immense gratitude to Doris Baker, former owner of Filter Press, for generously sharing her expertise in a thorough edit of the manuscript. Doug Lang, historian and editor, provided invaluable comments on all the biographies, giving both excellent writing feedback and fact-checking historical details. The late Skippy Rollins, a friend and talented editor, critiqued many of Julie's biographies. Marilyn Martorano's invaluable feedback on Maria Dolores Ballejos helped improve the authors' understanding of the Utes and Spaniards in Southern Colorado. Charles Lesage Jr. provided valuable feedback as an early reader, as did Barb Taylor and Cindy Martin. The members of Julie's Women Writing the West critique group, Nina Kunze, Betsy Lane, Katie Smith, and Holly Montgomery, all gave worthwhile suggestions on several biographies and the preface. Jan's husband, Earl, served as her first reader, providing valuable insight and spotting errors.

Doris and Tom Baker, former owners of Filter Press, deserve a special thanks for initiating the idea for this book by publishing Julie's children's biography, *Elizabeth Byers: Denver Pioneer.*

For making our dream come to fruition and reach our readers, we are grateful to Filter Press and the production staff, including Jordan Ellender for her excellent cover design; Laura Alderson, our tireless and very thorough editor, for her work on the final manuscript; Kara Duggan, a Filter Press intern who reviewed numerous pars of the book; and the Filter Press owners Julie and John VanLaanen, for accepting and publishing the manuscript.

About the Authors

Author J.v.L. Bell has a Bachelor of Science degree in Mechanical Engineering from Colorado State University and a Master of Science degree from Colorado School of Mines. She worked as a mechanical engineer for her entire career, including being an adjunct professor at Colorado School of Mines, but in her free time, she loved writing and researching Colorado history. In 2015, she left engineering and sold her first Colorado historical mystery, *The Lucky Hat Mine*, to the Hansen Publishing Group. In 2018, Filter Press bought her first non-fiction book, a children's biography about Elizabeth Byers. Her second Colorado historical mystery was published in 2019 by the Hansen Publishing Group, and her third was published in 2021. You can find out more about this author at her website, www.JvLBell.com.

Jan Gunia has a Bachelor of Science degree in Journalism from the University of Colorado, Boulder, and is a member of Kappa Tau Alpha, the national honor society for journalism and mass communication. Her passion for nineteenth century Colorado women's history began in elementary school and continues to this day. Her extensive research of Colorado pioneers has taken her beyond Colorado to Maine and Kansas, where she visited Augusta Tabor's former home and the Tabor land, respectively. While in those states, as well as in Colorado, she has conducted research at state archives, museums, local historical societies, and libraries.

Index

Burns, Robert, 229

Byers, Elizabeth, 226-59, 296,
293; children, 231, 241-43;
death, 253; Denver home
burns, 240; Frank (son),
231, 241, 250; Ladies'
Union Aid Society, 237;
living in the *News* office,
235; marriage, 229; parents,
228; *The Experiences of One
Pioneer Woman*, 233; travel
to the Rocky Mountains,
233-34; Valverde, 241, 244,
247

Byers, Frank, 231, 241, 250

Byers, William Newton, 139,
228-33, 237, 243, 245, 253,
255, 259, 286; affair with
Hattie Sancomb, 250, 251;
death, 251; kidnapping,
239

Camp Weld Council, 8-9

Canávish (husband of
Tsashin), 270-73, 275-82;
Anglo name, 270; conflict
with Meeker, 279

Captain Jack, 280

Carroll, William C.: rescue of
Tsashin, 267-68

Carson, Kit, 236, 270

Central City, 23, 26, 31-34, 42-
46, 48, 51, 58, 60, 62, 64-65,
68-69, 73, 75, 77, 81, 139,
196, 211; county seat of
Gilpin County, 30

Cherry Creek settlements,

227, 232, 234

Cheyenne, 1-3, 6, 10, 13-14,
16, 18-20, 62, 137, 185, 246-
48, 268, 293; 1851 Fort
Laramie Treaty, 6; 1861
Treaty of Fort Wise, 6;
Abiquiú Treaty, 6; Chief
Black Kettle, 8, 9; courtship
of Amache and John
Prowers, 4; Sand Creek
Massacre, 9; traditions, 2;
Treaty of the Little
Arkansas, 9

Chipeta, 263, 266, 283

Chivington, John, 1, 9, 245-
46, 248; Sand Creek
Massacre, 248

Christian Science, 129, 144-
49, 156-58, 295; Mary Baker
Eddy, 144-46, 150, 157-58

Civil War, 237, 272

Colorado Plateau, 262

Colorado Salt Works, 136-37,
139, 153-54, 158-59;
expansion of
manufacturing, 137

Colorado State Grange, 89

Colorado Woman Suffrage
Association, 87

Colorado's statehood bid
rejected, 63

Colorow, 280

Cozens, Mary, 22-49;
Catholic faith, 24-26, 28, 34,
37-43; in Central City, 30-
34; children, 30-32; death,

209

Call Tommy

(illegible handwriting)